PENGUIN BOOKS

ARE YOU A CORPORATE REFUGEE?

A counselor and consultant in private practice, Ruth Luban has spent the last twenty-five years developing workshops, treatment programs, and training for a wide variety of individual and corporate clients. She is also a lecturer and author often featured in regional and national media. Since 1988, she has specialized in the issues of midlife transition and professional burnout, developing *Choicepoints*, a self-assessment program for people in career, relationship, and life transition, as well as the audiotape series *Keeping the Fire: From Burnout to Balance*.

Are You a Corporate Refugee?

A Survival Guide for
Downsized, Disillusioned,
and Displaced Workers

RUTH LUBAN

PENGUIN BOOKS

PENGUIN BOOKS
Published by the Penguin Group
Penguin Putnam Inc., 375 Hudson Street,
New York, New York 10014, U.S.A.
Penguin Books Ltd, 27 Wrights Lane,
London W8 5TZ, England
Penguin Books Australia Ltd, Ringwood,
Victoria, Australia
Penguin Books Canada Ltd, 10 Alcorn Avenue,
Toronto, Ontario, Canada M4V 3B2
Penguin Books (N.Z.) Ltd, 182–190 Wairau Road,
Auckland 10, New Zealand

Penguin Books Ltd, Registered Offices:
Harmondsworth, Middlesex, England

First published in Penguin Books 2001

1 3 5 7 9 10 8 6 4 2

LIBRARY OF CONGRESS CATALOGING-IN-PUBLICATION DATA

Luban, Ruth.
Are you a corporate refugee? : a survival guide for downsized,
disillusioned, and displaced workers / Ruth Luban.
p. cm.
Includes bibliographical references.
ISBN 0 14 02.9632 8
1. Employees—Dismissal of. 2. Unemployed.
3. Downsizing of organizations I. Title.
HF5549.5.D55 L83 2000
650.14—dc21   00-029342

Printed in the United States of America
Set in Goudy Old Style
Designed by Jessica Shatan

To Jason and Gabe,
my best friends, my guiding lights

There is something in the pang of change
More than the heart can bear,
Unhappiness remembering happiness.
—EURIPIDES

ACKNOWLEDGMENTS

My heartfelt thanks to Morrie Warshawski, Jacqueline Austin, and Maria D. Laso Elders for their invaluable brainstorming, mentoring, and professional guidance in shaping this book—also for their brilliant metaphors! Thanks to my agent Gail Ross, who inspired and teased out of me the core concepts for *Corporate Refugee* and gently, but firmly, kept me on course. Thanks to my dear editor at Penguin, Jane von Mehren, whose patience and sage advice took me to the finish line.

Much love and thanks to my personal cheerleaders on this project: my sons, Jason and Gabe Luban, for their unconditional support; my mother, Elfi Gerstein (daughter of Leo); my dear friends Karen Delshad and Sharon Cohen; Dr. Ken Waltzer and my colleagues at Convergence Health; and the men and women of the Career Kevorkian Club whose insights and stories you'll read throughout these pages.

Finally, I sincerely thank Marcia Asbury, Dr. Michael Bonazzola, Doran Dibble, Steve Elders, Jeff Lampson, Ellen MacGran, Judy McLane, Richard Munk, Steve Pitzell, and Dr. Victoria Thoreson for taking the time to read and enthusiastically critique the manuscript.

The truism about there being a book in every one of us should have as its addendum, "but only with the love and support of great people."

CONTENTS

INTRODUCTION

How I Became a
Corporate Refugee

*Every act of creation is first of all
an act of destruction.*

—PABLO PICASSO

The roots of this book go back to 1989. I was in my tenth year of private practice within a corporate group of psychology associates in southern Oregon.

My specialty was eating disorders, and because no one else in the region was tackling the problems of anorexic teenagers, I had spun off several programs alongside my practice: intervention classes in the junior and senior high schools; residential treatment programs; and community-based health education seminars that took me out of town several times a year. Even though I did all the work of developing my own practice, I was paid only 40 percent of my clients' fees because the corporate group provided the overhead. Since I provided the sole financial support of my then teenage sons, I worked extra hours to fill in the gaps. To "balance" my life, I ran marathons and played in local tennis tournaments on weekends.

Clearly this pace could not go on indefinitely, but I was in denial. After a series of sudden losses, I crashed into career burnout. My father died. The house my family was renting was sold, and we were given only thirty days to vacate. My older son was graduating from high school, which was a celebration, yet I experienced it as a loss. Here he was leaving for college, and I'd been a working fool his entire life. Underpinning this cluster of losses was my utter exhaustion. I'd been pushing so hard for so long that I was disconnected from my body's distress signals. Finally, I had to walk away from all that I'd built and take time to heal my burnout. My employers immediately filled my spot, which further broke my heart and intensified my grief at having lost my home base of the past ten years.

My healing took two full years. Amazingly, I needed that long to recover my resilience and sense of self. The first year, I simply gave myself a chunk of savings and determined to do nothing until I could stop crying from all my losses. Doing nothing is not something I'd ever learned, having been a hard worker all my life. I was so overidentified with my work roles that I didn't know who I was without them. Furthermore, there were no ready answers for all the physical, mental, and emotional symptoms I was experiencing. At the time, literature on burnout was scarce. Much of the advice I received was reflexive and traditional. Medical colleagues treated me on a symptom-by-symptom basis, while vocational consultants urged me to get my resume together and simply change my career focus for renewal.

I tried desperately to honor the well-intentioned feedback from all these professionals. I applied for many jobs that made no sense for me. I felt so lonely, so outside the mainstream of work, and so lost that I stabbed at anything and everything that even vaguely promised rescue from my angst. Naturally, I was rejected by most of the employers I explored, or I rejected them when I recognized those jobs were clearly not a fit with my skills and talents. Finally, I simply surrendered to the necessary recovery time. In retrospect, I realize it was the surrender that sped my healing.

As I came out of the wilderness of that period, I began writing articles about burnout. It was the early 1990s, and radical downsizing was becoming the norm in corporate America. Seasoned professionals were being laid off in droves, and many were cast into the same no-man's-land I'd been traveling. Many had given so many extra hours to their jobs to meet the increasing demands of the workplace that, in addition to the huge personal losses that come with layoffs, they were also struggling with serious career burnout. Having studied my own process, coupled with my two decades of work in clinical psychology, I felt uniquely qualified to present burnout recovery and prevention programs to this group that I dubbed the Working Wounded.

I volunteered to speak at meetings of trade associations and community organizations. I gave interviews on burnout to local and national publications. I published *Keeping the Fire: From Burnout to Balance*, an audiotape program for burned-out professionals that received national attention and favorable reviews. By the time I'd completed my own recovery, I was in the national spotlight, crusading for burnout prevention.

Meanwhile, downsizings and mergers and acquisitions among corporate giants were multiplying at a dizzying pace as companies competed for market share and stock market gains. Consequently, more and more of my clients became casualties of this corporate battlefield. They complained of burnout, but their symptoms suggested profound identity crises and grief reactions secondary to job loss and change. Everything they'd previously counted on was suddenly being torn apart. Try as they might, they couldn't pull the fractured pieces back into a unified whole.

One day I was discussing my work with displaced workers during an interview with a radio reporter. Out of my mouth popped the phrase "corporate refugees." It seemed to perfectly describe my clients' internal experience as well as their outer recovery process. Like civilians in foreign war zones, corporate refugees are often innocent victims of forces beyond their control—from the shock of being involuntarily uprooted with little warning, through the terror of not knowing or of having little or no personal control, to the ultimate outcome of resettlement, possibly in a land not of their choosing. Their situation feels like a life-or-death experience, a survival of the fittest. With no intention of trivializing the experience of people made refugees by wartime atrocities, I see the *internal* experience of corporate refugees as uncannily similar.

The focus of my work moved from clinical burnout to the issues of the corporate refugee. The more corporate refugees I saw, the more I could see elements common to all of them. As committed, hardworking people, many were in the midst of projects they cared about or members of teams to which they felt a strong sense of belonging. All of them were dedicated to the greater whole that was their company, adopting its mission statement as their own. Yet they were being cast out of those "home" companies, largely through no fault of their own. They felt a tremendous loss of meaning, purpose, and identity. And they all experienced specific stages of recovery as they struggled to put their lives back together en route to finding another job and a new level of satisfaction.

The early stages of their expulsion from the corporate cocoon were fraught with shock, anger, and paralysis: Why me? What now? With time and support, these corporate refugees moved into a kind of wandering that felt egoless and groundless but was in fact the necessary winter that preceded their reentry into the vocational fray. Those who made full use of that fallow time to shed their previous roles and reclaim their core passions landed in new corporate homelands with greater wisdom, healthier personal boundaries, and a new view of the realities of the marketplace. Above all, I found that clients who took the necessary time to fully experience each recovery stage emerged with greater energy and feelings of self-worth than before they were cast out.

I became more and more impassioned on behalf of these clients. Having had my own experience as a corporate refugee, I identified with their predicament. Gradually I also came to realize that my sensitivity to their plight came from a deeper place, one based on my ancestors' history as refugees of the Holocaust.

I am the firstborn daughter of parents forced to flee their German homeland when Hitler was on his rampage. I grew up watching my parents and their friends struggle with assimilation in a foreign culture. They spoke German among themselves throughout the years of my childhood. My two sisters and two brothers frequently interpreted English words, idioms, and colloquialisms for them. We bristled under their Old Country customs, resented my father's urging that we learn German, and struggled with his continuing nationalist spirit (*Deutschland über alles*), which stood in contrast to my Viennese mother's lifelong rage against anti-Semitism and Hitler.

My father, Alfred, suffered harrowing experiences at Dachau before escaping while in his early twenties. After a lengthy period of evading capture in Europe, he found a benefactor to facilitate his emigration to America. Never able to feel at home in his new country, Alfred yearned to return to the forests of his homeland. Over time, he somehow compartmentalized the heartrending fact that his parents had been killed by Hitler and that his extended family also had been eliminated. His opportunities to begin life anew in the United States always looked suspect to him; he told us over and over how the Nazis would rise again in America: "We will never be safe." He could not relax, and, by extension, he rarely allowed us kids to relax. We had to work, work, work! We were never grateful enough, in his view, for having been born in America. We could never understand the depths of his pain, which seemed pervasive and unrelenting.

Ironically, my mother's father, Leo, a gifted furrier from Vienna, was also at Dachau, though he and Alfred never met there. Leo's experience was more physically abusive than my father's. When Leo got out of Dachau through the miracle of sponsorship by some remote American relatives, he was forty-eight.

Leo was a tradesman, an entrepreneur, and an extrovert. In contrast to my father's inability to recover from his refugee experience, my grandfather was determined to make lemonade out of lemons. He immediately set about finding work as a furrier in New York City. He supported his family of five on nickels and dimes until he could build an income large enough to rent a decent-sized apartment. He learned English. He blessed the freedom in America and urged all around him to do the same. He did contract work until he could rent a small loft to begin a fur business of his own. When the furriers' union refused to let him join (he was "too old") and then intimidated him out of business (because he was nonunion), he found a small shop to rent in New Jersey. His long days at work were then framed by a lengthy commute from New York.

Still, he grew more successful. A competitor in Newark saw Leo's industriousness and proposed a business partnership. Leo trustingly went for it, only to discover that this man was selling stolen merchandise. Heartbroken, Leo left the partnership. By then he'd been in America nearly nine years. His three daughters had married, and two were living in other states. At fifty-seven, Leo had to reinvent himself yet again.

He made his way to Los Angeles, where his youngest daughter and son-in-law were contract furriers. They gave him work, which he leveraged in a very Leo-type way: If it took 45 skins to make a fur coat, Leo figured out a way to use 44 and keep one skin for himself. When he had collected enough extra skins, he would make a coat of his own design and sell it for pure profit. He used this strategy, lived frugally, and soon was able to get back into business for himself.

He opened a small fur shop in a palm-tree-lined village that attracted him: Beverly Hills. His shop turned out to be one of the few where movie stars could find fur coats that met their wildest whims. He catered to prima donnas. It thrilled him to see them happy. I'll never forget my strolls with him through the streets of downtown Beverly Hills during the mid-1960s when I was in college. He'd pop into all the shops of his fellow tradespeople: the seamstress on Doheny, the tailor on Rodeo Drive, the jeweler in the hotel lobby— not all refugees, but people with whom he could identify, craftspeople working with their hands, with pride, and with great joy. He had found a community of like-minded folks plying their trades like himself.

Leo made money. He learned about real estate. He coached my father to "buy duplexes, Alfred. Real estate ownership is the wave of the future. You'll make enough money to be supported in your old age." My father refused. He constantly told us how crazy my grandfather was, how reckless and unknowing. Yet even to my young eyes, my grandfather was making a healthier adjustment to his new country than my dad was. Leo was making a new life, building a supportive community around himself, blessing his freedom, and celebrating every new risk that proved successful—and by now he was more than seventy years old. He worked until he was nearly ninety, and died—financially comfortable and proud of all he'd accomplished—at ninety-four.

Meanwhile, my father was miserable. When Alfred first arrived in America from Germany in 1939, he was hired by a shoe corporation based in Columbus, Ohio, that gave refugees low-level sales jobs to help them get established. Alfred gave his entire life to the shoe business. A distant relative of Albert Einstein, my father had considerable mathematical and scientific curiosity and skill. He worked quickly and efficiently. He could easily have earned an MBA and fulfilled his potential in his new country. Instead, he was stuck in his anger, in the excruciating loss of his homeland and the unresolved, never-expressed grief over the loss of his parents (he was an only child). He retired at age sixty-eight, and four years later, after three years of debilitating strokes, he died.

Growing up with these two father figures was deeply formative in the development of my character. Temperamentally a glass-is-half-full kind of person like my grandfather, I tried desperately to be the family cheerleader, always presenting the bright side of things to my depressed parents. I also, unwittingly, internalized their grief. I didn't understand until much later in my life that it was *their* burden that made me incapable of seeing Holocaust movies or references to refugees without feeling drained and immobilized. I remember routinely being stuck in my seat at the end of such movies as *The Pawnbroker* and *Schindler's List*. Each time the movie ended, I was unable to stand; I felt paralyzed. An usher had to literally tell me to leave as my friends waited outside.

Finally I realized I'd become the embodiment of what happens to refugees. They are first paralyzed by man's inhumanity to man, by precipitous loss and change, by all sense of personal control being taken away. They have to be guided (as by the usher) to take the next steps back into the world. If they are lucky, they find benevolent guides through this reentry. Over time, and with soul-searching work, they become their own cheerleaders through rebirth.

Not accidentally, I've felt called to guide fellow travelers along the refugee path. My own experience of their realities, and the wish to celebrate their healing, fostered my career path in psychology. I've worked for more than thirty years in a variety of social-service capacities. I've talked with literally hundreds of people who've endured a variety of personal and career transitions. Most recently, I've focused on those who've suffered but survived—and ultimately thrived—as the result of corporate downsizing.

In America, our work-addicted culture programs us to define ourselves by the work we do, the salaries we earn, and the lifestyles afforded by our careers. It demands that most of our waking hours be dedicated to those identity-based jobs to maintain ourselves and our families. When those jobs are suddenly taken away through no fault of our own, there are precious few props to keep the displaced worker afloat. The popular wisdom says to get another job as fast as possible. Well-meaning human resources people hand the corporate refugee over to outplacement counselors, some of whom are hypercritical or insensitive to the emotional paralysis and resistance that are *normal* during post-layoff shock.

THE REFUGEE EXPERIENCE

Refugees never intend to leave their home country. They assume the holy soil in which they were born will also be their final resting place. In between, they will enjoy the familiarity, pleasures, and comforts of all that comes from their forebears: native language, communal customs, familiar terrain. Their joy in life will come from a deepening connection to these gifts while they improve and expand them for their progeny.

When they are made to leave their comfort zone for new territories because of persecution, repression, or rejection, these citizens suddenly have no birthright. They can no longer count on the protection of their home countries. The elements of choice and control, previously taken for granted, are ripped away. They seek refuge or asylum in a new environment they hope will be safe, secure, and prosperous, but find such places with widely varying degrees of success.

At best, their path is fraught with trauma. Suddenly rootless, refugees must regroup quickly and adjust to new terrain, language, even food. They must adapt to new customs and values as they let go of the traditional beliefs, taboos, and social stigma associated with their prior cultures. While struggling with loss, they must focus on the present and use all their survival skills to heal the trauma, violence, and loss that accompanied their move. Internally, refugees must be prepared to deal with periods of depression, waves of intense self-doubt, and bouts of self-pity. They have to develop support systems that will sustain and validate them along their way. And ultimately, they must reinvent themselves vocationally to regain a sense of self-worth and self-esteem, not to mention control over their lives.

Similarly, today's corporate refugee in America came of age during a time when corporations promised an unimpeded career path. Included in this covenant were loyalty, professional growth, personal renewal, financial stability, a life for one's family, and a pension through old age.

Now, however, no matter how many hours a dutiful employee puts into the job, no matter how many personal sacrifices are traded for the promise of a solid future, none of these efforts count when it comes to the exigencies of larger corporate or cultural economies. Downsizing, restructuring, and reengineering—relatively new terms that enter the twenty-first century already as clichés—along with the constant mergers and dissolutions of corporate entities, are the true determinants of our future.

In contrast to our parents' generation, we are being taught—almost hammered—by our educators, media pundits, and employers to be prepared for a lack of job security, a multiplicity of careers within our lifetime, and the need to constantly retrain and reinvent ourselves to be fit for the marketplace of the new millennium.

We are reliving, again and again, the refugee experience.

A Corporate Refugee is the brokenhearted (and, often, broken in general) outcast from the original paradigm, casting about the wilderness, awake—maybe for the first time—to his or her mortal plight and thereby experiencing what might be called a "spiritual emergency." Extreme stress and burnout exacerbate the role and identity losses that come with excommunication from one's "home" company. Further compounding the trauma are the onset of financial losses, questions about the future well-being of one's family and dependents, and a true identity crisis that can be paralyzing.

It's tough not to personalize this state of affairs or not to feel isolated and alone, even if others received their walking papers simultaneously. This book offers asylum for the Corporate Refugee and a blueprint both for psychological recovery from being cast out of the job and for surviving and thriving in one's chosen "new country." We'll look at who Corporate Refugees are, what's common or unique to the experience, how you can best prepare for the loss and change that come with corporate defection, and, ultimately, how you can develop a new resilience and greater sense of self for any future journeys through occupational change.

I learned from Alfred and Leo that there are two paths out of refugee status: one, a life journey fueled by anger, victimhood, and fear of moving onward; the other, Leo's, a proactive, optimistic path enriched by each lesson learned along the road from victim to victor.

May this book inspire you along Leo's path into a future you couldn't have imagined were it not for your first having been made a Corporate Refugee.

ONE

Downsizing:
The New "Normal"

The first step . . .
shall be to lose the way.

—GALWAY KINNELL

"We should call this group the Career Kevorkian Club!" Jessica blurted out as she scanned the room filled with fellow support group members. She followed her reference to the Michigan doctor who assisted many in ending their lives with, "Every one of us nearly gave our soul to a corporation that sucked us dry. Instead of rewarding us, they let us go. The only saving grace would be the mercy killing of our jobs."

The group burst into nervous laughter, not sure if Jessica really meant mercy killing, assisted suicide, or just plain murder. But slowly, one by one, the participants nodded in knowing agreement, and the label stuck. Each week someone in the group would ask, "So, who is the next among us to be *Kevorked?*" Or, in response to the all-too-familiar sob story of a new member, one of the veterans would muse, "Uh-oh, sounds like he needs to be *Kevorked.*"

Frank certainly would agree. Frank, fifty-two years old, was a senior engineer and vice president of technical services for a large

I

conglomerate, his only employer during his twenty-six years in the workforce. Frank was comfortable at his job—so comfortable that he describes himself as having been "asleep at the wheel" when the changes began.

His first brush with downsizing was the elimination of several positions at his company and the relocation of those remaining from Indianapolis to North Carolina. Frank, a lucky survivor of this first purge, agreed to a transfer even though his wife did not want to move. A year later, the company implemented another restructuring and yet another relocation. This time, Frank's wife refused to move. Frank, fearful of losing his job and benefits, commuted to Chicago while his family remained in North Carolina.

The final downsizing was the most heartbreaking. Frank and several other engineers were called to a meeting. Those being retained were led to one room. Those being downsized, which included Frank, were taken to another room and told they had ten minutes to clean out their desks and leave the premises. When one worker protested that he carpooled to work and had no way home, the meeting facilitator said someone would take the carpoolers home. Frank says he will never forget feeling like a criminal as he hurriedly threw his belongings in a box and left the company forever.

Looking back, Frank realizes there were many signs that further changes would follow that first reorganization. With each move, corporate managers were offered severance packages to leave "voluntarily." Rumors spread that threats of involuntary removal accompanied those "offers." Frank had stayed because he had invested so much time in the company and would soon be eligible for a healthy retirement pension. In the end, he was dumped, with no pension, a year short of earning his retirement benefits.

Frank is a victim of the new workplace reality: corporations would, he says, "sooner choose the young guys fresh out with their MBAs, willing to be transferred every year if necessary, than

> Who told you that you were permitted to settle in? Who told you that this or that would last forever? Did no one ever tell you that you will never feel at home in the world?
>
> —STANISLAW BARANCZAK

THE NUMBERS DON'T LIE

 In 1999, 55,000 to 70,000 workers per month, totaling approximately 750,000, were laid off, compared to only 100,000 in 1990. One in ten employees lost their jobs due to mergers and acquisitions, up 35 percent from 1998.

honor the years of blood, sweat, and tears put in by people like [me]." He identifies with the realities of refugees—people who are forced to leave their homeland because of persecution, repression, or rejection. Left with little choice or control, they must quickly adjust to new terrain, new language, and new customs.

STAGES OF LOSS AND RECOVERY

Dr. Elisabeth Kübler-Ross, in her now-classic book *On Death and Dying*, identified five stages of recovery that follow the death of a loved one. Her work was groundbreaking, not only for its attention to the then taboo subject of death and dying, but also for its suggestion that healing from loss takes time and includes definable stages. While certain primitive cultures compassionately allow a year of recovery time after a profound loss, we Westerners are given only a day or two off from work or school when someone close to us dies. Then we're expected back at our desks, and back to "normal." In fact, humans require far longer periods of recovery to return to optimal levels of physical, mental, and emotional functioning. Kübler-Ross suggested that we recover from profound loss only after passing through five stages: denial, bargaining, depression, anger, and, finally, acceptance.

William Bridges also writes about loss and has examined the process in many contexts, including that of career loss. In his seminal book, *Transitions: Making the Most of Personal Change*, written in the wake of his own career shift from college professor to gentleman farmer, Bridges explains that change occurs externally as an event, a moment in time. But its *impact* occurs internally and takes longer to process because of the shock and grief involved. He calls this process *transition*. In Bridges's transition paradigm, we experience, knowingly or not, three stages after a loss before we are truly ready to begin anew: the Ending, of the old way of doing and being; the Neutral Zone, a time of being "stuck in neutral, unable to go forward or backward"; and the New Beginning, when a new pattern of doing or being takes hold. Each stage is a process that takes time to complete and varies with each individual.

Like the stages of grief following a death, the stages experienced by Corporate Refugees can be placed along a similar continuum. There has been a "death" of one's job, with concurrent internal and external losses that must be grieved.

Along with any job or work role comes a structure. The physical part of that structure includes the nuts and bolts of the job itself, the team of coworkers, the hierarchy of decision-makers, and the physical environment in which one performs the work. Additionally, there are invisible aspects of that structure, including a sense of shared goals, the culture of the organization, the rewards for a job well done, and the psychological incentives toward further growth and creativity.

Over time, because we spend most of our waking hours in this work structure, the physical and psychological elements of our jobs become instrumental to our feelings of self-worth, productivity, financial well-being, and concept of the future. The job is so loaded with meaningful attributes that its loss is not simply the loss of a paycheck or of the work itself; it is the loss of a *structure* that literally and figuratively supported us and gave us a sense of self, a sense of meaning and purpose. Without that structure, we are, as Bridges put it, "between trapezes," hanging in midair, not at all sure whether we're going to catch the next bar or go crashing into some abyss.

Sometimes this blow is compounded by previous losses that have not yet healed. Many Refugees report experiencing frequent changes at the workplace before being let go, so that, for example, there is not enough time to recover from budget cuts in one's department before staff reductions occur. Then, as the worker is adjusting to the greater responsibilities that come with a reduced workforce, a new manager or CEO arrives with a whole new set of demands, and the transition process begins all over again.

Employees who identify with work at the expense of identifying with themselves will not survive in the new corporate workplace. It no longer matters if a worker is a good corporate citizen. It no longer matters if the worker is loyal, dedicated, driven, overworked, underpaid, or self-sacrificing. Nowadays, anyone can be discarded by a company.

Today's America is full of Refugees, a new breed of uprooted and unsettled workers. Some workers have been forced out due to downsizing; many are victims of an onslaught of mergers and acquisitions that have reached record numbers. They are our neighbors, our friends, and our relatives. They are ourselves—if not today, then almost certainly in the future.

THE HEADLINES
Nearly 28,000 workers laid off at Boeing in Seattle and Long Beach; 15,000 at Compaq Computer Corp. of Houston; 14,500 throughout the United States because of the British Petroleum–Amoco merger; 9,900 at Mitsubishi and 21,000 at Nissan, both Japanese companies employing workers in many countries.

Brad

Now thirty-four, Brad had been at a health care billing company providing tech support for six years when it was bought by a larger company. Although the employees were told in advance of the buy-out, they weren't prepared for the radical job cuts that came soon after the announcement. Brad describes the new owners as "having to lower the head count so it would look like a better buy."

At first, displaced workers were offered no severance, but they banded together and fought for it. Despite the group's best efforts, Brad ended up with only two weeks' salary for his six years of service.

For most of the laid-off workers, including Brad, this was their first experience of job loss. They were angry but proactive, believing their technical skills in a strong job market positioned them for easy recovery once recruiters were alerted to their plight. To celebrate their meager severance awards and bring closure to their loss, the laid-off employees held two "survival parties," for which Brad made piñatas in the shape of the president of the company. "People got a lot of release bashing their former boss in this playful way," Brad said. "Plus we got to see that it wasn't personal—this was a great group of people, all victims of a business decision that was out of our hands."

This first job loss became a gift as Brad recognized how much he disliked the medical-billing industry. A technology whiz, he polished his computer-based animation skills and got a teaching job at a technical college. Two good years followed, during which Brad developed close relationships with his fellow teachers and his boss, until, suddenly, that school was bought by a larger one. No notice was given to either set of employees until the day they were merged. Brad felt a strong sense of *déjà vu* as his job was reconfigured. At the time located in Hollywood, Brad and his colleagues were told on a Friday to report the following Monday to a new office in Burbank, thirty-five miles away. Their arrival totally shocked their new colleagues, who hadn't been told the new workers were coming.

The original group had been a tight team with much camaraderie. Once merged, however, members of the group were dispersed to three disparate areas and not allowed to see each other on a daily basis. They were not given desks, and when they tried to use existing workstations, the Burbank employees would chase them away. Brad coped by constantly assigning himself new tasks and focusing on his teaching. "When I was teaching, I was fine. But between those classes, I was miserable."

Six months later, Brad was unceremoniously downsized out of his job. His team of teachers was given no warning of an impending job change. In fact, on the day Brad was fired, his boss had asked him to use his connections to get the school licensed on a particular software. Brad made the calls and successfully arranged the licensing process. Later that day, he went in to celebrate with his boss his quick consummation of the deal. Instead, this same boss told Brad that he no longer had a job. Brad was able to get some personal satisfaction by immediately interrupting the licensing process, but he had to leave the premises the same day with no severance, no notice, and no outplacement help.

Brad was numb with shock. He thought he'd made a good career choice a couple of years before when computer animation was the hottest field around. Not only had there been a huge hiring boom, but the field also requires artistic and technical skills, both of which are his passions. Teachers had been in great demand, and students were often hired right out of the classroom by large studios paying huge salaries to young people willing to work 60- to 80-hour work-weeks.

When some of the animated films did poorly at the box office, however, more and more production companies consolidated or went out of business. The result was a glutted marketplace. Many animators are still in shock at being in constant demand one week and expendable the next. Brad says, "Though I love teaching, I've basically been preparing my students to take all the jobs I could qualify for. Now that the industry needs fewer trained animators, I see that I would have been better off sinking roots in a production company where I could stay put, instead of training the very people who would take the few remaining jobs."

Carol Lloyd, in her book, *Creating a Life Worth Living*, calls Brad's role "the midwife syndrome." Such jobs, Lloyd says, "put you in the role of fostering and developing other artists . . . you're cleaning up after the lion when you want to *be* the lion . . . [thereby] neglecting yourself as an artist." Even though these jobs paid the bills, a creative professional like Brad loses more than his job when the layoffs come: he becomes cynical about the medium itself, not to mention his own identity as an artist in his own right.

Although Brad again came up with a plan to find work as an animator in a production company while pursuing his creative passions for music and book writing, he's now in the throes of grief after three job changes in three years. He feels fearful financially, so he's uncomfortable taking much time off. Yet his self-worth is shaky, and he dreads going out on job interviews. He's angry but doesn't know "whom to be angry with, since the industry as a whole seems to be wiping out."

Jessica, Frank, and Brad, along with millions of other Americans, are Corporate Refugees, innocent victims of business forces beyond their control. Displaced from their jobs as corporations merge, die, shift, and change, these hardworking, dedicated employees become fearful wanderers. As the number of yearly job-cut announcements grows, it becomes harder and harder to avoid joining the ranks of this group. Many displaced workers have experienced multiple job losses and no longer trust corporate employers.

Are You a Corporate Refugee? is designed to show the way for this displaced workforce to survive and thrive. It will alert you to signs that you may no longer fit in your corporate culture and may soon be discarded. It will help you survive the turbulent time immediately after leaving or losing a job, guiding you through a five-stage path to personal and vocational renewal. The chapters are designed so that no matter what stage you are in when you pick up the book, you will glean information to help you move forward in your journey. Here are the recovery stages you'll learn about:

Stage 1: On the Brink. The period when you know that something is amiss and that Refugee status is imminent.

Stage 2: Letting Go. The phase during which you leave the workplace, become a Refugee, and learn how to grieve.

Stage 3: In the Wilderness. The period of time during which the Refugee is wandering, desperate for a new home.

Stage 4: Seeing the Beacon. A time of great ideas, false starts, and gradual enlightenment, when the wanderer finally encounters the light that augurs a new world ahead.

Stage 5: In the New Land. The period of renewal when the Refugee has found firm footing in a new reality, one that begins a brand new cycle.

HOW TO USE THIS BOOK

As you explore the stages and find your place along the Refugee journey, you can maximize your progress and your healing by making the following commitments to yourself:

Expect to Be Transformed
Determine that your Refugee journey will be a defining experience in your life. The best attitude is one that rebuilds your basic resilience

and hardiness, rather than dwells in victimhood or gets stuck in grief or shame, and which educates you not only about your own unique ways of handling job loss and change, but, more important, prepares you for the likelihood of ongoing shifts and changes in the marketplace of the new millennium. This way you'll have a template for recovery should your career bring future Refugee experiences your way. Intend for transformation to be an outcome of your loss, and you won't be surprised when it shows up at the door.

Find Your Place in the Refugee Journey

Learning and working through the stages will facilitate your optimal recovery. Each stage is defined by its entry point, its process, and the completion that moves the Refugee into his or her next stage. Although the stages are delineated with internal and external signposts, they are, in truth, fluid and organic, often overlapping one another.

Study the signposts and be clear about their meaning in your particular experience. Perhaps you've already passed the Brink and are fully dealing with Letting Go. If you recognize that you've done considerable grief work, you might feel the Wilderness is your present home. Feel free to move ahead to the chapter(s) that speak to where you are in your journey, but don't be afraid to look back at descriptions of the earlier stages if you find yourself unable to move forward.

Replace Uncertainty with Structure

Each stage of the Refugee journey is riddled with uncertainty. To help you deal with such uncertainties as well as the loss of structure that was provided by your prior job, you'll find in this book Interim Structures designed specifically for each stage of the Refugee journey. Each Structure has three components: Daily Rituals, for maintaining your basic health; essential Actions, to move you through each stage; and optional After Hours strategies, to deepen your healing and expedite your recovery. As you complete the work of one stage and move into the next, you'll find that each Interim Structure builds upon the work you have accomplished to that point.

Try as many Actions as possible within each Interim Structure. They provide subtle, profound, and overarching support as you move through your entire recovery experience. When you've completed your journey and arrived in the New Land, many of the Daily Rituals and healing strategies you learn will become lifelong tools to keep you physically, mentally, and emotionally balanced. With ongoing practice, you will stay steady on your feet long after your Refugee experience has passed.

Test Your Readiness for the Next Leg of Your Journey by Dipping into the Backpacks

At the end of each chapter, you'll find a Backpack for the Road. These Backpacks contain questions to test your readiness for the next stage of your journey. Your responses to the questions will not only tell you where you stand as each stage winds down but will also become a document of your travels as you move closer to the New Land.

Remember, each stage of the Refugee journey is a process that takes its own sweet time. If you rush forward prematurely, you'll be catapulted back for lack of readiness. Only by fully experiencing each of the Interim Structures will you get back on the road as quickly as possible. It's in your best interest to take the time each stage demands.

Roadblocks and Pit Stops

Every difficult journey has potential roadblocks that test your tenacity or tease you into shortcuts that can become dead ends. This book anticipates those roadblocks and provides Pit Stops between some of the more difficult stages—both to nourish your flagging spirit and to suggest concrete steps you can take while your psychological recovery work continues. Contrary to the Interim Structures, which are essential actions, the resources offered in the Pit Stops are optional.

Tools for the Road

For each leg of your journey, three types of supportive tools are provided to maximize your Refugee experience and guide you to a gratifying New Land:

- Facts for thought, represented by ☞, offer current, enlightening information.

- Resources, represented by 💡, contain further readings, networking opportunities, and online resources to expedite the suggested action steps.

- Inspirational quotes, represented by ☀, provide encouragement to stay the course and open your imagination to the unlimited possibilities that lie ahead.

Voyagers discover that the world can never be larger
than the person that is in the world; but it is impossible
to foresee this, it is impossible to be warned.

—JAMES BALDWIN

TWO

Stage I:
On Your Turf . . .
Or On the Brink?

The bond between a man and his profession is similar to that which ties him to his country: it is just as complex, often ambivalent, and in general it is understood completely only when it is broken.

—PRIMO LEVI

Annie, age forty-seven, is a sales and marketing executive for a real estate development organization on the brink of disaster as its stock value plummets under threats of a takeover or buyout. A longtime employee who has landed many big deals for her company, Annie earns a great salary. She has always enjoyed her job—that is, except for the past year, when she began to feel railroaded by a new boss fifteen years her junior. Despite having recently spent 60-hour workweeks to close two huge deals, Annie received a performance review of 1.5 (out of five), along with "slandering put-downs," from her boss. When Annie pressed for details, she was given vague and negative answers. She called two attorneys, both of whom said that until she was fired she could not sue for damages. Annie crafted a brilliant rebuttal to her review and copied it to the head of human resources. Still, while awaiting a response, Annie is in shock and pain—she is On the Brink.

Greg, forty-three, is a twenty-five-year veteran of a large telecommunications company. He commutes one hour each way to

13

a job that is becoming harder and harder each year as downsizing reduces the number of people in his work teams. Even with these negatives, Greg fears losing the security of the big company. He used to believe that, by refusing promotions, staying specialized within his engineering niche, and producing more than his requisite numbers from year to year, he was protected from the corporate chopping block. But now warnings of his ouster surround him as longtime colleagues are "packaged out." Each day Greg draws closer to the Brink.

On the Brink—Stage 1 in the journey of the Refugee—is marked by signs within the company that things are changing. Over time, job descriptions or expectations change unpredictably as more and more work is piled on, more and more responsibilities are assigned for which workers may not be technologically or experientially prepared, and too little time is devoted to recovery from previous changes.

Word comes down that budget cuts are needed. Workers hear that news as code for "Watch out! Our jobs are at risk." Whole departments might be cut if it is determined they are not producing bottom-line results. Some workers become proactive and update their resumes. More often, people go into shock or denial and are unable to make any decisions, in spite of persistent intuitive rumbling. The possibility of their becoming Refugees may flit through their thoughts, but more often, disbelief takes over. Typically, there is a long period of holding on that is characteristic of being On the Brink.

Some of this holding on is encouraged by the mixed messages from management. Rumors of downsizing build, but they often are the fodder of the complaint mill rather than an impetus for our making any changes. We become so attached to our work that even if we have lots of complaints, the complaints become part of our deeply held identities. As dedicated workers, we feel we are doing the best possible job, often with amazing numbers to prove our contributions to the company's growth. Surely, we rationalize, our jobs will be protected from the chopping block; we are too valuable to be eliminated. Ironically, this thinking pervades even those who have suffered previous Refugee experiences with other companies.

Employees may query management as to the future of their jobs, yet many people aren't told the full story because upper management feels the timing is not right. Instead, we get reassurances from our supervisors, which lead us to relax and feel safe, even though we may be axed after all. Or, managers assure us of our indispensability in the morning, only to hand us a pink slip with our paycheck in the afternoon. Employers say this is done to prevent hostile employees at termination time. After all, they say, what if disgruntled outcasts go on a destructive rampage or put a virus in the computer before leaving the company? In all fairness, some companies terminate employees with more notice and concern. But more often than not, workers are displaced with little notice or choice.

Sherry

Sherry, fifty-four, devoted twenty-three years to climbing the ranks of a nonprofit, community-based hospital system. During the last several years, she was a corporate vice president in charge of so many functions it would take three people to replace her. This hospital was known for its rehabilitation program, treating seriously brain-injured patients and stroke victims, trauma patients, and the indigent who came in repeatedly after street fights, falls, and other injuries. Sherry had authority over all the managed-care and business development areas of the hospital. She was also in charge of case management throughout the continuum of care, covering therapists (rehab and social service), nursing, three outside clinics, home health agencies, and administration. She sat on three boards that took up many of her evenings—to the point that her husband felt neglected. Nevertheless, he was incredibly proud of his high-powered mate of thirty years. Most nights he fell asleep while Sherry sat up in bed, with piles of work.

At the hospital, Sherry was a bright light for staff and patients alike. So charismatic and gifted at organizational development, she was always a part of the recruitment of upper management. Sherry designed team-building and information-sharing programs that resulted in her facility becoming the shining star in an eighteen-hospital system.

During Sherry's tenure, the hierarchical system of president, vice president, and descending ranks was transformed into a highly creative management structure called "the Office of the President." Sherry and one counterpart were the two senior VPs under George, the president whom she had helped recruit and to whom she became a "working soulmate" (her words) over the years. Under the two VPs sat directors who each supervised their respective branches of the hospital. For nearly a decade, this system worked exquisitely well, with growth and an *esprit de corps* that were the envy of competing hospitals, many of which courted this one for merger potential.

Then came trouble. The hospital's parent company purchased three hospitals whose revenues weren't adequate to carry their own weight. When a joint venture with yet another hospital system failed, a directive came down that all divisions, particularly rehab, had to become solvent by the end of the calendar year. As Sherry worked feverishly to make the deadline, her colleagues voted to bring in an external consultant to expedite the process and suggest potential cost cuts. After a national search for the right consultant, the team voted for the least expensive applicant, with Sherry as the lone dissenting vote. She had a bad feeling about this consultant, whom she saw as "a steamroller, mean-spirited, and insensitive to the needs of our special population of patients."

To add insult to injury, George, Sherry's supposed "soulmate and best friend at work," told the consultant all of Sherry's objections, immediately setting up a difficult working relationship. George also decided the executive level should set the stage by modeling the changes that lower divisions would have to experience. As fixed staff was reduced, and the Office of the President was reorganized back to the old hierarchical model, Sherry and her counterpart were constantly reassured by George that they were essential and would stay on board, albeit with reorganized duties. Many of their previous responsibilities would be outsourced.

Things happened fast, and Sherry had less and less access to George. Still, she trusted her friend and felt she could rely on his reassurances. One day, while giving a speech at an important meeting on Medicare downtown, Sherry was paged and told that she was needed at a meeting at the hospital. This hastily called session, which included all the top managers, came at the end of a Friday, which seemed curious to Sherry. But she had no time to question it. Instead, she focused on her speech and then rushed through weekend traffic, barely getting back to the hospital in time.

In George's office, Sherry found herself to be the focus of the meeting! Alongside George sat the new consultant and the hospital's chief financial officer. They showed her a reconstituted organizational chart and explained her new role. Unbeknownst to her, Sherry's counterpart VP had been laid off that afternoon. On this new chart, Sherry's role was down at the third tier, reporting to the CFO, who previously had been at her same level; her job now included many of her counterpart's prior responsibilities. To top it all off, her title was to be controller, the job she had had twenty-three years earlier when she first came to the hospital. All line authority and case management responsibilities were taken away from her. The departments she had nurtured and made famous within the region were gone from her job description. Sherry was in shock and told them she needed the weekend to decide whether she would accept the new position.

When Sherry walked out of that room, she felt paralyzed with disbelief and deep betrayal. How could George have deceived her all this time? She walked numbly to her office, where her entire staff sat waiting to hear the news. They naturally thought she'd be put in charge of everything and were prepared to celebrate her new role. Instead, they joined in her dismay and left the hospital that evening feeling like shell-shocked war casualties.

Over that weekend, Sherry racked her brain to figure out why she didn't see this coming. Her husband was furious at George, whom he knew well after entertaining him and his family countless times in their home. They cursed George's spinelessness in being unable to look Sherry in the eye during the meeting and for making himself unavailable afterward.

Sherry's husband had long been begging Sherry to cut back or just quit this taxing job so they could have more time together, but Sherry's commitment had always been astounding. She couldn't imagine quitting, not until this weekend. By Sunday evening, Sherry had determined that this would be her exit. She felt it would be too heartbreaking to watch staffs be decimated, her own roles shredded, and the patients subjected to substandard care. There was no choice but to resign. Before she did, however, Sherry had a sudden intuitive need to go to human resources and look at her employee file. She wanted to see what future employers might see.

What she saw added salt to her open wound. There were no negative reviews in there. But Sherry discovered that she—who had the most responsibilities at the VP level, the longest tenure of any executive on staff, and supposedly the "most favored confidential status" with George—was the second-lowest executive in pay! All those years of extra work and effort had garnered her none of the benefits Sherry thought she deserved: pay raises that recognized her contributions to the hospital, the truth from George about what was coming down from the reorganization *vis-à-vis* her job, and some appropriate closure from George and the physicians she had served.

Veronica

Veronica, on the other hand, admits she could have predicted her job loss, but she preferred to rationalize its unlikelihood. A clinical psychologist at the same hospital as Sherry for seven years, Veronica was the only Ph.D. left after many cuts to the social services and rehab departments. Through almost daily staff reductions, Veronica hung on. She was there when Sherry was reeling from the decisions being made at the VP level. Yet Veronica remained certain she'd be spared somehow.

Although Veronica kept long hours at the hospital to get everything done, she was not paid overtime. To make ends meet, she developed a small private practice that she operated on weekends. When the inevitable end came, it was her private practice that kept Veronica sane.

Instead of receiving notice and a severance package, Veronica was told that some irregularities mentioned in a patient's deposition, plus a single complaint from another patient's family, were grounds for her firing. The deposed patient turned out not to be hers, but even when the responsible person was acknowledged, there was no apology from management. Similarly, the second patient complaint was immaterial: the family of a brain-injured patient had wanted Veronica to disallow smoking in hopes that it would force the patient to quit. But because of the patient's traumatic injury, Veronica had suggested that a smoking cessation program should occur later, so further trauma would be reduced and the patient's healing could proceed more easily. The family made a formal complaint. This six-month-old episode nevertheless became grounds for Veronica's dismissal. Colleagues, including Sherry, told her that the outside consultant was looking for every possible way to cut costs, and that firing staff was cheaper than laying them off with severance. An attorney suggested that Veronica's vindication would cost more in legal expenses than it could potentially resolve. He advised cutting her losses and moving on.

Both Veronica's and Sherry's grief includes the "shoulda coulda woulda's" of wishing they'd seen this coming. But when one is in the trenches while downsizing and reorganizing are going on, it's natural to be hopeful, to assume our commitment and value to the company will be recognized and our job spared. Eventually though, people On the Brink realize they are approaching the edge of the cliff, and soon the question that looms ominously overhead, like Damocles' sword, is, "Will I jump, or will I be pushed?"

SIGNPOSTS

Constant change has caused many workers to try and "go with the flow" to keep their jobs even though they may hate the types of changes taking place. They rationalize this behavior by claiming their need for a paycheck, their attachment to retirement or health benefits, or their family's dependence on their incomes. Yet the healthiest solutions for people in this stage are to pay attention to the signs of potential change and to *come out of denial*. Here are some indicators that should serve as warnings that your job is likely to be impacted by radical workplace changes:

- Workers learn of company changes in the morning paper.

- People stop talking openly and directly to each other, whispering gossip in the halls instead of working.

- You get left out of important meetings you once attended.

- Your boss has no time to meet with you.

- There are more closed-door meetings.

- Resumes are accidentally left in the copy machines.

- "Voluntary" severance packages are announced.

- Rumor mills thrive.

- Older executives and supervisors are hounded into taking a severance package.

- Frequent reorganizations occur, even if just within departments or divisions.

- Perks, such as expense accounts, assistants, and budgets, get reduced or eliminated.

- Vacancies are left unfilled.

- Vague reassurances come from the human resources department but clearly sound hollow.

• In companies where you can't take it with you, the number of people taking sick leave goes up. They know they won't be getting a check for their accumulated sick days, so they call in sick Monday through Friday until it's used up.

• You're asked to write a job description.

• Budgets are cut, causing managers to compete for funds; sometimes there are frenetic screaming matches when, for example, marketing argues that it's a more important department than engineering and therefore deserves the higher dollars.

• New software is installed that has the potential to cut jobs.

• After mergers are announced, damage-control teams enter the workplace to assure employees that there are no plans for layoffs.

• You read the business plan for the coming year, and your role is nowhere to be seen.

In addition to these visible markers—or to the changes you've already had to adapt to during turbulent reorganizations of your workplace—internal signals are trying to get your attention. Rather than rationalize or deny them, be alert to such indicators of trouble on the horizon as:

• constant feelings of powerlessness in a frequently changing workplace;

• self-doubt and fear that you'll not be able to begin again, having already given up so much for your job;

• the lure of "golden handcuffs" (a retirement package), which causes you to constantly calculate the Rule of 75 (in which you are granted lifetime insurance and profit-sharing when your age and years of service total 75) or the amount of time you have left until you are fully vested in your retirement benefits;

• staggering workloads and extended hours eventually causing overwhelming feelings of preoccupation and exhaustion;

• feeling that if you don't work overtime, you may lose your job;

• a free-floating anxiety that you don't vocalize, based on feeling not trusted, communicated with, or valued;

• a feeling of *déjà vu:* since sequential job losses have occurred to many people, there are losses of self-confidence and meaning when the external signals show up again;

• the blahs, in which, while waiting for the ax to fall, you lack motivation and worry about either your diminished interest in the work or your inability to do the work you like in a more supportive environment;

• the fear that you've lost connections to the structure that once felt reliable and to coworkers who seem not to be telling you everything;

• the Chicken Little syndrome, in which you fear the world is about to end and that disaster, financial destitution, and loss and change are just around the corner;

• suffering from sleep disturbances, appetite changes, and frequent colds and flus, even if you were previously hardy and resilient;

• questions from your family about your work situation, resulting in the burden of carrying their fears of loss and worries about money on top of your own.

All of these markers signify the beginning of chronic unrest and uncertainty—hallmarks of the Refugee experience. The ground is shifting; a nomadic existence seems imminent. While the natural inclination is to cling to the known, there are clearly serious fractures in the foundation that used to support you. The structure is unstable; it may crash at any time. It's therefore essential that you build a temporary structure that will provide some semblance of safety and control.

STABILIZING THE GROUND BENEATH YOUR FEET

Since most people On the Brink are still working, there is an external structure in place. It includes a given number of hours on the job, plus the requisite time necessary to manage the essentials of daily living, such as food shopping, laundry, home maintenance, time with family and friends. For most of us, this is a very full day—so full that adding more activities seems nearly impossible.

When you are On the Brink, however, you must face the realities of your situation to prevent a later collapse. Most people in this stage have options but don't create the time and necessary focus to explore them. Far more constructive, however, is a gradual implementation of actions that will stabilize you during this frightening stage. While this means adding yet more tasks to your already hectic schedule, you'll be rewarded by their profound impact on your difficult Refugee journey. If you incorporate the suggested actions as soon as possible, you'll protect your health, your finances, your relationships, and your career—not to mention your emotional well-being as a Refugee. There are three categories of actions suggested for this stage as well as for those to come:

- The Daily Rituals—four fundamental behaviors that will gradually become the infrastructure for your entire Refugee journey.

- Actions—proactive strategies designed to expedite your passage, especially through the Brink stage.

- After Hours—supplementary options to augment your work during this stage.

Taken together, these components comprise an Interim Structure you'll come to rely on as you move through the Brink and subsequent stages. Rather than feeling helpless to affect the changes happening around you, you can, instead, take charge of the Brink.

As you embark on the Interim Structure that follows, establish your goals for this stage. Ideally, they should include:

- coming out of denial about the possibility of losing your job;

- developing daily self-care rituals that will fortify your health and help you deal with the uncertainties of being On the Brink;

- creating time for introspection, networking, and brainstorming about your options.

THE DAILY RITUALS

Your Morning Journal

Buy yourself a journal with a cover that contains imagery symbolic of your inner journey through the Brink stage. It may be a blank book to remind you to stay open to any possibilities; it could have an inspirational image or message you want to read each morning as you write; or it could be a spiral-bound Mickey Mouse notebook to remind you not to take yourself too seriously.

You may need to get out of bed a half hour earlier than usual to give yourself the time, but it's best if you can "journal" first thing in the morning, before your day gets away from you. First thing each morning, sit peacefully at your desk, at the kitchen counter, or in your garden, and write whatever occurs to you. You might

For an in-depth explanation of the benefits of daily journaling, read *The Artist's Way* by Julia Cameron (J. P. Tarcher, 1992). "The morning pages (sometimes the mourning pages) acquaint you with yourself in a new way. You are free to feel and be exactly as you are in the moment. The pages are completely accepting. Do not tame your pages. Extreme emotions, judgments and reactions all are part of what the pages help clarify and ground."

AN OVERVIEW OF THE INTERIM STRUCTURE
FOR STAGE I: ON THE BRINK

Goals While On the Brink

- Come Out of Denial
- Develop Daily Self-Care Rituals
- Create Time for Introspection, Networking, and Brainstorming

Daily Rituals

- Your Morning Journal
- Watch Your Diet
- Physical Fitness for On the Brink
- Decompression Ritual
- Get Those ZZZs

After Hours

- Moonlighting
- Crafty Stressbusters

Actions

I. Find Out What's Really Happening in Your Company

- Reconnaissance
- Become an Intrapreneur
- Justified Paranoia

II. Seize the Day While There's Still Time

- Network, Network, Network
- Get Organized
- Retool
- Use Your Benefits

III. Get a Grip

- Financial Preparation
- Simplify
- In and Out
- Circle the Wagons

IV. Jump Ship?

anticipate and write about your coming workday. You might analyze the inner and outer markers that suggest your job is at risk. You might tune in to your emotions and simply write what's there. Commit to filling one page in your journal (more is okay!), then get on with your day. There's no need to read what you've written from day to day; just dump your feelings onto the page, close the book, and you've met your commitment.

If you feel empty, stay committed to this exercise and write a statement of your emptiness enough times to fill the requisite page: "This is a stupid exercise; I feel numb and empty." It's unlikely you will write such a sentence more than ten or twenty times before some additional feeling or awareness pops up. The point of journaling is to give you a forum for expressing and externalizing the stress you experience as you endure the Brink. As a creative writer, Brad, whom we met in chapter one, thrived on the work he did in his daily journal. Venting his feelings and experiences in writing not only was cathartic, he says, but also saved his marriage from getting bogged down by his continual complaints. He vented in the journal, then moved on, knowing he could vent more the next day. The journal is not the only place to vent, since you may share your feelings with family, friends, and colleagues, but writing in a journal has many benefits beyond mere venting, including:

- the freedom to express anything and everything that occurs to you, in whatever manner and language you feel like using;

- the privacy to be yourself without consideration for other people's reaction to your thoughts or feelings;

- the insights you'll gain as deeper feelings find their way onto the blank page;

- opportunities for creative self-expression that you may not have been aware you were capable of had you not been forced to express yourself in writing.

Above all, your journal will become an indispensable healing tool throughout your Refugee journey, not only as a document of your progress but also as a place to do written exercises that will be suggested in later stages. Now, while you're On the Brink, is the time to become habituated to the use of your journal by writing at the same time each day.

Watch Your Diet

Your diet has great impact on your daily health as you deal with the stress of the Brink. Better to focus on healthful nutrition and replace overeating with exercise than to wear your job stress in the form of extra pounds that will further lower your self-esteem.

Emma

Nurses at the hospital at which Sherry and Veronica worked have been "quaking in their boots" while department after department is cut in waves of downsizing. Because they need their jobs, most have determined to hang on in hopes they'll be deemed essential and maintained. Emma, one of the dedicated nurses in the now skeletal rehab department, describes the great quantities of food the nursing staff orders in for each shift.

"This is how we manage our stress, I'm afraid," Emma reports. "When we talk about what's happening all around us, we try to assure each other it'll be okay. After all, Jason works round-the-clock at the expense of nearly neglecting his kids. Surely they'll see his dedication and spare him from losing the job he relies on to support his family. Then there's Kathy, who's the lone recreation therapist left in our department. She already puts in 12-hour days, taking patients out into the community to teach them how to use their wheelchairs during trips to the grocery store and doctors' offices.

Who will do that if they cut her? We shore up by feeling indispensable, yet we're eating our stress into numbness. Is that denial?"

Yes, that is denial! There's no question of Emma, Jason, and Kathy's value to the patients in their care. But downsizing is not about you; it's about cutting costs.

Are you denying the reality of your situation through overeating? Look at how and what you are eating as you move through this stage. Focus on nutrient-dense foods, such as vegetables and fruits, to maintain your energy, boost your immune system, and reduce your risk of weight gain. If you consider yourself a "junk-food-junkie," now is the time to gradually implement healthy eating patterns that will keep you well-nourished and nutritionally balanced from this stage onward. For snacks, trade pizza, potato chips, cookies, and high-fat foods for low-fat muffins, whole-grain crackers and pretzels, and foods high in fiber, such as dried fruits, raisins, and fig bars. For your meals, avoid processed foods including packaged, quick-fix products and fast foods; instead, emphasize lean meats and fish, fresh vegetables, and whole grains such as brown rice, beans, and legumes. Take charge of your diet, knowing that poor food choices combined with the stress of being On the Brink can put you in danger of illness, fatigue, and possibly even more serious conditions such as heart disease, hypertension, and diabetes.

FOR QUICK NUTRITION EDUCATION

• The American Dietetic Association provides up-to-date research, menu ideas, books, and newsletters at their Web site www.eatright.com.

• At Meals for You (www.mealsforyou.com) you'll not only find recipes and menus subdivided into such categories as weight loss, vegetarian, or gourmet, but you can also get a specific shopping list for your chosen meal, nutritional information, and preparation times.

• For healthy take-out food, visit Food.Com (www.food.com), which partners with more than 12,000 restaurants nationwide to bring your order to your door within 30 minutes of your e-mail request.

Physical Fitness for the Brink

Most of us collect stress in our bodies, whether or not we are aware of it. During the Brink, feelings of shock, denial, and free-floating anxiety multiply the daily stresses and compromise the immune system. Commit to regular exercise to externalize your stress, help you sleep, and keep you in touch with your body's signals of distress. Set up a system to make yourself accountable for working out. It could be ritualizing an exercise routine so it's scheduled for the same time each day. It could be arranging for partner workouts so you have someone with whom to share and be accountable. Joining an evening athletic league is another good way to get you to show up for fun exercise. You're not likely to let down a friend or team that depends on you. Exercise adherence rates are highest for partner-based workouts and lowest for videos and exercise tapes.

It's also important to practice all four of the components of fitness: cardiovascular (aerobic) exercise, strength training, flexibility workouts, and balance work. If you are new to such a regimen, treat yourself to a one-time assessment with a fitness trainer to get a baseline for ongoing work throughout all the coming Refugee stages. Learn the essentials of breathing, postural alignment, and muscular awareness. Take advantage of free introductory offers at health clubs for this purpose. If you haven't been working out regularly, this may sound like a frivolous suggestion, but in fact, you'll be delighted by how much better you'll feel and by how dramatically exercise can reduce your stress.

At a minimum, the following exercise strategies should be undertaken during the Brink stage:

- Ten minutes of movement at least twice each day, such as walking up and down stairs and stretching, neck and shoulder rolls while standing or sitting at your desk, and basic whole body stretches.

- On the weekends, more extended exercise sessions, such as cycling, hiking, or seasonal sports such as skiing, waterskiing, skating, swimming, tennis, and golf.

- Slow body movement, such as tai chi or similar focused movement routines.

LOCAL RESOURCES

Bicycling clubs or organized rides are sponsored by local bike shops. Hiking trips along local paths can be arranged using local trail maps or through the Sierra Club, state parks, and city recreation centers. Yoga, tai chi, and body movement classes are available at the YMCA/YWCA and listed in local recreation guides and newspaper listings.

The bottom line is that you make the commitment and prioritize exercise routines. Write them into your daily calendar so they become as important as the rest of your appointments.

Here are some exercise remedies *specific to the symptoms* many people suffer On the Brink. As you experiment with these, add others and keep the list posted on your refrigerator or bathroom mirror. When such symptoms occur, simply refer to these options, and DO THEM.

- For free-floating anxiety: Do extended bouts of cardiovascular work or interval training. Also, any gross motor movements will work, such as stomping and shaking your hands and your body. Body movement classes encourage all of these movements, but feel free to do them in the privacy of your own home.

- For feelings of apprehension, even about exercising: Just do it! Tackle new exercise modes with consistent but bite-sized diligence. Get in touch with your own personal power: find out where in your body your fear is located, then use deep breathing or screaming or stomping your feet to externalize the fear and thereby release it. Acting and dance classes are great for this as they teach you how to access and express emotions through movement.

ACT YOUR WAY OUT OF ANXIETY AND FEAR

Acting classes can be found in the Yellow Pages (under Drama Instruction) as well as in local adult education guides, trade papers, and online indexes.

- For anger: Push hard through a strength workout.

- For bodily tension: Try power yoga or sports stretching classes or videotapes.

Decompression Ritual

While flirting with the Brink, most workers are obsessed with the stresses of their jobs. We often work long overtime hours in the hope that we'll be seen as more committed, as so valuable that we surely should be spared a layoff. We often bring work home, or do nothing but shoptalk with family or friends, who quickly feel neglected or bored by the obsessed worker.

It's essential to establish a daily behavior that separates the work portion of your day from the nonwork hours left for yourself and your family. Your decompression ritual could be something physical, such as a stop at the gym for a fitness class or workout, a walk in a park or quiet neighborhood, or something calming, such as yoga or a meditation class.

Another decompression strategy could be to claim the first twenty minutes after you walk in the door at the end of your workday as your own. Request that your family not ask for your attention. Rather, go straight to your bedroom, change out of your work clothes, and maybe stretch out for a short nap or take a hot bath. Alternatively, you could lean back in an easy chair, listen to relaxing music through headphones, and practice deep breathing to release the stress of the day. Twenty minutes of deliberate decompression will do wonders for releasing the stress of the day's events and worries.

DECOMPRESSION IDEAS

•Don't wear a watch during the evening or weekend.

•Change clothes as soon as you get home from work.

•Leave your briefcase/pager/cell phone in the car, or at least by the door. Don't let them intrude on your home life.

•If you must work at home, do so only in one place, preferably out of the way. Don't take work to bed, or spread it at the table while you eat.

•Start your decompression ritual before you leave the office. Cover the computer. Tidy your desk. Take off your tie or put on sneakers. Turn the calendar to the next day, and then go home.

Get Those ZZZZs

Along with good nutrition and regular exercise, sleep during this stage is critical. Nothing undermines health like inadequate sleep. Not only is the immune system further compromised (your stress level is already taking its toll), but also efficiency, mood, attention span, driving reactions—basically all of our day-to-day functioning—depend on good rest. Be conscientious about getting to bed at the same reasonable hour each night. Aim to get a minimum of seven—preferably

DID YOU KNOW . . . ?

Those who sleep fewer than six hours a night don't live as long as those who sleep seven hours or more.

eight—hours' sleep nightly, and take relaxation breaks throughout the day, ideally ten minutes every two hours.

At first glance, incorporating the Daily Rituals of journaling, exercising, healthy eating, and decompressing at day's end may sound overwhelming. Slow down and realize that you are probably already doing some of these behaviors but not in a focused way. Simply choose which of the rituals you want to implement first and focus only on that for a week or two. For example, begin your day with your journal, and, once that ritual has become comfortable and reliable, keep it going and add at least ten minutes per day of focused aerobic exercise. As you maintain the exercise ritual, your body will slowly demand longer workouts and you'll achieve the goal of a thirty-minute routine before you know it.

Once your journal and exercise rituals have been established, focus on your food choices:

•Are you launching your day with a healthy breakfast?

•Do you leave your workplace for a healthy lunch rather than eat on the run or at your desk?

•Do you plan your dinner menus so they are low-fat, high-fiber, well-balanced meals that you can enjoy peacefully with your family or by yourself?

Finally, design your daily decompression ritual based on the unique stresses of your job, your energy level, your preferences, and the demands of your family. Introduce and habituate this final ritual—or maybe combine it with your exercise routine—so that your day becomes punctuated

SLEEP TIPS

For great information about sleep and tips for overcoming sleep disorders, visit www.sleep-net.com or read *The Promise of Sleep: A Pioneer in Sleep Medicine Explains the Vital Connection Between Health, Happiness and a Good Night's Sleep* by William Dement (Dell, 2000) or *Sleep Thieves: An Eye-Opening Exploration into the Science and Mysteries of Sleep* by Stanley Coren (Free Press, 1997). If you respond to gentle, guided, auditory suggestion, try *Easing into Sleep,* a powerful audiotape program by Emmett Miller, M.D.

READINGS IN NUTRITION

See *Jane Brody's Nutrition Book* (Bantam, 1989) and E. Somer's *Age-Proof Your Body: Your Complete Guide to Lifelong Vitality* (Quill, 1999). Both books assess your diet for optimal health, sleep, and stress management.

by the self-nourishing benefits of your Daily Rituals. In no time, they will become automatic behaviors for self-care.

ACTIONS

It's tough to wait for the ax to fall while you are On the Brink. Rather than waiting passively, take preemptive steps to stabilize your health and spirit through this uncertain stage. The Actions to take while On the Brink are divided into four categories:

• First, size up your situation within your workplace.

• Second, seize the day, get organized, and use the benefits you still have on this job.

• Third, get a grip and shore up those emotional ups and downs.

• Finally, decide whether it's time to jump ship.

I. Find Out What's *Really* Happening in Your Company

Reconnaissance
Educate yourself about your company's situation, your place within that situation, and your options. Obtain "competitive intelligence," such as information about similar companies and what's going on in your industry. This cataloging of information not only informs you of present and future realities but also allows you to depersonalize what's happening, reminding you that you are merely a cog in a machine that's constantly changing.

Assess your support system at work. Determine who your allies are, those people who see what's going on the same way you do. How much of your feelings of foreboding have you shared with them? Would any of these people be helpful to you at this time? Are there resource people you should consult for support or to learn what your rights are, such as human resources staff or employee assistance counselors?

Become an Intrapreneur

Consider becoming a free agent *within* your own company or industry rather than remaining stuck in your current job description. Study the organizational chart of your company. Given your skills and experience, in what other departments or divisions could you find another job? Develop a project you might "sell" to a supervisor in another part of the company. Even if nothing comes of it, such a practice will prepare you for selling yourself to another company should this job end. On the other hand, it might land you something even better—and safer from potential layoff—within your own company.

Marty

Marty, longtime assistant to the vice chairman of a large fitness and sports equipment company, felt he was languishing in his job and that his malaise would inevitably lead to being laid off when impending budget cuts came down the pike. Having asked other departments for projects to capitalize on skills he wasn't using, he suddenly realized he could fashion a position for himself. His love of travel, his knowledge of sports, and his experience as an event planner combined to suggest a position in the Olympic events department. Marty also fashioned a public relations campaign the company could develop in Asia, where its reputation was flagging. Marty packaged these skills into two job descriptions and peddled them to the powers that be, figuring that either one would satisfy him more than his present position. Who knows, he ventured—if the company didn't go for these ideas, maybe he could perform the same roles in a different corporation.

Justified Paranoia

Be careful about whom you listen to. Take heed from Sherry's story (page 15), plus those of countless other Refugees who believed reassurances from colleagues, supervisors, or human resources departments. Too often these people will only tell you the short-term half-truth (or lie) because it's all they're allowed to say, when the long-term truths are what you're seeking. Choose your mentors and confidants carefully and conscientiously to make sure you don't get trapped in rumor mills. Trust your intuition and implement strategies to pave the way for a healthy Letting Go (Stage II) if your inklings prove prophetic.

II. Seize the Day While There's Still Time

Once you've determined what course the company appears to be on, take charge of the time you have left within your current job. Get organized and capitalize on the benefits that you still have while On the Brink.

Network, Network, Network

Don't wait for the hatchet to fall if you can preempt it through contacts. Whom do you know outside of the company but in your industry? Check in with them to explore options they might offer. Find recruiters who specialize in your industry, and add your resume to their files. If they find you a new job, you can always say no if things at your company stabilize. Call everyone who knows you and your accomplishments. Become familiar with online career sites. Join trade associations in your industry and study their newsletters for word of other possibilities.

Becky

Becky, forty-two, a member of the Kevorkian group (see page 1) and a former chief operating officer in a biotech firm, has been unemployed for a year. Prior to her departure from her job, the group had urged her to join trade associations and beef up her relationships with key people in her industry. At the time, she was so wrapped up in the day-to-day demands of her work that she rationalized against networking during her downtime: "I had so little quiet time, the last thing I wanted to be doing evenings was sitting in networking meetings." She also believed recruiters would easily market her talent to employers when she was ready, so why worry. Instead, when she was finally laid off, Becky found that recruiters are now called "retained search firms" and work primarily for employers, hiring for specific openings only. The worker has to do all of the actual networking recruiters used to do, including mailers and cold-calls to prospective companies. Even banking one's resume with specialized recruiters is now the candidate's job. Becky has planted her resume with more than fifty recruiters who specialize in biotech, but so far, no bites. Her biggest regret, she says, is having delayed the networking she's now doing.

Be unabashed in looking for other job options, even if your current position ends up safe for a while. Networking is the surest way to find new possibilities, particularly while you're still employed and possibly beating the rush of others in your company who might be laid off as well. Better for you to be one person networking today than one of thirty next month!

Get Organized

During that steady flow of signals that presage a potential layoff, get into gear. Revise and update your resume. Make a copy of your Rolodex or update your Palm Pilot or its equivalent. If the ax falls and your job instantly ends, are you prepared to empty your desk into a single box and be escorted from the building? Use this unpredictable time to organize your files and the personal belongings that are in your workplace.

GUERRILLA NETWORKING

Organize networking dinners, parties, "cocktail hours," or salons and incorporate some of these ideas:

• Plan to meet at 6:30 P.M. on a Tuesday, Wednesday, or Thursday so people can come right from work and leave at a reasonable hour.

• Have a dinner buffet or potluck at home for a dozen people, or meet at a quiet restaurant for their happy hour specials.

• Invite people who represent a variety of occupations for meaningful brainstorming but no more than eight to ten so that everyone can contribute.

• Avoid inviting coworkers, couples, or business partners so people feel free to be candid.

• Encourage people to drop off or post business cards as they enter. Use the cards you collect for future parties.

Liza

When Liza, a meeting planner for a large entertainment company, was laid off in a recent sweep of her department, she was given ten minutes to pack and leave. As a meeting planner, she had many tools of her trade stored in her office cabinets and closets, including directories, voluminous file folders of resources, presentation equipment, and items collected over a decade spent working from this location. Clearly there were too many to collect quickly, let alone fit into a single box. When she protested that she needed more time—and more boxes!—she was told to take what she could and that the rest would be "messengered" by company staff. It has been a month since her layoff, and still Liza has not received her belongings. She has decided to contact an attorney—although she cannot afford it—to help her collect her personal equipment.

Retool

Become adept at brinkmanship and seize opportunities to bring your skills up to speed. Learn new software or how to operate new equipment; enroll for any training programs that will add new skills to your resume. If cost-cutting has eliminated company-funded training, look into online courses or those offered in your community.

Are your English speech, grammar, and spelling skills up to par in case you have to present yourself to new employers? If not, don't be shy. There are many community-based classes filled with interesting people like you who are often there for similar, career-changing reasons.

How about your public speaking and presentation skills? Public speaking is the most intimidating challenge for most of us, yet the inability to speak up with confidence can be a sure ride down—rather than up—the corporate ladder.

Use Your Benefits . . . While You Still Have Them

Have you had a physical recently? Eye or dental exams? Do you have unused vacation or sick time that might go away with your job? If so, consider taking some of those paid days off to assess your options away from work.

GET SCHOOLED

• The American Management Association offers literally thousands of business seminars on topics that range from information systems and sales management to finance and public speaking, with tuition ranging from $100 to $2000. For information, call (800) 262-9699.

• For English language skills, look for listings in community college, YMCA, and vocational school catalogs.

• Public speaking skills are taught at Toastmasters International. To find a chapter near you, call their headquarters at (800) 993-7732, or visit their Web site at www.toastmasters.org.

• Many continuing education classes are offered online, from specific skill building all the way to achieving a graduate degree in the field of your choice. A good resource for exploring this option is offered by News Radio Channel 4000 in Minneapolis/St. Paul, Minnesota, via their Web site at www.wcco.com/education.

• Find computer classes through the Learning Annex, your local community college, and online.

III. Get a Grip

The Brink is a challenging time emotionally. The first feeling that haunts most of us is fear—about money, about the future, about the unknown. Don't let these fears paralyze you. Instead, take the following actions during the Brink to shore yourself up:

Financial Preparation

Assess your savings immediately, and build up as much cash reserve as you can to see you through potential hard times. Don't put this off until the pink slip arrives. Be proactive. After paying your monthly fixed expenses, immediately put a set amount into savings and make this a priority until you have at least six months of living expenses set aside. Avoid using credit cards. Pay as you go with cash and become debt-free as soon as possible. Maximize your 401(k) contributions. Increase your withholding tax to set up a greater income tax refund for next year.

Study your investments and make any rearrangements necessary should you have to dip into them later:

•Are there any securities that have not performed well enough to string along? Would they be best sold now, with the cash preserved in a money market account?

•What are the rules for your 401(k)? Are there provisions for borrowing against your plan? If so, what are the repayment options? What happens to such a loan should you lose your job?

•Do you have a life insurance policy with cash value you could borrow against if necessary? If you're unsure, contact your insurance agent and find out what the process would be to borrow in this way. Again, this is simply preparatory; the more aware you are of your financial resources, the more comfortable you'll feel.

•How about a home equity loan for a future line of credit? If you anticipate losing your job, with reemployment an unknown, now would be the time to line up this option. There is no obligation to use those dollars, but knowing they're there can be reassuring.

> ## DID YOU KNOW . . . ?
> Home equity loans are based on *simple* interest and operate as second mortgages for up to 125% of the equity in your home. By contrast, credit cards charge you *compound* interest daily, which means you actually pay up to three times more for the money you borrow on your credit cards than through a home equity loan. The downside of this strategy is that any equity you've built in the ownership of your home will be used as collateral for this kind of financing. For advice on debt consolidation, including a calculator to determine home-equity financing, visit www.cnnfn.com or www.quicken.com.

Simplify

When you are On the Brink, it's time to look at the complexities in your life and reorganize and reduce them. Are you overcommitted on evenings and weekends, or so tired all the time that you can't sink into your feelings and set goals? Reduce your calendar clutter. Do you come home to stacks of papers and magazines you've long postponed reading or filing? Outer chaos mirrors inner confusion, so set aside time to eliminate those piles and give yourself the feeling of being organized and up-to-date instead of overwhelmed and inefficient. Cancel some subscriptions, get a refund, pocket the savings, and go to the library.

> ## THE PHILOSOPHY OF SIMPLICITY
> *The Simple Living Guide: Sourcebook for Less Stressful, More Joyful Living* by Janet Luhrs (Broadway Books, 1997) and *Voluntary Simplicity* by Duane Elgin (Quill, 1993) are great books for inspiring a less materialistic lifestyle.

In and Out

Feelings about job loss vary depending on each person's unique situation. If you've been working in your dream job, the potential loss of this position can be devastating because it's so connected to your talents and passions. If, on the other hand, you are ready to leave your current position, or are getting transferred, or have the option of retiring, feelings about the impending change will likely be at least partly positive. Most corporate workers On the Brink of becoming Refugees have no choice about their impending exile and therefore feel angry, hurt, and confused. It's best to allow all these feelings to flow through you and create a system for expressing them. Some excellent repositories for your negative feelings can be your journal, outside-of-work meetings with coworkers to share perceptions and compare notes, and venting and brainstorming sessions with friends and significant others. Find or start an appropriate support group that meets regularly; it can be a great forum for sharing your feelings and receiving feedback on a regular basis. The most important thing is to know that your feelings will be all over the map as you endure this stage. Determine to be aware of the feelings but get them out in healthy ways rather than risking illness or injury by suffering them silently.

GROUP SUPPORT

See Barbara Sher's book *Teamworks* (Warner Books, 1989) for some examples of powerful, easy-to-facilitate networking parties or groups. Note particularly her outline for "Success Teams."

Circle the Wagons

How strong is your nonwork support system? Have you shared your concerns with your family? Don't keep anxiety or job stress completely to yourself. It'll cause exhaustion, irritability, and detachment from the very people you need the most right now. It's important to talk about what's going on and shore up your nest of caring companions. They are a powerful support team should job loss or change occur.

IV. Jump Ship?

After you've confirmed the likelihood of impending job loss, explored other opportunities within your company, and contemplated working for a competitor or becoming a new competitor in your own startup, it may be time to think about moving on.

Ron

Ron had given ten years to a 100-year-old banking institution with people who had long tenure and a deep sense of loyalty. A newer bank tried but failed to buy Ron's company. For about three months afterward, nothing happened, but the rumors flying around the company grew. His peers were frozen in a wait-and-see posture because they had been promised a "retention bonus" if they stayed through any future mergers. As Ron saw it, if the bank didn't push to grow, the only possibility left was that it would be acquired. Yet he could see no growth efforts being made. As a result, Ron decided to get out. "It was risky, because by job searching, I might have been seen as disloyal and canned before I was ready to leave, but it seemed a no-choice for me at the time."

He decided to search for a job online during his evening hours. In addition, Ron called some recruiters and confided his needs. Almost immediately, he landed job offers and selected a consulting position with an international accounting firm. He would be doing systems engineering, just as he had for the bank.

Ron is now making the same amount of money, but there is a downside: As a consultant, he's doing project work that requires travel away from home. He misses his wife and baby, and he sees why his colleagues with families were trying to maintain the status quo, yet he feels sorry for those who grabbed the retention packages. "They have to stay another year and three months, 'doing time' to get the money. They're bored, unmotivated, and wasting opportunities in this great job market. They're jealous I've been able to jump ship and grow." One year after Ron left the bank, it was acquired, and all of his former colleagues were laid off. Ron saved himself but feels sad for those who stayed. "They thought they were clinging to financial security, but they ended up losing all around. Not only did they endure the emotional trauma of all that change, their loyalty wasn't even rewarded when the chips fell toward yet another corporate takeover."

Before you jump ship, assess your situation and determine that you are leaving for the right reasons. If, like Ron, you have paved the way for a good opportunity, clearly you are making the right decision. If you have enough savings to support you during a job search without a consistent paycheck, be aware that some industries have plentiful job opportunities and you'll be reemployed quickly.

Here are a few additional questions to ask yourself before you jump ship:

DID YOU KNOW . . . ?
If you jump ship, you wouldn't be alone. *U.S. News and World Report* reported that jumping ship was a viable solution for 17 million Americans in 1999, up 6 million from 1994.

DID YOU KNOW . . . ?
Outplacement counselors suggest this rule of thumb: Expect one month of job searching for every $10,000 you desire in salary—for example, six months for a $60,000 job.

• Do you have transferable skills that will serve you well in today's cutting-edge, lean-and-mean corporate environments? If your answer is "I think so," get a reality check from key people in your target industry. If your answer is "I don't think so," use the remaining time in your current position to update your skills before you jump ship.

• Have you been passed over more than once for promotions while the company hired considerably younger staff? If so, it may be time to jump ship.

• Is the work meaningful to you, particularly in its relevance to both your industry and your values? Could you easily find similar work elsewhere and still derive this sense of meaning if you jump ship?

•Could you market yourself for a new job while hanging on rather than jumping ship prematurely?

•Might your job be eliminated and later outsourced or contracted out? If so, are you in a position to negotiate that option for yourself?

If you decide to jump ship, make a graceful exit. Give more than two weeks' notice, complete your work or find your appropriate successor, and resist the impulse to vent your frustrations on your way out. Better to be remembered for your contributions and maintain your contacts. You may end up returning in a different capacity or consulting to this very company. Who knows—the person you hired and trained may someday jump ship and hire you for his or her new startup.

> Never burn bridges. Today's junior prick, tomorrow's senior partner.
> —SIGOURNEY WEAVER

AFTER HOURS

Whether you decide to stay on your job until further notice or to jump ship for a better opportunity, the Brink inevitably takes its toll. Consider the following after-hours options that might mitigate the stress of job insecurity and give you a greater sense of personal control.

Moonlighting

Can you think of any opportunities that might provide extra income in the event of a layoff? Often such after-hours jobs evolve from longstanding avocational interests that have nothing to do with being On the Brink. But during this stage, they might be a great opportunity to stabilize you emotionally, financially, and maybe occupationally. Here are several such examples:

•Brad, whom we met in chapter one, is a writer of mystery novels and a singer as well as a computer animator. Throughout his Refugee journey, he maintained both avocations as ways of balancing his life, singing in studio sessions and writing on the side. Both of these creative sidelines brought income when he was laid off.

• A software engineer purchased an old limo, made a hobby of restoring it, and determined to open a sideline limousine service that he could beef up should his job disappear.

• An attorney whose firm is positioned to merge and let go of some lawyers is indulging his love of the outdoors by taking a part-time job at an adventure equipment store. When assured of confidentiality, he rhapsodized that he wouldn't mind working in that environment full time, so relaxing is it compared to litigation.

• An administrative assistant at a rapidly changing television studio has been struggling with insomnia as she witnesses whole departments being cut. Instead of worrying all night, she gets up and makes beaded jewelry. She has made so many pieces that she has decided to sell them at annual Christmas craft shows. She's also realizing that her jewelry-making could become a lucrative sideline business.

What passions, talent, or sideline abilities might you parlay into part-time income? Now might be the time to develop these.

Crafty Stressbusters

Craft-based hobbies are known to be great stressbusters. They can be particularly calming and balancing during the chaos of the Brink. Beyond providing stress management, a meaningful craft outside the workplace offers the Refugee hands-on interaction between one's inner creative urges and a tangible outer product. There's a sense of control over the process, joy *during* the process, and closure at the completion of the project that offsets the feeling of no control over the workplace.

As long as you remember that your hobby or craft is not a performance, it can be enormously gratifying. Park your perfectionist tendencies when it comes to outcomes and focus on the *process* of creation. It may lead you in directions you couldn't have imagined, including new friends or a cottage industry if you really get hooked on a particular creative outlet.

ONWARD PAST THE BRINK

Once the Brink stage has been resolved, the Refugee inevitably moves into Letting Go. The entry point to this next stage is the ending of the prior job. Most of us resist Letting Go. It's uncomfortable to deal with loss. The fastest way to get through the discomfort is taking some time out to grieve. In fact, that is the work of Letting Go. If you feel panicked by that prospect and want to avoid a free fall into sadness, or if you want to launch a job search concurrent with your Letting Go stage, take a detour into the Pit Stop that follows (page 48).

DID YOU KNOW . . . ?

In a 1995 study commissioned by the Home Sewing Association, psychologists at New York University looked at heart rate variability, blood pressure, and perspiration rates to determine the stress-reducing properties of sewing. Statistically significant benefits were found in people who concentrated on designing, creating, and completing sewing projects. Other crafts, such as woodworking, ceramics, needlepoint, and various hands-on hobbies, have likewise been found to bring people into a pleasurable zone that acts as a tranquilizer.

BACKPACK FOR THE ROAD

Before your Refugee journey inexorably moves you into Letting Go, let's gather the gifts and lessons learned On the Brink.

1. List the signals and signposts you've gathered along the Brink.

_____

_____

_____

_____

_____

2. Now pick some of the signals you've listed above, and list the opportunities each might provide. For example, if you see yourself being left out of meetings (signal), you might list networking, brainstorming, or updating your resume as the opportunities you should follow up. Be as specific as possible in your opportunities list: Network with whom? Brainstorm with whom? Where? When? Update which parts of your resume?

Signal   **Opportunity**

_____

_____

_____

_____

3. Do you see yourself going in and out of denial as you sink into your Brink? Ask someone outside of your workplace to be your buddy. Assign him or her the task of listening to your accounts of what's going on at work and keeping you awake to the likely outcome. Denial can delay your journey and lead to depression if the Brink stage becomes prolonged.

4. Which Daily Rituals have you not yet incorporated into your days? Create a small schedule below; then place a copy on your refrigerator and in your calendar to prod you to prioritize exercise, nutrition, rest, and decompression.

_____

_____

_____

_____

5. Which Actions for the Brink have you not yet explored? Why? What do you need to move you into action on these? List them below or in your journal.

_____

_____

_____

_____

6. Before moving forward on your Refugee journey, make a To Do list. Include organizing your finances, finding out about ongoing health insurance and your rights to unemployment benefits, and a belt-tightening meeting with your family. Set a timeline for the items on your To Do list.

**To Do List for Moving   When I'll Take This Action
Past the Brink**

_____

_____

_____

_____

_____

_____

_____

Copy this list and put it where you'll see it daily. Don't be afraid to add to it as time goes on.

Now is the time of departure. The last streamer that ties us to what is known, parts. We drift into a sea of storms.

—DEREK JARMAN

The Job Search

Don't Jump Up and Grab a Job . . .
But If You Must, Here Are Some Tips

To deal with fear and foreboding—handmaidens of the Refugee journey—you've implemented a healthy Interim Structure while On the Brink. Nevertheless, you find yourself obsessed about lost income and the urgency of finding new employment if this job ends. Even as nature is pushing you toward Letting Go, your mind is urging you to take action toward new employment and to do something—anything—to break your fall. If a new job could be found immediately, you reason, maybe the emotional roller coaster will stop.

Here are some proactive antidotes that you can implement to assuage those feelings of helplessness and launch a job search before Letting Go. As you peruse these ideas, remember that the rest of the Refugee stages still have to be lived. Even if you find a new job in fairly short order, there will be recovery work to do before you return to a sense of balance and control. Look at this section as a pit stop designed to augment the actions you've already taken, but not to the exclusion of continuing your journey through the rest of this book.

KNOW YOUR RIGHTS

The first order of business is to learn about your rights should you be terminated. Do you feel there are discrimination and/or wrongful termination issues that require legal advice? Do you know how

48

to negotiate a separation package, apply for unemployment compensation, and extend your health benefits?

Update Your Job-Hunting Skills

If it's been a while since you've had to search for a job, you might want to begin by developing your job-hunting skills. The marketplace is changing so quickly that key assumptions of the recent past have gone by the wayside. For example, unlike our parents' one-job, one-company era, the current marketplace embraces the term "strategic job hopping." Workers are being coached to have a career master plan and to switch jobs as often as necessary to get to their goal.

ADVICE ABOUT YOUR RIGHTS
NERI, the nonprofit National Employee Rights Institute, offers a book titled *Job Rights and Survival Strategies: A Handbook for Terminated Employees;* at a cost of $19.95, it offers advice by employment lawyers Paul H. Tobias and Susan Sauter. To order, call 800-HOW-NERI or e-mail ptobias@igc.apc.org. *Firing Back: Power Strategies for Cutting the Best Deal When You're About to Lose Your Job* (John Wiley & Sons, 1997), by Jodie-Beth Galos and Sandy McIntosh, also offers excellent advice on all aspects of job termination.

Another maxim that's losing luster is that it's easier to get a new job if you're still in your old one. Nowadays, employers don't hold it against the job seeker if he or she is unemployed during a search. Mergers, acquisitions, and constant downsizings have catapulted many talented professionals into unemployment before new positions can be located.

The key to a successful search requires updating your job search skills and understanding the prevailing attitudes among those who are doing the hiring. The *Wall Street Journal* and the *Washington Post* offer a great number of articles and links to help job hunters systematize their search.

Launch an Online Job Search

The Internet has become an amazing career search resource. Not only are there literally hundreds of job databases you can access, but there are also sites that walk you through resume-writing and interviewing strategies specific to your industry. You can research potential employers, find trade associations, and chat with other job seekers for tips and leads.

The idea behind online job boards is that employers pay a fee to post available positions and receive resumes. In addition, they offer "virtual job fairs" you can "attend" from home. It's free to the job seeker, so you have nothing to lose. You can post your resume in the evening and have e-mail or phone interviews the next day.

JOB SEEKERS' ONLINE TREASURE TROVE

Access the *Wall Street Journal* and *Washington Post* (including their archived articles) online at www.public.wsj.com/careers/ and www.washingtonpost.com. You'll find a veritable treasure trove of links to employers, advice columns, and resources that you may never have thought to explore. Similarly, *Fortune, Inc., Entrepreneur, Fast Company,* and most other business magazines provide updated market information, both on- and off-line. Before going online, clarify exactly what you are seeking. If you haven't explored these resources until now, you'll be overwhelmed by the quantity of information.

If you aren't online via a home-based computer, you might check with your local library to see if you can get on the Internet through its system. There are Internet cafes and local stores that charge nominal hourly fees for your online time. Outplacement packages often include access to computers too.

Before you begin your search online, study the world of online job markets by perusing some of the sites listed below. Learn how to search the databases efficiently, such as by industry, by region, or by keywords. Also, keep in mind that in the ever-changing world of the Internet, a site listed here at publication time may be gone by the time you read this book. But you can be sure that more will crop up in its place.

www.learnthenet.com

This site provides a primer for online networking and job searching on the Internet. If you have never used online databases to peruse job listings, start here to learn the ropes.

www.monster.com

Even if you are a newcomer to the world of online job searching, this site makes the process easy. In addition to a huge and very current list of jobs all over the world, the Monster board is the granddaddy of career search Web sites. You can search by region, industry, or specific employer. There is also a talent market for independent contractors and consultants. Built on the online auction model, this site allows you to list the skills and other offerings on which employers will bid. You can also upload your resume and order its transmission as specific jobs become available. There is even a process whereby job listings that match what you are seeking can be e-mailed to you automatically!

HUNDREDS OF ONLINE SITES

For help navigating the hundreds of job-search sites, take a look at these recent books:

•*CareerXRoads 2000* by Gerry Crispin and Mark Mehler (MMC Group, 2000) provides a directory of more than 500 Web sites for job seekers along with a free e-mail update service.

•*Job Searching Online for Dummies* by Pam Dixon (IDG Books Worldwide, 2000) lists meta-sites and helps you save random searching time.

www.100hot.com/jobs

This site is a great find. It lists the top 100 online sites for job postings all over the world. This list is updated every 72 hours, based on daily traffic patterns used by job seekers at more than 250,000 Web sites. There is a huge sidebar index that provides state-by-state listings of, for example, online recruiters, telecommuting jobs, Navy jobs, software jobs, television industry jobs, etc. Monster.com is always on the "hot" list, as are several of the following sites.

www.careermosaic.com

In addition to the resources mentioned on monster.com, careermosaic offers thirty-five partnerships that are industry-specific job sites, such as www.healthopps.com; www.accountingjobs.com; www.EETimes.com (for engineers); and www.HRPlaza.com (for human resources jobs).

www.joboptions.com

Here you can search by job title.

www.mbafreeagents.com

This site specializes in management positions at "virtual" companies looking for the short-term project help often needed by start-ups, such as developing business and marketing plans.

www.netshare.com
Specializing in confidential senior executive recruitment, this site was named a "best search site" in 1999 by *Fortune* magazine.

www.careerlab.com
This site provides the usual postings of resumes, cover letters, and networking opportunities, as well as access to (fee-based) vocational testing services.

www.jobstar.org
A comprehensive catalog of jobs in California, this site is funded by California State Library grants. It offfers good hints for searching other states' databases as well.

www.computerjobs.com
This site boasts "hourly updates" and lists a variety of career-oriented content, including lists of jobs organized by region and skill set.

www.dbm.com/jobguide/local.html
The Riley Guide is a national jobs list categorized state-by-state.

www.liszt.com
This site teaches you how to use mailing lists for your job search. It offers advice, discussion groups, and 91,000 mailing lists.

These search sites are being used by employed as well as unemployed workers. People already working but looking for more interesting or higher paying jobs may not risk posting their resumes, but they use the search system to see what's out there. From an employer's standpoint, such applicants are desirable because they're being proactive about their careers.
   If you decide to post your resume, be sure to:

•Include keywords on your resume that truly reflect the work you want.

• Indicate the word processing program in which your resume is written, and request that your resume be posted in that program to prevent fouled-up formatting when it's downloaded.

• Include a link to your own Web site if you have one.

What About Consulting?

If you are experienced and deeply networked in your field, consulting might be the appropriate next step for you. Not only are there tax advantages to self-employment, but also there is a tremendous amount of freedom when your time is your own. It's essential that you do some serious soul-searching before launching a consulting practice, particularly if you've never been self-employed before. Ask yourself the following:

• Have you identified a market niche that would match your skills?

• Have you developed a business plan showing how your offerings would meet the needs of that market?

• Have you done enough homework, including studying your competition, researching your chosen niche, understanding the nature of the work itself, and clearly identifying who might hire an individual for their needs versus a large, well-established consulting firm?

• Have you studied your finances to determine how much of your savings will go toward your startup? How much income will you need in the first or second year?

TEST YOUR CONSULTING POSSIBILITIES ELECTRONICALLY

"E-lancing"—marketing your consulting services or finding assignments online—might provide a quick barometer for how viable consulting is for you. Check out these sites:

• www.elance.com, where you can bid on listed projects.

• www.ework.com and www.iniku.com provide a virtual office through which contractors are connected with projects.

• www.advoco.com and www.ithority.com offer short-term assignments—including those in which you answer others' questions in your area of expertise—for which you get paid.

• Can you get a line of credit?

• Are your family members on board? Will they be able to tolerate your working long hours the first year? How much support do they need from you or you from them?

• Do you have sales skills? Can you wear several hats or will you need staff?

• Do you have the emotional strength to weather the trials of startup? Consider your level of self-discipline, time management skill, tolerance for ambiguity, and ability to tolerate rejection.

• Are you willing to put in extraordinary hours to launch your practice, even if this means letting go of some current commitments? Are you physically fit enough to handle the long hours and focused work?

• Is your personality such that working solo will be comfortable for you? If you've been team-based in your job, this is a critical question. Many professionals who leave corporate settings for self-employment feel lonely and isolated.

• Finally, is your network deep and current? Have you shared your idea for the business with trusted colleagues who might become clients?

TO LOCATE A COACH

The International Coaching Federation is a trade group of 1500 executive coaches, many of whom specialize in industries in which they worked before becoming coaches. To locate chapters and coaches in your geographic area, contact them at (888) 423-3131, or online at www.coachfederation.org. Be sure to get references before signing on with any career counselor or coach since many states do not have a licensing standard for these professionals. The book *Guide to Executive Recruiters* by Michael Betrus (McGraw-Hill, 1996), updated every year, is a directory of thousands of recruiting firms and recruiters, listed geographically and by occupational specialty.

Need a Coach?

There is a whole world of career centers, executive coaches, and recruiters you can access for traditional—and nontraditional—career counseling, should you desire that kind of support. In addition to job search sites, the Internet provides instantly accessible resources you can explore in private and during off-hours while you live through your days On the Brink.

BOOKS TO INSPIRE YOUR JOB SEARCH

Here are some books to add direction to your job search. The first list targets niche or specialized markets. Books on the second list give strategic advice for your job search.

Finding Jobs in Specialized or Niche Markets

Civil Service Handbook: Everything You Need to Know to Get a Civil Service Job, 13th edition, by Hy Hammer (Arco Publications, 1998). Includes job descriptions and sample test questions with answers.

Green at Work: Finding a Business Career that Works for the Environment by Susan Cohn (Island Press, 1995). A guide to "green" jobs, including contacts for green companies.

Greener Pastures: How to Find a Job in Another Place by Andrea Kay (Griffin Trade Paperback, 1999). If geography is your first priority, this book advises how to do a long-distance job search.

High-Tech Careers for Low-Tech People by William Shaffer (Ten Speed Press, 1999). A step-by-step guide for getting a job in the high-technology world with little or no background or training.

Household Careers: Nannies, Butlers, Maids and More: The Complete Guide for Finding Household Employment or "If the Dog Likes You, You're Hired!" by Linda F. Radke (Five Star Publications, 1993). Job searching advice for household employees.

Inside Secrets of Finding a Teaching Job by Jack Warner, Clyde Bryan, and Diane Warner (Park Avenue Productions

Publications, 1997). Advice for teachers from experienced educators.

Sunshine Jobs: Career Opportunities Working Outdoors, 2nd edition, by Tom Stienstra, Robyn Schlueter, and Janet Connaughton (editor) (Live Oak Publications, 1997). Advice about many outdoor occupations.

Teaching English Abroad: Talk Your Way Around the World!, 4th edition, by Susan Griffin (Vacation-Work, 1999). Lists short- and long-term opportunities, real-life experiences, salaries, red tape—and you don't have to be a trained teacher for this work.

Books Offering Strategic Advice for Your Job Search

Creating a Life Worth Living by Carol Lloyd (HarperCollins, 1997). Offers inspiring and practical career advice for artists, inventors, and innovators. Designed as a course, this book suggests "day jobs" for aspiring artists while they pursue their true passions.

The Health Care Executive's Job Search by J. Larry Tyler (Health Administration Press, 1998). A "how-to" book on conducting a job search in the health care industry, focused on senior-level positions.

Is It Too Late to Run Away and Join the Circus? by Marti Diane Smye and Richard Chagnon (IDG Books Worldwide, 1998). Smye works for Right Associates as a change management specialist. Provides worksheets for discovering a new career.

Making a Living While Making a Difference: A Guide to Creating Careers with a Conscience by Melissa Everett (Bantam Books, 1999). Compelling stories and guidance for principled job seekers and those trying to change the circumstances of their current jobs.

Running from the Law by Deborah L. Arron (Ten Speed Press, 1996). Gives disgruntled lawyers many career-change options and fascinating case histories.

60 Seconds and You're Hired! by Robin Ryan (Penguin Books, 2000). A concise approach to packaging yourself and figuring out what your marketable strengths are.

SOME INFORMATION AND SUGGESTIONS FOR OLDER WORKERS

Unquestionably, the number of mergers and acquisitions, coupled with the advent of high-tech, has created tremendous job opportunities for younger workers, often at the expense of older workers who are presumed to cost more in salary and in health and pension benefits. In fact, age discrimination in the current workplace stems from employers' belief in myths that are quickly being dispelled, both by significant studies refuting these fallacious assumptions and by the shortage of qualified workers of any age.

YOU'RE NOT ALONE
By 2003, for the first time ever, there will be more workers over age forty than under, reported *Fortune* magazine in its February 1, 1999, issue.

Nevertheless, many Refugees have to battle some of these mistaken beliefs about older workers, all of which are untrue:

• Older workers have higher rates of absenteeism.

• Older workers stifle creativity and have a harder time grasping new concepts.

• Older workers have lower levels of commitment, motivation, and overall work skills than younger workers.

• Older workers increase the health care and pension costs of an organization.

• Older workers take longer to train, are less flexible, and are less likely to keep up with new developments than younger workers.

Studies by the National Council on Aging (NCOA) in 1999 and the Society for Human Resource Management (SHRM) in 1998

DID YOU KNOW . . . ?

• The Age Discrimination Employment Act (ADEA) protects workers over age forty, stating that ability and not age must determine hiring and firing practices.

• The Federal Older Workers Benefit Protection Act of 1990 makes it illegal to target older workers for cutting benefits programs. It regulates legal waivers employers may ask you to sign when offering a "golden parachute" (early retirement) program.

resoundingly refute these myths and provide encouraging news for mature workers:

• Extensive research has found no relationship between age and on-the-job performance. A 1993 review of 185 research studies found that older workers may actually have higher motivation and job satisfaction than their younger peers. This was confirmed in a 1998 Older Workers Survey by the American Association of Retired Persons and the Society for Human Resource Management, in which older workers were found to be more reliable and have higher levels of commitment to their organization than younger workers.

• InfoWorld, a subsidiary of CNNInteractive, reports that the average workweek for workers of all ages is forty-eight hours, so don't let anyone suggest that younger workers put in more hours than older workers.

• Today, Americans over age fifty-five make up 10 percent of the workforce but account for 22 percent of the nation's job growth since 1995.

• Older workers are changing jobs at an annual rate of 4.1 percent—more than double the 1.8 percent of the general population.

• Between 2000 and 2010, the fastest-growing age group will be those between ages fifty-five and sixty-four.

• By 2005, those age fifty-five and over will represent nearly 20 percent of the workforce.

• Fifty-one percent of older women are working, up from 43 percent in the early 1990s.

•Almost 60 percent of working Americans over the age of nineteen expect to work at least part time after the age of sixty-five.

•Of those aged seventy to seventy-four, one in eight is employed full or part time.

•A Hudson Institute study warns of a "severe" labor shortage by 2010 as baby boomers begin to retire and fewer young workers are available because of the slow population growth during 1966–1985.

•A survey of human resources professionals found that 62 percent of them were hiring retired employees as consultants or temps.

So, take heart—these numbers talk, and you are very much needed in the workforce. The key might be in how you package and present yourself to potential employers. In addition to the resources suggested in this book, you might add the following:

IF YOU THINK YOU'VE BEEN DISCRIMINATED AGAINST ON THE BASIS OF AGE . . .

Call the Equal Employment Opportunities Commission (EEOC) at (800) 669-4000 to locate the office nearest to you.

•For written information on your rights under the law, get free publication #D12386 from AARP titled "Age Discrimination on the Job." See Resources section for mailing address of AARP.

•If you think your benefits have been targeted on the basis of your age, contact an employment attorney through the National Employment Lawyers Association (NELA). See Resources section for address.

•Be prepared to dispel age-based notions and reassure employers that you are flexible, energetic, and committed. Give examples the interviewer can relate to.

•Emphasize your skills rather than your years of experience. Many older workers feel they've been rejected based on age when, in fact, they lack the skill set and technical expertise the employer is seeking. On the other hand, if you're applying to a young company, your depth of management experience would be attractive, so be clear in advance as to which approach to use.

MORE ADVICE FOR OLDER WORKERS

For more in-depth exploration of these findings, as well as advice, job listings, and links for older workers, see NCOA and SHRM Web sites at www.ncoa.org.maturityworks and www.shrm.org.

• Sometimes age discrimination is manifested when an older worker is rejected for being "overqualified." This is often code for "too expensive." If you've lost a high-paying job, determine in advance of any interviews how much less salary you are willing to accept and be prepared to discuss this issue during your meeting.

• Present yourself as someone who is comfortable working for someone younger than you.

Given the many avenues you can take toward your next career move, the critical issues for a Refugee are deeper than the job search *per se.* You need time to determine what you truly want in your next job. You need time to process and heal from the loss of your last position. And you need rest.

This pit stop is meant to alert you to some of the tools that are out there to support your career path. But the more important next step is Letting Go of what's been lost.

MONSTER.COM'S SPECIAL TOOLKITS

To address the special needs and desires of older workers, the venerable online job database monster.com has created several new "toolkits" located at:

• http://content.monster.com/olderworkers/

• http://content.monster.com/careerchangers/

• http://content.monster.com/military, for people transitioning out of the military

• http://content.monster.com/nonprofits, which offers information on nonprofit careers.

Each toolkit includes forums for asking questions of experts, news relevant to each niche, and referrals to the current Internet and print resources.

We have to stumble through so much dirt and humbug before
we reach home. And we have no one to guide us.
Our only guide is our homesickness.

—HERMANN HESSE, STEPPENWOLF

THREE

Stage II:
Letting Go
(of the Old Reality)

What you really value is what you miss, not what you have.

—JORGE LUIS BORGES

We all have characteristic ways of handling endings, whether they are the termination of the single life when we marry, the loss of freedom when we have a child, the dissolution of old friendships when we move, or the savoring of the last luscious moments of a long-awaited vacation when it's time to return to work. These endings are moments in time, followed by periods of adjustment with considerable emotional content. Similarly, the Refugee's actual departure from a job is an *event* that takes place at a specific moment in time. That departure may be preceded by anticipation, buildup, decision-making, or the beginning of grief.

Hence, such endings are more complicated than simply one thing stopping and another beginning. They are more like the abrupt confusion of being shipwrecked. All the assumptions about where we were heading—such as how a certain career path would end in healthy retirement, or how investing in a learning curve might facilitate starting one's own project—and the financial,

61

vocational, emotional, and mental structures that went along with a planned future have run aground. In their place are tremendous emptiness and severe disorientation. What now? How will I survive? Your feelings are likely to be a mixture of panic, rage, shock, confusion, and enormous unease.

Suddenly there is a new reality, one that does not include the familiar structure of a job with a sense of belonging and well-known turf. Lost are many of the props that give our lives meaning: our professional role, status, identity; sense of security and self-worth; faith that things will continue in a certain way; belief in our skills and competencies; and a sense of meaning to what we get up in the morning to do each day—in some cases, even *why* we get up each day.

Emotionally and spiritually, this stage resembles dying. It's a spiritual emergency that requires releasing the life—in this case, work life—we recently had and surrendering to uncertainty. Whereas the action in On the Brink was coming out of denial, the action in Letting Go is surrender. It's not easy. And it's not quick. It happens only gradually, with waves of fear punctuating periods of tenuous calm. Each time we try to relax into accepting reality and moving forward, we fear the emptiness and uncertainty of an unknown future. Rather than release the past, our instinct is to cling to our old identity, to anything we feel we can still control.

SIGNPOSTS

During On the Brink, there were many subtle external markers that triggered apprehension, denial, and bargaining. Because you still had a job, there seemed to be concrete actions you could take to stave off unemployment. During Letting Go, however, the primary external marker is the actual ending of your job. Increasingly, workers are being laid off so precipitously these days, Letting Go sets in as soon as you are asked to pack your desk and leave the building. Even if there were recognizable signs before this moment, denial or rationalization can no longer be invoked to cushion the expulsion.

Some workers receive two or more weeks' notice to wind down and hand off work before walking out the door for the last time. In such cases, Letting Go also begins with the notice of termination, but at least there is time to say good-bye to coworkers, to the work itself, and to the structure that felt reliable just yesterday.

If you can, find ways to mark the end of the job. For example, throw a party like the piñata parties described in chapter one. Any such forms of closure have great positive impact on Letting Go. They allow for commiseration, recognition for a job well done, and validation of collegial relationships to help the departing workers know this layoff was not their fault. Thus the shock of termination might, to some extent, be integrated by the time one is without employment. If no one organizes a going-away party or farewell happy hour—because others may themselves be in denial—plan one for yourself. Identify people with whom to vent feelings about your impending loss of colleagues and job duties. Exchange phone numbers and home and e-mail addresses with the people with whom you wish to stay in contact. Set up a dinner date or luncheon for a couple of weeks after the final day.

With notice, you may also get a head start on your job search. You might receive company-sponsored outplacement coaching that could result in immediate reemployment, though most displaced workers say it's rare to land another good job so quickly. Feeling proactive might make the transition easier, but not necessarily.

Lauren

Lauren hopes to be proactive. An assistant casting director for a large TV and movie studio, she's in her second week of a four-week notice that her job has ended. Two years ago, Lauren experienced a "happier Letting Go" when she was recruited from another large studio by a previous boss who defected and wanted Lauren to come along. Lauren jumped at the invitation because it promised promotional opportunities. And the new job delivered. Whereas she had previously been limited to casting feature films, here Lauren was immediately given casting responsibilities in three divisions—television, motion pictures, and interactive video (for which she did voice casting). Lauren received a generous expense account with which to scout for talent by attending local theater, movie, and comedy events, renting videos, and traveling to view promising new performers.

It sounded good. But over time, the reality proved far more stressful and thankless than that of her previous job. She and one counterpart, both working under her corporate-level boss, had no assistance other than occasional interns who "took more training and hand-holding time than they were worth," Lauren recalls. Lauren also dealt with "tons of mail for attending showcases, people wanting to apply for acting positions, and time-wasting calls from people in marketing who sat around with nothing to do." She attended frequent meetings and casting sessions during the workday. Evenings and weekends, when she wasn't scouting new talent, were filled with reading scripts, listing possible people to play parts, organizing and maintaining thousands of audio and video titles, and trying to keep everyone happy. "Animators only work on one project at a time, so they treated me as if I too had only their project and was readily available. I was constantly juggling, scheduling, and rescheduling meetings because of conflicts among all three departments that thought I belonged only to them."

Lauren's workdays began early; she always worked through lunch and was often at her desk until it was time for some evening performance she was required to attend.

Still, Lauren loved the work. She felt she was "learning a ton" and clearly believed she was indispensable because of her drive, initiative, and accomplishments. When she finally became overwhelmed and asked her boss for an assistant, the response was criticism. Lauren's boss, who had provided no training, mentoring, or management to help Lauren learn the basics of her job, told her to budget her time better. There was no recognition of all that Lauren had accomplished. Instead, there came a warning about budget cuts. Looking back, Lauren says the first pangs of *On the Brink* began during that meeting. Instead of heeding her inner inklings, Lauren personalized the criticism and got into therapy to "figure out how to manage my time and do my job better."

Six months later, the entire animation division was deemed unprofitable and was shut down. High-level executives in animation were bought out of their contracts, but Lauren had no contract, no union, no legal recourse, and no stock options. Still, she figured, "they're not going to save money by getting rid of me, so I'll lie low and be okay." Again, that small inner voice was saying, "Cut your losses, Lauren, and get going toward something new." But her job was so demanding, there was never time. And Letting Go is never easy or enticing. Lauren was On the Brink and—as is so common at that stage, as we learned in chapter two—in denial.

Finally the dreaded meeting occurred. Lauren expected her yearly review. Instead, she walked in and her boss beckoned Lauren to sit beside her on the couch, an unprecedented behavior as this boss always held court behind her desk. She blamed the CFO for cutting Lauren's job, saying she had tried to fight it but that it was out of her hands. She said she dreaded bringing the news to Lauren, especially since she'd been the one to bring Lauren here from her prior job. She said the best she could get for Lauren was vacation pay and four weeks' notice.

Lauren walked out of there shocked and "paralyzed for twenty-four hours." Lauren's counterpart was also forced out, but she had a husband with a strong income, whereas Lauren is single and has a large home mortgage.

Lauren is now valiantly networking, collecting great references, and saying it'll be easy to Let Go of this job. "It's chaotic; there's constant change; no one appreciates what you do here. I can't wait to wash my hands of this place."

Nevertheless, grief is setting in, now that she's said her good-byes and handed off her files. There are nightly tears and frequent insomnia. Lauren goes in and out of denial and anger. She has been calling around, networking, and talking with recruiters, but pilot season is over so there will be no new jobs in television for several months. Given the frenzy of her work just a few weeks ago, having time on her hands is somewhat uncomfortable for Lauren. She finds herself preoccupied with her old role.

"I'm proud of my work. If I had to do it over again, I can't imagine doing anything different. I refuse to look for anything but casting. Besides, I'm too old to do something different now." Lauren is thirty-one.

Internal markers are the most poignant during Letting Go because the overall experience is one of loss, anger, and fear. Sometimes people are lucky and find another job fairly quickly, but there will still be Letting Go adjustments because of the loss of the old and the shock of the new. Even if you quit your job, you are likely to feel rejected by the once-safe womb of community that you enjoyed at your workplace. This is a natural byproduct of having spent years building collegial relationships in an environment in which you probably felt a warm sense of mutual respect and belonging. Even if you didn't always like it there, you'll likely remember it with a fond nostalgia. Lucy, who had spent many years working as credit manager for a department store, described an empty feeling in the pit of her stomach every time she drove by the building. She had come to think of this building as her "home." In fact, she had spent many more hours at her office than in her real home. After leaving the company, it took her a full year before she could drive past the building without crying.

Some workers take their premonitions of layoff seriously while On the Brink and confront bosses about the future of their jobs. Reassured that their jobs are safe, they feel tremendous anger and betrayal when they later get "packaged out" anyway. These employees want to Let Go, because they literally hate the dishonesty with which the layoffs were handled, but first they must process their anger and loss.

Melissa

Melissa, thirty-six, is a case in point concerning feelings of betrayal. An attorney for a large national HMO, she was caught up in the consolidation of two regional legal departments into a single national entity. As other lawyers were laid off, she had a gut feeling that her job was also in jeopardy. For six months, Melissa went to her boss repeatedly, asking to "be told rather than ambushed." Each time, her boss reassured Melissa that her job was safe, yet it never rang true. Frustrated, Melissa simply continued to do her work. But when Melissa went in for her annual review, the first words out of her boss's mouth were, "You're being let go." Melissa had taken half of a Valium, hoping to be calm during the anticipated storm. Instead, Melissa screamed at her boss for all the previous deceptions. Her boss replied curtly, "We weren't allowed to tell anybody."

Enraged, Melissa refused to sign the severance papers on the spot. She studied them for days, hired legal counsel, and sent "searing letters back and forth, trying to squeeze every penny out of them that I could." In the end, this single mother of two young teens felt backed to the wall and signed in order to get what severance she could. She let the human resources people know how angry she was. When they pushed outplacement counseling at her, Melissa told them to "shove it." She felt deeply betrayed and wanted none of what she felt was gratuitous charity from this employer. "I'll never rely on a business or a corporate entity again. My best advice to anyone who senses an impending job loss is to trust your gut," Melissa says. "Don't believe a word they tell you. The whole process of downsizing is so emotionally debilitating, you're better off leaving on your own rather than waiting for the ax. Even though we all talk ourselves into holding on for all the possible money, the emotional agony is simply not worth the price."

Ted

Ted, forty-five, would be among the first to agree. After sixteen years as a manager in various capacities related to data processing in a large, national telecommunications company, he was in line for a prestigious national position. But just as Ted's promised appointment was to come his way, the very person who'd asked Ted to reach for the position held him back. No reason was given. Ted called a meeting with this VP, presented his pile of excellent reviews, and showed how he'd exceeded statistical expectations in each department he had supervised. Still no reason was given for his being passed over. Ted was so upset, he had to walk out in order to control his anger. Later, Ted learned that his rejection was not personal, but a bottom-line decision, and he continues to resent his boss for not having told him that. To add insult to injury, Ted's old position was also eliminated.

Ted was given thirty days to find a new job in the company, which he did. It was an internal consulting position on the national level. The salary and title represented a demotion from his prior position, but since his personal obligations included child support, alimony, and a twelve-year-old still living at home, he felt grateful to have found a job to maintain his benefits and seniority. The work itself was also creative.

A year later, after Ted had settled into his new position and was in the midst of building his team networks, he got wind of a downsizing effort in his department. Historically, data processing had been essential enough to be left unscathed by downsizing, but now people were being given involuntary severance packages.

"I'll never forget that day," Ted says. "I thought my job was outside the purview of the downsizing process since it was deemed critical to transitioning people through all the cuts. My wife, who also works for the company in a different department, phoned me in the early afternoon to ask if I'd been saved from 'being tapped.' After assuring her all was well and hanging up the phone, my supervisor tapped me to come to the boss's office. They told me my function was being eliminated. I said, 'How come? I'm in the middle of a funded project.' She had no answer, just said I could pack up and leave today or come back Saturday to pick up my things. And by the way, I had thirty days to find something else in the company if I so chose.

"'Can I walk around the company and do some networking to see what's available?' I asked, still in total shock at having been essentially fired. 'No,' she said. Then I asked, 'But how am I supposed to network to find another job?' 'Don't know,' she replied. 'Don't care' seemed to be the implied follow-up."

Ted took his grievance through channels to rebut the involuntary separation. He needed only five years to qualify for a pension (people eligible for early retirement were volunteering to leave and getting bonuses, severance, and pensions), but the human resources official refused to convert his involuntary separation to an early retirement program. Ted is certain his cut and others like his were related to age. Ted was earning in the mid-$60,000s, and, like him, most of those severed had long tenure with the company and would be expensive to support all the way through their pension benefits.

When all was lost and Ted was forced to take the involuntary package, he experienced another frustration: "They throw three inches of paperwork in front of you and give you a short time to choose among a few options: a lump sum, a rollover into your IRA, or monthly pay-out of a severance payment.

"You're shocked, confused, unable to stand up straight let alone figure out all the numbers and what they mean. After sixteen years of blood, sweat, and tears for this company . . ." His voice trails off. "You just can't think straight to make those decisions.

"They took my badge, so I couldn't use the facilities to network for another position. They said we could use terminals in a certain area of the company to check for job listings, but there were no telephones available to follow up on postings. They gave us three days of outplacement counseling, but when you're shell-shocked, trying to write a resume is the hardest thing to do."

Adding to the emotional roller coaster was the fact that a month prior to his termination, Ted had graduated from a company-sponsored college degree program. He was valedictorian of his graduating class, with a 3.9 GPA. Ironically, the company president had sent Ted a letter of congratulations with a statement about people like him being the kind of employees the company is happy to send through school. They even gave him a $250 award for being an exemplary student. But because they had laid him off, the award had to be mailed to him!

It's been two years since that horrific experience, and Ted is still bitter. "There was no good reason for me to lose my job. I never provoked anything. I expressed myself professionally. I was open to change." Sadly, Ted adds that his colleagues from all those years in the company deserted him too. "Everyone left there is crouched in their cubicle waiting to be tapped. Like animals who have to look out for themselves, they're superstitious about talking to you . . . like my job loss is contagious."

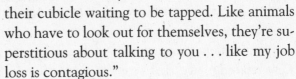

ONLINE MONEY MANAGEMENT RESOURCES

• www.frugalliving.about.com is a Web site loaded with suggestions for belt tightening and frugal living.

• www.quicken.com has budgeting software that's updated annually. Microsoft Money and Your Money are other popular software packages for the same purpose.

• www.fool.com, which includes the "Fool's School," interactive step-by-step advice on how to build a budget and develop investment strategies.

• www.money.mpr.org offers online tips and downloadable budgeting software originally presented by "Sound Money," a show on Minnesota Public Radio.

There is no easy answer for the displaced worker who's received mixed messages prior to being let go. Lauren, Melissa, and Ted were lied to in ways that are unfortunately all too common. Such practices leave you feeling powerless, humiliated, and bereft of meaning after working so hard.

It's extremely difficult for the Refugee not to personalize the loss of a job through feelings of resentment and paranoia. Even before a job loss, when staff changes presage job cuts, the Refugee is likely to feel resentment toward new management and be wary of younger workers who come in at lower salaries, frequently eager to replace tenured professionals. Then come the precipitous announcements.

"Why me?" asks the employee who has just been ejected. "I saved the company so much money over the years, and worked so many extra hours, and got top evaluations year after year, yet this is how they thank me? Why didn't they can so-and-so, whose record pales in comparison to mine?" Retrospectively, the Refugee looks around the former workplace and sees a hotbed of sexism, discrimination, and ageism. Still, the Refugee grasps at straws, even consults with an attorney to check on wrongful termination rights—anything to avoid the surrender to change that Letting Go dictates.

Once the Refugee gives intellectual acknowledgment of the surrender demanded by Letting Go, fears surface that can become obsessive. "My success wasn't really mine; it was only because I was part of a company, a team. I'm afraid I don't know how to be creative alone." Fear that people will judge us for having lost a job can reduce self-esteem and cause a paralysis that keeps us from applying for new jobs. Financial fears can be overwhelming, sometimes out of proportion to one's circumstances. Somehow, grieving the lost paycheck feels more tangible than surrendering to uncertainty about the future.

Jessica

Jessica, the woman who dubbed her support group the "Kevorkian Club" (page 1), was the operations manager for a large food-manufacturing firm. After thirteen years of dedicated service, she accepted a severance package. Jessica was fed up with the lack of support from her superiors. She had been rocked one too many times by the successive "reengineerings" of her plant. During her On the Brink phase and before leaving the company, Jessica busied herself with unselfish acts of goodwill. She met with every single person in her charge, tightened their job descriptions, pointed them in new directions, mentored people toward personal career goals, and used the power of her position to arrange for raises and promotions where appropriate. Her coworkers bid her farewell with a lavish party, and she floated away on a cloud of love.

For Jessica, Letting Go didn't click in until a few days later, when she looked around and suddenly realized she had nowhere to go and nothing particularly pressing to do. Before leaving her job, Jessica had assumed she could easily develop a consulting practice because of how well known and respected she was in her industry. She had culled an international reputation, winning many industry awards, and had contacts who would be thrilled, she thought, to access her expertise as soon as she was a free agent. Yet the phone was mysteriously quiet. The consulting practice was not happening by itself, and she suddenly realized she didn't know how to begin to create it. Despite her best efforts, Jessica was sad and lonely most of the time. Even though she *thought* she had a plan, she *felt* adrift, lazy, and unmotivated.

Eight weeks into her six-month severance period, Jessica began to panic about her financial situation. Then came a call from Tom, a colleague from the old company who had stayed in touch and was now strategically placed in company headquarters. Tom alerted Jessica to a new position at the corporate level—a job for which she was more than qualified. And it would pay more than her previous job had. The downside was that Jessica would have to move from the West Coast to the company's headquarters in New Jersey. After two trips East for interviews and to check out New Jersey, Jessica decided to take the position.

When Jessica announced her plans to the Kevorkian group members, they were incredulous. Was this the same person who had complained bitterly about this company during her On the Brink experience? The same Jessica who loved her California apartment so close to the beach? In any event, the group wished her the best, and threw her a good-bye-and-good-luck party.

On her second day in New Jersey, Jessica woke up to the reality of what she had done. The people at corporate headquarters and the problems in New Jersey were no different from those at her old position. One week later, Jessica decided to quit and move back to

California. Imagine the surprise of the Kevorkian group when Jessica appeared at the very next meeting after her farewell party!

CLINGING

Jessica experienced many of the issues common during Letting Go. She was afraid of "becoming unglued," of the disintegration of her self-image that would come from separating herself from work. The disruption of the first few weeks of unemployment was enough to unhinge her from the path of Letting Go and boomerang her right back into a situation just like the one she had so abhorred. Luckily, Jessica had the courage to realize and remedy her mistake. She returned to California and took the time to grieve her old identity. Eventually she reemerged as a college instructor. Jessica will still have to dip into savings to make ends meet until she develops some business consulting on the side, but she can now look back wistfully on her Letting Go trauma and savor the lesson of her "week in corporate."

Like Jessica and Lauren, many Refugees have a tendency to cling to anything that might keep them safe during their Letting Go period. Imagine being pushed from a cliff's edge (On the Brink) down a steep decline (Letting Go) coated with olive oil. You careen down this slide with no sense of where or how you'll land. You try to climb back up, or stem your fall—to no avail.

Like Ted, whom we met earlier in this chapter, the Refugee may try clinging to the old work community by taking another job within the company, even if that job is a demotion. This clinging might be compounded by rationalizations: "I can't survive without my major medical insurance, my 401(k) plan, my company car, my expense account." Or, "I've always had people in the company to help sort out issues like writing proposals, dealing with health insurance, contacting clients, and the myriad other items that we take for granted while employed. How can I ever manage those things alone?"

It's very difficult to let go of roles that had given us a handle for

Most of us are about as eager to be changed as we were to be born, and go through our changes in a similar state of shock.

—JAMES BALDWIN

navigating daily life. As a result, a Refugee may grasp at his or her old identity as a software engineer, artistic director, or social worker, even if he or she is burned out or no longer interested in that type of work, or if in fact the job has become obsolete. Sometimes ex-managers project their managerial persona onto their families and become bossy or controlling in areas they previously left to their mates or offspring. Sometimes these behaviors and roles have become so ingrained, we don't even notice our attachment to them.

CLUSTER OF LOSSES

A common characteristic of Letting Go is the experiencing of a "cluster of losses." Losses at this stage appear to come in groups, either coincidentally or because we've been so busy *doing* that we've suppressed awareness of inner and outer losses that have already stacked up. Suddenly the loss of one's job coincides with the loss of one's health, the pain of marital discord, the loss of motivation to create a holiday celebration for one's family, the loss of sexual desire, as well as external losses such as the death of a relative or friend, the sale of one's house, the ending of a relationship. As the shock of present loss resonates with the grief of past, even childhood, losses, we may reexperience the disorientation and aloneness of those times. It's essential to allow the grief to flow through you (as suggested in the "Dutchboy Syndrome" strategy elaborated on page 99). Whether the grief feels more related to the past or to your current losses, the emotions are occurring in present time. Let them out of your body. Feelings are energy; pent up, that energy causes greater harm than the sadness that comes with its release. Ultimately, this grieving stage is transient, although knowing that does not make living through it any less excruciating.

IT'S NOT ALL BLEAK

Since work is so central to life in this culture, many of us—when times get tough for any number of reasons—resort to our work as a means of feeling productive. If you've used work as a tranquilizer or tool for avoiding other issues in your life, the notion of losing that tranquilizer can be terrifying. On the other hand, think about how much stronger and happier you will be when you reclaim the inner strength you lost through your attachments to the job or title. Though Letting Go is a necessary passage to effect detachment from what felt essential before, the payoffs are far greater than you can imagine right now. Here are just a few:

•If you've gradually merged your life and your identity with your job, you might have developed blinders to other possibilities out of fear of rocking the boat. By Letting Go, you'll see how resourceful, resilient, and creative you can be outside of the job description to which you've been tied.

•Maybe you've developed a specialization within your field to the exclusion of other interests and talents. With Letting Go will come release from those limitations and the opportunity to rediscover dormant skills and passions.

•Heightened communication and healing will occur in all of your relationships as you move through this stage.

•Your ability to deal with loss in new and creative ways will strengthen you for future losses of all kinds and save you from the stress of avoiding and denying difficulties along life's highway.

•A career track that provided regular raises might have hypnotized you into a sense of financial security that scared you from reinventing yourself when boredom or burnout set in. By Letting Go, you can be honest about such feelings and move on.

Ultimately, new opportunities will surface after you've negotiated all the recovery stages—opportunities that you couldn't have seen from the vantage point of your old job. As dark as your days may feel during Letting Go, take one step at a time and know that it's not all bleak: there will be a happy ending.

FINANCES

While On the Brink, you organized your finances in anticipation of an undetermined period of unemployment. Now is the time to solidify your budget, based on severance, unemployment benefits, and/or savings.

Severance packages are not automatic. Employers are not required to provide severance pay, unless it was guaranteed by a written contract when you were hired. Typically, longer-term, higher-status employees receive the best severance packages. Whatever the case, severance packages are often negotiable.

The standard severance formula is a week of salary for every year of service, often with a two- or three-month minimum. If you've worked for your company for several years, don't settle for a mere three-month minimum. Get an attorney who specializes in employee issues to draft a letter demanding enough severance to compensate more generously for your many years of service and support you through a period of retraining. Larger packages are sometimes offered in installments rather than a lump sum. If you have a choice, consider taking the lump sum so you can walk away from this employer and not look back. Then safely invest that money where it will earn interest yet be liquid enough to tap as you need it. Consult with your financial advisor regarding installment versus lump-sum payments to be sure about what's best for your particular tax situation.

Similarly, pension dollars are a critical issue. Your accountant and attorney will be essential advisors in determining what your best options are and how to receive or roll over pension money. Because of the huge tax consequences of receiving your pension money directly, you're most likely better off having your employer deposit it (roll it over) into a self-directed Individual Retirement Account (IRA) via your broker, banker, or mutual-fund advisor. Better still is the option (if offered by your employer) to leave your 401(k) or profit-sharing plans where they are until your retirement, provided the company is solid and you feel the plan is well managed.

Be sure to continue company-based health insurance as you enter Letting Go. Your employer is required to extend your medical benefits but not to pay your premium. The COBRA plan (Consolidated Omnibus Budget Reconciliation Act of 1985) allows for eighteen months of employer-provided health insurance, for which you'll pay the premium at a group rate plus 2 percent for administration fees. Do not hesitate in this regard. Yes, it's an expense you're not used to having to pay out of pocket, but it's essential to cover yourself and your family until you have new coverage in a new work situation. If catastrophic illness hits during a time you are not insured, much more than your job will be lost. Or, if you are part of a dual-income family, get yourself added to your spouse's insurance coverage.

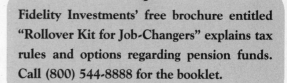

Fidelity Investments' free brochure entitled "Rollover Kit for Job-Changers" explains tax rules and options regarding pension funds. Call (800) 544-8888 for the booklet.

Did your company provide life insurance coverage? Was there any accumulated cash value at the time of your job loss? If so, you might be able to borrow against that cash value if you need the money, or simply take out the cash if you prefer. Your employer is not likely to continue the policy, but you are entitled to convert it to an individual policy with your family as beneficiaries.

Once you have negotiated the best severance package and determined your unemployment benefits, it's time to draft a budget that will sustain you during an indefinite unemployment. If you are part of a family, have a family meeting to agree on interim spending allowances. Reduce expenses wherever you can. For example, you may want to lower your long-distance phone bills, eliminate the extra phone lines in your home, and cut off premium cable channels. Engage family members to help you list all the expenses you now have; then, item by item, brainstorm no-cost ways of achieving the same goals. For example, how can you work out without a gym membership? How can you eliminate a dry cleaning bill? If you find that you will need to dip into savings and that makes you nervous, establish a budget that shows you concretely what the limits of such dipping must be. If you know you'll be short of funds and have relatives willing to help financially during this period, consider accepting their support graciously with the knowledge that not only will this time of need be temporary, but you'll also have opportunities in the future to reciprocate. Don't let your pride prevent you from buying some very necessary recovery time right now. Your future depends on it.

SOME BOOKS THAT TEACH FRUGALITY

•*Miserly Moms* by Jonni McCoy (Holly Hall, 1996). Provides suggestions for how to live on one income.

•*The Complete Tightwad Gazette: Promoting Thrift as a Viable Alternative Lifestyle* by Amy Dacyczyn (Random House, 1999). The gold standard for money-saving tricks and tips.

•*Your Money or Your Life* by Joe Dominguez and Vicki Robin (Penguin, 1993). Presents a strategy for simplifying your life and thus lowering your need for income.

GO COLD TURKEY

Take deliberate time off during this stage. We all know that rebounding from a relationship by entering a new relationship too quickly has the potential to preempt healthy recovery, not to mention jettison you into a potentially worse relationship. When a relationship ends, you need to take as much recovery time as possible. The same is true when a job ends: you need time to reclaim YOU. Unless a compelling new career opportunity forces you to act fast, take as much time off as you can afford.

INTERIM STRUCTURE FOR LETTING GO

Because this stage catapults the Refugee into unknown and unstructured territory, an easily managed, reliable vehicle is needed with which to navigate the Letting Go obstacle course. If you don't create an Interim Structure for yourself, you're likely to feel desperate isolation, disorientation, anxiety, and vulnerability. Over time, these feelings can result in a free fall so destabilizing that the benefits of Letting Go cannot be experienced. In some cases, self-defeating behaviors such as binge eating, compulsive spending, excessive drinking, or oversleeping become habitual, vain attempts to numb the pain of Letting Go.

What follows is a suggested Interim Structure that provides the psychological environment most Refugees need in order to move through the trauma of Letting Go—a self-nourishing framework within which grief and surrender can safely occur. The suggested strategies build upon the Interim Structure you developed during On the Brink: Daily Rituals, Actions, and After Hours options to take you into the next stage. The absence of your job opens up lots of available time, so you can practice the exercises as often as needed to facilitate a healthy release. A natural, yet potentially self-defeating, corollary of having time on your hands is negative self-talk, which can sabotage your progress at this time; therefore, the Interim Structure for Letting Go also includes a component called Watch Out For . . . to support you past such potholes.

> ### THE IMPORTANCE OF SELF-CARE
>
> Studies quoted in the *American Journal of Public Health* (January 1998) report that unemployment creates health risks. Even a serious *threat* of unemployment triggers physiological effects linked to heart disease.

As you move through this stage, be gentle with yourself. Even though the process of grieving is natural and healthy, there will be some rough days as you experience the loss of the familiar structure. Think of this stage as releasing the old to make room for the new. Affirm the following objectives for your Letting Go experience:

- Surrender to feelings of sadness and anger that are natural components of Letting Go.

- Gradually release the past job.

- Prevent self-destructive or numbing behaviors.

THE DAILY RITUALS

The Interim Structure for Letting Go begins with the Daily Rituals you launched during On the Brink with some changes specific to the work of Letting Go. If you didn't make these rituals a part of your daily routine during the Brink, now is the time to do so.

Your Morning Journal

Assign yourself the task of filling a minimum of three pages every morning just after you wake—just three pages and then on with the

AN OVERVIEW OF THE INTERIM STRUCTURE
FOR STAGE II: LETTING GO

Goals During Letting Go

- Surrender to sadness and anger
- Active grief work to release the past
- Prevent self-destructive or numbing behaviors

Daily Rituals

- Your Morning Journal
- Feed Yourself with Care
- Exercise Mindfully
- Daily Purpose
- Remains of the Day

After Hours

- RIP
- Dis' Old House
- Catch the Spirit
- Bless Is More

Actions

I. *For Emotional Release*

- Breathe!
- Hello, Heartache
- Die a Little
- Shake Your Fist
- Give Thanks
- Get a Physical

II. *To Reclaim Your Natural Rhythm*

- Metaphors Be with You
- Simmer
- Weekly Support Group
- Soft Pillows

III. *Watch Out For . . .*

- Spillover into Family
- Don't Be a Do-Bee
- Waste Not—WPT Not
- Dutchboy Syndrome
- Avoid Anesthetics
- Static Negativity
- Social Withdrawal

day. If you remember dream fragments, jot them down without concern for what they might mean. If you're angry, feel free to express yourself using any kind of language you like. Complete sentences are immaterial for this process; just put the words on a page with as much honesty as possible.

If you greet the empty page feeling empty yourself, bring your awareness into the present moment and tune into your senses. What do you *see* around you at this moment? Write that down. What do you *hear* that's in your house, or outdoors? Write that. How does your body *feel* right now? Write. Soon your senses will have brought you into the moment, and your pen will take off, writing almost on its own! Even if you become aware of just one feeling expressed in one sentence, keep repeating it until you have filled three pages. Do not reread your entries; just fill the pages and move on.

Your journaling may begin as a ritual that is purely an act of will and not a heartfelt enterprise. No matter; do it anyway. The simple act of pouring words onto the page is a form of meditation, a daily practice with untold physical and emotional benefits. Keep your journal private. Soon it will become an intimate friend, a receptacle for your innermost feelings, needs, wishes, and dreams.

Feed Yourself with Care

Following your morning journaling, make yourself a healthy breakfast. Take the time to savor what you are eating. Don't eat standing up at the counter! Again, use your senses to stay in present time as much as possible. If your mind wanders into the past, contemplating your old job, or gets anxious about the future, stressing about your To Do List, gently bring your attention back to the food you are chewing, its textures on your tongue, the nourishment it's bringing to your health and well-being.

During your working days, you might have felt strapped for time and skipped meals or eaten on the run. Now is your opportunity to

> **BENEFITS OF JOURNALING**
> In James Pennebaker's book *Opening Up,* in which he reports on a series of studies investigating the healing effects of writing, a group of unemployed people were asked to write their *deepest thoughts and feelings about losing their jobs.* Eight months later, they had twice the success in finding a new job than those who just wrote about their job-seeking plans.

return to the sensual aspects of mealtime. Light a candle and set a place for yourself; include a place mat and cloth napkin. Take a meal out to the garden, deck, balcony, or nearby park. Learn your body's needs during this fragile time. Maybe you need more fiber, more greens, more grains. Your immune system is surely compromised by the stress of Letting Go, not to mention your time On the Brink. Even if your diet is reasonably healthy, your cholesterol or LDL/HDL ratios might be abnormal. A simple blood test will tell you if you need supplements. Healthy eating along with proper supplementation can do wonders to rejuvenate both your resilience and your mood.

FINDING HEALTHY COMFORT FOODS

"Comfort foods" are those that have soothed us all the way back to childhood. To guard against high-fat versions of such foods, explore these resources for creative comfort foods low in fat:

• *Healthy Homestyle Cooking* by Evelyn Tribole (St. Martin's Press, 1994).

• *Moosewood Restaurant Low-fat Favorites* by the Moosewood Collective (Clarkson Potter, 1996).

Exercise Mindfully

After breakfast, take a walk or exercise at the gym for at least thirty minutes. (If you prefer, this can be done before breakfast.) It is essential that you get your body moving during the early part of each day. Aim to raise your heartbeat to an aerobic level. This brings your awareness into your body and helps foster the secretion of endorphins, the chemicals in our brain that help fight depression. As you work out or walk, notice how your body and spirit feel:

• Are you tired?

• Are you sad?

• Can you appreciate the sights and sounds around you as you move?

• Is there grief, fear, or anxiety to be dealt with, or do you feel perfectly calm?

Whatever the feelings, acknowledge rather than avoid them. Remember that anything denied is doomed to return. Better to embrace even the toughest feelings and give them your attention. Don't try to resolve any negative feelings or solve difficult problems. Instead, work on *allowing them*, assuring yourself that these feelings are a normal and necessary part of Letting Go and will pass.

Daily Purpose

After your morning rituals (journal, breakfast, exercise), design a purpose for the day—just for this one day, not for the vast future, not even for tomorrow. Enter your feelings at this moment, and ask yourself what you most need today— and resist the knee-jerk response of "I most need a job."

> **EXERCISE AGAINST DEPRESSION**
>
> Many studies show that exercise has antidepressant effects. For example, in a 1988 study by the U.S. Surgeon General, the relative risk of depression was 27 percent lower for men who played three or more hours of sports each week.

Do you most need to be outdoors? If so, in what setting? Do you crave intellectual stimulation or entertainment? Companionship? If you can't seem to clear away your fears to identify what you truly need at the moment, try asking it this way: If you were financially independent and money were not an issue in your life, what would you most want for yourself at this moment?

Once you have focused on your need, design a loose structure— for this day only—and get dressed accordingly. Explore a park or museum that you postponed visiting during your aggressive days of work. Wander through a bookstore or library and find pleasure reading books and magazines you've so long neglected. Go to a lecture listed in the morning newspaper, see a movie matinee, sit peacefully at a sidewalk cafe with a cup of herb tea—all delicious pastimes rarely experienced by busy worker bees. Take advantage of the fact that you are free on a weekday, and revel in paying matinee prices, or in not waiting in line at the market or for the treadmill. Whatever you do is likely to be different each day. Deliberately make some of your activities relational and others solitary.

Remains of the Day

This exercise is a variation on the decompression ritual you began during On the Brink. During Letting Go, your "work" is not gainful employment; nevertheless, it is stressful. Make a list of relaxing experiences you most enjoy, such as:

- a hot tub or bubble bath surrounded by candles;

- stretching out on a sofa or chaise listening to music;

- contemplating beautiful images in an oversized book of photography or work by a favorite artist;

- putting in time on the hobby or craft project of your choice;

- snuggling with a mate, or pet, or a great book.

At the end of the day, create a sacred time for any one of these experiences. Ideally, you will ritualize this time so that you do it at the same time every day and before you get too tired to appreciate it. As you discover additional experiences you enjoy, add them to the list of activities you can choose to do at this time of day.

Writing down your list of potential relaxation activities grounds them as options for you on days when you feel foggy. The list also acts as a reminder of the last task of your day, similar to closing down the office when you used to leave work. In essence, *you* are your workplace now and giving yourself a gentle, sensual winding-down at the end of each day is very healing. It's also a self-nourishing ritual that will continue to be useful when you return to a career-based lifestyle.

POETICALLY GUIDED RELAXATION

Physician, poet, and author Emmett Miller has produced several powerful audiotape programs of guided visualization for relaxation, sleep, and change management. Try three longtime favorites: *Letting Go of Stress, Rainbow Butterfly,* and *Accepting Change and Moving On.* To purchase these, and to review Miller's entire collection, write or call: Source, P.O. Box W, Stanford, CA 94309, (800) 52-TAPES.

ACTIONS

For Emotional Release

Emotional release is the heart of your work during Letting Go. The following strategies are meant to help you surrender to and deal with your feelings. The more of these Actions that you use repeatedly, the quicker will be your progress through this stage. Don't be surprised if these actions give rise to emotions that run the gamut from the sadness of loss to the frustration and anger that come with powerlessness. All of those feelings are normal and necessary to support a healthy Letting Go.

Breathe!

Get an audiocassette program of guided visualizations to teach you conscious breathing for relaxation, centering, and stress reduction. Use a portable cassette recorder so you can situate yourself in a quiet place and practice with your tape at least once daily until you naturally notice the stress in your body and learn to use your breathing to center yourself. Not only will breath work soothe the anxiety that occurs during Letting Go, but it will also help you stay in present time rather than reliving the past or worrying about the future.

In spite of our natural, exquisite potential for harmony, we don't stay in balance easily. Such balance requires alignment of our bodies and minds, a dynamic process maintained by deep, relaxed breathing. Unfortunately, our cultural style has inspired a level of striving and driving that focuses us on our minds rather than on our bodies; hence, we operate at a staccato beat that helps us maintain a maximum intellectual speed. This speedy functional tempo has led to our breathing very shallowly. Gradually, shallow breathing lessens our ongoing sense of connection with our bodies, and we become aware only of what's going on mentally. Physical and emotional distress can mount, yet we focus on *doing* because we are disconnected from *feeling* the dis-ease building within us.

THINKING TIME
VS.
FEELING TIME

Stephen Rechtschaffen, in his book *TimeShifting: Creating More Time to Enjoy Your Life*, introduces the concept of thinking time (that staccato-paced, somewhat breathless style that occurs when we're mentally focused) and feeling time (the relaxed, body-based rhythm that drives our emotional awareness). He teaches readers a simple method to recognize and shift between these states.

Returning to simple, relaxed breathing instantly resumes the mind-body-spirit connection nature gave us. Ideally, we need to inject these meditative moments into every day of our lives, but it's particularly essential that while you are in the Letting Go stage you conscientiously work to breathe more deeply.

Barbara

After graduating *magna cum laude* with a degree in English literature, Barbara got an entry level job with AT&T in the '70s. She worked her way up the ranks of companies, including Xerox, Apple Computer, General Electric, and Pfizer, doing everything from sales and marketing to managing and training. A gifted conceptual thinker and hands-on manager, Barbara's leadership qualities won her corporate and regional honors, including four national awards for outstanding sales production at a large U.S. bank. She designed and built training departments, originated a mortgage insurance sales department that became, at the time, the largest in the state of California, and increased her bank's customer satisfaction rating from 80 percent to 95 percent during her tenure.

You can imagine her shock when this senior vice president and regional sales manager had to leave her job as the result of a huge reorganization in the early '90s. Barbara's first reaction was total shock and denial: "This cannot be happening. Look at my numbers!" During her On the Brink stage, Barbara spent long days networking among company colleagues, trying to find a spot in their departments to avoid leaving the company. At the same time, she was acutely aware of physical and emotional exhaustion, symptoms she had suppressed during nine years of putting out fires. Barbara's wake-up call came in the form of breast cancer that eventually bought her an additional year of severance and disability insurance payments. Only when she was prostrated by illness and forced to let go of her huge job and her obsessive overidentification with her professional persona could Barbara surrender to grief and change. In retrospect, Barbara says, the process of Letting Go was her most powerful life experience, "far beyond any of the honors and accomplishments work ever gave me."

As Barbara worked on using relaxation techniques to ease her Letting Go experience, the deepened breathing brought up spontaneous emotions that surprised her. She gradually recognized long-standing marital problems and feelings of emotional isolation and sadness that she'd completely suppressed in order to stay focused on her professional life. In fact, Barbara realized she'd "buried" herself in work "to avoid dealing with what was really making me sick."

Deliberate breath work brings awareness back into the body and spirit in ways that force us to *feel* what's going on with us. For Barbara, full recovery from breast cancer came with a renewed connection to her body and spirit. She decided to work part time as a consultant in the banking industry and use the balance of her "work time" to provide volunteer career coaching to fellow cancer survivors. Not only does she describe this as "a way to give back, it's also a blessing for me. I get to be reminded daily of my own need to ritualize mindful breathing techniques and keep myself 'hooked up.'"

Hello, Heartache

Because grief and fear are the handmaidens of Letting Go, they must be honored. It takes courage to befriend tough feelings and recognize them as messengers with great knowledge for you, but the payoffs are invaluable. This practice will speed your healing. It also will teach you about suffering in general, about how we contract and harden against it, which tends to deepen the pain. If you learn to surrender to suffering, you'll experience your heart moving into compassion. Then, miraculously, there's release. In Tibetan Buddhism, this practice is called *tonglen*. Following are some simple variations on that concept that you can practice to aid you during Letting Go.

First, notice the sadness approaching. This is akin to the way an aura precedes a migraine headache. When migraine sufferers pay attention to that aura by stopping what they're doing to relax deeply, they can often ward off the debilitating pain. The heartache that comes with the Refugee experience can be dealt with similarly. As that familiar sadness approaches, stop what you're doing. Sit in an easy chair, resting your arms at your sides, and lean your head back. Close your eyes, take a few deep breaths, and invite the

> Your pain is the breaking of the shell that encloses your understanding.
>
> —KAHLIL GIBRAN

feeling to join you in the room. As it appears, focus on your breathing, keeping it deep, slow, rhythmic. No matter how uncomfortable you may feel, continue the focused breath work, counting your breaths if it helps you stay in the moment. You'll soon see the miracle in this process: The sad feeling will come, gently leave its message, and then go away.

Another way to use this strategy is what author and philosopher Ram Dass called "inviting your grief to tea." Have your journal and a pen beside you or on your lap. Begin by doing some gentle breathing to get centered. Then, in your journal, write out a dialogue with your fear. You can name the fear: call it NoJob, or NoMoney, or Fear of the Future. Better yet, visualize the fear and personify it with a human name. Then, as if you were a playwright scripting dialogue, write out what you and your fear character say to each other. Continue the dialogue until it reaches some kind of closure. You'll know when that is. Your fears have messages for you, and finding those kernels takes work. The more you practice welcoming these dark moments, the more you can learn from them.

A GIFTED TEACHER OF *TONGLEN*

In her books and audiotapes, author and Buddhist teacher Pema Chodron lovingly explains the practice of *tonglen*, as well as the use of compassion when our world seems to collapse from loss. See particularly her audiotape and book *When Things Fall Apart: Heart Advice for Difficult Times* (Shambhala, 1997) and her audiotape program *Good Medicine: How to Turn Pain into Compassion with Tonglen Meditation* (Sounds True Audio, 1999).

Die a Little

Once you've practiced conscious breathing and focused relaxation, you are ready to try "practicing the art of dying," an exercise suggested by Marion Woodman, a gifted Jungian psychologist. The idea is to use any opportunity life presents to connect with our mortality—such as time away from work or downtime due to illness—as a wake-up call to the many exquisite choices we have each day, choices that are life-giving yet overlooked due to chronic busyness.

The process for practicing the art of dying begins with setting aside a time when you can be alone, quiet, and uninterrupted. Put your journal beside you; get comfortable yet be alert; allow your

Dying is something we human beings do continuously, not just at the end of our physical lives on this earth.

—ELISABETH KÜBLER-ROSS

breathing to become deep and rhythmic as you let your eyes close. Allow an image of yourself as you are at this moment to present itself on an imaginary movie screen. See the clothes you are wearing, the chair in which you sit, the characteristics of your surroundings. Now gently imagine your spirit wafting up, out of your body, and allow your body to "die." See this image as peaceful and natural, the moment of your death against the present context of your life. Now watch an imaginary movie of what happens next: Whom have you left behind? What have you left behind? How will the lives of those around you carry on? What did you leave unfinished?

From this vantage point, where you no longer have the power to impact anyone or anything, what looks important to you? See a typical *workday* in your recent life, only you are not there. See the frustrations, the joys, the people involved, the ways you used to cope. Now see a typical day in your *home* life, only without you. Who is there? How do they spend their time without you? What do they say about you? As you experience this movie in your imagination, how is your heart feeling? What do you wish you had done or said before your "death"? What looks important to you now, from this perspective?

PRACTICING THE ART OF DYING

When you feel stuck in current reality, knowing the state you want to experience but unable to effect it, Stephen and Ondrea Levine's book *Who Dies?* (Anchor Books, 1989) is a powerful resource. The Levines teach meditative practices that shift us out of limited thinking and help us "die into life."

Gently allow whatever emotions you feel to simply be there. . . . Keep breathing deeply. . . . When you're ready, imagine your spirit returning to your body, open your eyes, "return" to the room, and immediately write in your journal any insights you saw and felt. This is a powerful meditative practice that allows us to see our lives against the larger context of our mortality, to reclaim core values and priorities, and to see choices that may have previously been masked by temporary fears or concerns.

Shake Your Fist

Anger is emotional energy that is an arm of the stress response. Anger mobilizes us toward fight or flight when we sense danger. It's meant to be a short-term physical state that can be rapidly dissipated through action. The classical image is one in which a child is pinned beneath a car or heavy object, arousing a mobilized parent to be flooded with enough energy to have the strength of several people—enough to lift the car and free the child. Similarly, combat arouses the physical and mental states of anger that foster intense and immediate action.

When anger is expressed and dissipated through action, it subsides and an emotionally neutral state returns. On the other hand, if anger is not externalized, it can result in chronic hostility that is more damaging to our bodies than most other mental states. So it's not whether we get angry that's important, it's how long we stay angry, and what we do before we calm down. Anger itself is normal and appropriate, neither good nor bad. What's essential is that we accept our anger, develop healthy means of venting it, and heal any leftover resentment that can damage health.

Anger during Letting Go is not only a normal reaction to the stress of job loss but also a good sign of healing. Suppression of anger will cause depression, while expression, in healthy ways, can move you toward forgiveness and new beginnings. Here are a few strategies for healthy anger management:

• Physical expression of some kind, ideally constructive (such as exercise) rather than destructive (breaking objects) can reduce the agitation that comes with anger. It might help to punch a punching bag or hit a tennis ball or racquetball against a backboard to externalize the anger. Take a tennis racquet and hit the top of a mattress for ten minutes, long enough to get sweaty and feel the emotional release. The bed won't get hurt, nor will the tennis racquet, but the release is great.

• Screaming can be therapeutic—in the shower or in the car while driving on the freeway where no one can hear you (but drive safely!).

• Shallow breathing often accompanies the arousal of anger in our bodies. Focused deep breathing to open up the lungs and break up the contraction in your stomach and chest can be very healing.

•Expressing your feelings to someone who understands your anger or in your journal are excellent tools for release. Such expressions may require repetition, but the anger will dissipate. The critical factor is that you watch how you rate, or "frame," the anger. If you frame the situation as catastrophic and stoke its fire, the anger will not easily dissipate. If you vent the emotional energy, coupled with relaxation practice, you'll soon see the lessons available from it and be free to heal.

Give Thanks

After anger is expressed and its residuals dissipate, gratitude can surface—gratitude for the good things that came with your old job as well as the opportunity to move on. In your journal, write thank you notes to anyone who's had any impact on your life during this transition, even to your former boss or company. You don't have to mail these. They are meant to be an expressive process that helps in Letting Go. If it feels artificial, take inexpensive paper, fold it in half, and use it like a note card. Be honest as you write, and truly acknowledge what you got from each individual. This is not meant to deny or overlook any resentments or disappointments your former boss or colleagues may have caused you. It's about *balancing* your view of them. Remember, this was a business relationship and surely something was gained.

Get a Physical

In some cases, a Refugee feels extreme anxiety or depression that might require temporary medication. Sleep difficulties can also surface during this stage as your psyche wrestles with loss and transition. Visit your doctor and have a complete physical—blood tests and all. In this way your physician can rule out any medical problems. Then, if indicated, the doctor may prescribe the short-term

A hundred times every day I remind myself that my inner and outer life depends on the labors of other men, living and dead, and that I must exert myself in order to give in the measure as I have received and am still receiving.

—ALBERT EINSTEIN

use of an antidepressant to help you sleep and function optimally during the Letting Go period.

Don't be afraid or ashamed to ask for help. Physiological changes do occur during major change. Some can be addressed with proper nutrition, vitamins, or herbal supplements. Others may require medication, but rest assured, it is usually just a temporary prescription for a passing state. Having the ability to seek medical advice is another reason you'll be glad for the health coverage allowed by COBRA.

TRY A VIRTUAL PHYSICAL

To assess your health from a variety of perspectives that combine the best of conventional and alternative medicine, visit www. healthy.net. You'll receive a personalized profile of your nutrition, sleep, fitness, and emotional, behavioral, and physical health along with a customized action plan for your healing. Referrals to recommended practitioners are available as well as real-time consultations with experts in Eastern and Western modalities.

To Reclaim Your Natural Rhythm

The venting process that is Letting Go takes time, the length of which differs from person to person. As the gamut of emotions gradually flows through you, try not to deny or avoid any feelings; otherwise, you may get stuck in sadness or anger, thereby prolonging your time in Letting Go. The following Actions, in addition to the Daily Rituals, will help you reclaim your own unique, natural rhythm while enhancing your ability to let go.

Metaphors Be with You

Develop a powerful guiding metaphor to which you can return easily whenever you need fortification during difficult moments. Metaphors are creative comparisons that allow us to infuse our inner conflict with new meaning. They open up new ways of viewing current reality. The intent of a guiding metaphor is to give the creative part of our brain a bridge through which the confusion that comes with our loss can gently move toward a new reality.

You might think of such metaphors as: a snake shedding its skin, a butterfly emerging from a cocoon, Homer on his odyssey, a lunar eclipse, the Native American medicine wheel. Note that each of these metaphors includes the pain that comes with letting go of the old structure, along with the promise of new life on the other side. The idea is to choose a metaphor that contains an inspiring and instructive story that touches you on a deep, visceral level. Let this metaphor then become your psychological guide through the ambiguities of this phase of your journey.

If a metaphor doesn't readily occur to you, here is a simple way to find one. Put yourself in a comfortable position and close your eyes. Contemplate the state of your reality right now, both external and internal. Allow your breathing to become slow and rhythmic, so that your body becomes fully relaxed. As you notice places in your body that remain tense, take your breath to those areas: inhale deeply, as if you're bringing fresh healing oxygen to them, and exhale, imagining the tension leaving your body with your breath. Inhale through your nose; exhale through your mouth. Breathe in calm; breathe out anxiety.

As you relax, notice where in your body you feel the confusion, fear, pain, or other emotions associated with your current situation. Is it in the pit of your stomach? Or in your forehead? Or in your arms? Just notice where it seems to lodge and let it be there. If you had to give that emotion a visual image, or a sound, or a phrase, what would it be? What is that image doing? Does it change as you focus your attention on it, or does it remain the same? Next, allow your image to tell you a short story about itself. What does it say? It might be a familiar story like a fairy tale or the lyrics to a song . . . or it could be a colorful phrase or saying that seems to stand alone while embodying your identified feelings.

Kirk

Kirk, thirty-eight, lost his job at an automotive plant. Always a happy-go-lucky guy, Kirk tried to avoid feelings of fear and foreboding during Letting Go, saying he'd never experienced them and "didn't want to go there." His resistance manifested itself in hives and frequent stomachaches. Finally, a guiding metaphor occurred to him while he was swimming with his children: he saw an image of a graceful mallard duck who, to the casual observer, appeared to be calmly gliding across the water while just beneath the surface and unseen to the viewer were two webbed feet furiously treading away! It was a stark reminder of his own apparent outer calm negated by the extreme inner turmoil Kirk felt during the Letting Go stage. When Kirk needed a handle to guide him through a wave of grief, he visualized his mallard, which he named Mike. He would first zone in on Mike's outer calm, then have Mike stop the anxious water treading, and *voilà!* Mike was able to glide peacefully across the water without strenuous activity.

Simmer

Instead of maintaining a steady emotional boil—whether it's raging at your loss or racing through your day the way you used to when you were strapped for time and deadline-driven—learn to simmer. Retire the alarm clock and allow yourself to wake naturally, when your body is rested. Stay in bed a while, tune into your body, and simply notice the ebb and flow of your breathing. Empty your mind. Luxuriate in the peaceful beginning of a new day. Allow your feelings to flow. You may want to do your daily journaling while simmering in bed. Letting Go includes letting go of the fast pace demanded by your prior work life to create the space for a new cycle to evolve. But watch that you don't malinger in your jammies all day "because there's no clear reason to get up." Simmering is about reclaiming your natural rhythm . . . period.

Roland

Roland, forty-nine, was the founder and artistic director of an international film festival. Over a fifteen-year period, he transformed his passion for Asian and Pacific Island films from a fledgling project funded by tedious, annual public-arts grants to a $10 million self-supporting enterprise that garners record attendance and community recognition year after year. With its success came corporate sponsorships, which soon led to corporate interests ruling the board of directors. Finally, Roland was forced to leave his post as founding director, to be replaced, as he put it, "by a suit."

Although the city gave Roland great recognition during the last festival under his aegis, he felt "put out to pasture"—without income. His transition into Letting Go was soothed by a couple of consulting projects, but after those, plus some vacation travel, he was hit by grief and nostalgia. Many longtime "friends" were no longer in his life now that he had no festival connections to offer.

Roland embraced the idea of jettisoning the alarm clock and SIMMERING before leaving the luxury of his bed each morning. He could use that simmering time to recollect and study his dreams, he realized. In his previous vocation as a storyteller and performing artist in local schools, Roland had found a treasure trove of metaphors and archetypes by recording and contemplating his dreams. This process had been lost to him for more than a decade as the festival's administrative demands required that he jump out of bed and use every waking minute for work. In truth, Roland was naturally nocturnal, forced by business into a diurnal lifestyle. Now he could resume his natural rhythm and recover his creative core. Roland began writing about his dreams, recording his reveries, and developing a book of memoirs. Ultimately, a new career as a writer and critic was born of his determination to SIMMER.

Weekly Support Group

A weekly support group or counseling opportunity is an important Action during Letting Go. It provides you a chance to talk things out with people more objective than your immediate family. Not only will loss and grief move through your system more quickly, but talking about your pain is also the single most effective way of mitigating those terrifying feelings of ambiguity and not-knowing. We are social creatures and benefit enormously from commiseration and reassurance. It is particularly beneficial for you to hear

FINDING SUPPORT GROUPS
The Self-Help Clearinghouse lists mutual self-help groups and contact numbers in the United States, Canada, and internationally at its Web site, www.mentalhelp.net/selfhelp/clrnghse.htm#states. There is also a list of groups under the "Toolkits" section of the *Wall Street Journal* Web site at www.wsj.com.

about and be reminded of the extent of powerlessness that also pervades others during the stage of Letting Go.

If you have not yet found a support group that's unrelated to your job, here are some ways to begin:

• Look in your daily newspaper for announcements of group meetings.

• Call your local college career office to explore their offerings. If you are female, there are Women's Opportunities Centers on virtually every college campus. Their offerings are free and often varied.

• Trade associations are another option, though they may serve better for networking than support. Nevertheless, members of trade associations may know about an appropriate support group.

• If all these leads fail to turn up the appropriate group, start one of your own. A well-placed classified ad in a local paper will amaze you when you receive calls of like-spirited job seekers who are also struggling with Letting Go.

If you aren't comfortable with an ongoing group, consider a one-day gathering of your prior work team of colleagues who were displaced at the same time as you were. While outplacement programs often provide a day of "venting" for displaced workers, after that it's up to you.

THE HEALING IMPACT OF VENTING

Following the recent Balkan wars, three Chicago psychiatrists set out to collect stories from refugees with the intention of creating a public document to preserve Bosnian culture. As the refugees expressed their anger, depression, nightmares, and stories of violence they had experienced, their posttraumatic stress symptoms dropped by 47 percent. The key to this dramatic drop appeared to be the public nature of their testimony, given that they are a people who are community- and family-based (rather than individualistic, as are many Western cultures). By collecting and sharing their stories, participants felt they were contributing to future generations. Similarly, when whole departments or work teams are displaced, their collected stories, recorded even in a temporary way, can expedite healing.

Soft Pillows

Within your plan of each day's activities, inject moments or experiences that will function as sanctuaries from busy-ness. Rhonda, a journalist, described these moments of respite as "soft pillows." While on the job, she had always been driven by constant dead-lines. She was forever saying, "Sorry, I don't have time for lunch with a friend . . . I don't have time to go to the gym . . . or to medi-tate . . . or to pray." Between jobs, Rhonda was finally able to choose how to fill her time and punctuate those activities with "soft pillows" of rest, wandering, painting, or simply sitting in the garden to contemplate nature's pace.

WATCH OUT FOR . . .

As you move through the work of Letting Go, one of your goals is to avoid numbing yourself with self-defeating habit patterns that can be extremely harmful at this time. Stop engaging in any of the following behaviors if they pertain to you:

Spillover into Family

Job loss can be difficult on the entire family. It's tough for loved ones to suppress anxiety about lost income, uncertainties about the future, and concern about the sadness projected by the grieving worker. All of these feelings are normal and appropriate. Healing is a process for everyone, and talking openly about everyone's feelings is the best therapy. Encourage all family members to express themselves. Brainstorm about ways to maintain family spirit, household responsibilities, and plans for the future.

Children can become particularly fearful, since you are their lifeboat. They have a propen-sity for blaming themselves if anything goes wrong for Mom or Dad. Assure them this job loss is nobody's fault, neither yours nor theirs. Allow them to be open with you when they

RESOURCES FOR FAMILY BALANCE

•*Living in Balance: A Dynamic Approach for Creating Harmony and Wholeness in a Chaotic World* by Joel and Michelle Levey (Conari, 1998) has a section on the spillover of job stress onto family, and how to achieve work-family balance.

•*Good Enough Mothers* by Melinda M. Marshall (Peterson's, Princeton, NJ, 1994) gives working moms permission to be imperfect through exploration of the necessary tradeoffs, creative compromise, and the testimony of powerful role models.

•Or try these Web sites: www.familiesandwork.org—resources of the Families and Work Institute, and www.workfamily.com—a clearinghouse of resources and links for everything from childcare and eldercare to work-family programs.

DID YOU KNOW . . . ?

Although workaholics appear to be dedicated, driven overachievers, they are acting out a compulsive need for control and power. Work becomes their drug to the point of profound personality change, loss of feelings, and clinical depression. For indepth understanding of this complex addiction, read *Workaholics: The Respectable Addicts* by Barbara Killinger, Ph.D. (Firefly Books, 1997).

worry. If your unemployment is prolonged, you might consider telling your children's schoolteacher or guidance counselor that this stress is occurring, in case your children display sadness or academic underachievement at school.

If the stress of job loss and job seeking becomes burdensome to your marriage, you should seek couples counseling. Sometimes financial issues loom large in marital problems, and job loss can exacerbate these concerns. It can also bring forth other difficulties that had never been adequately processed before. If you have free counseling sessions available to you through an Employee Assistance Program, now is the time to take advantage of them and get support through this difficult time.

Don't Be a Do-Bee

Be careful not to load up your To Do list as a way of drugging yourself with overdoing to avoid dealing with feelings of worthlessness, loss, and the pain of not knowing what's next.

Joan

Joan's been a busy bee all her life. The third of twelve children, she was the little mother of her siblings and the peacemaker when her parents battled. There was never enough money for food, let alone toys. Joan learned to entertain herself with books, crafts, and taking care of others. She started working during junior high school, married at seventeen, and was the mother of three by age twenty-two. There has never been a day without work. Indeed, Joan, now forty-five, won't *give* herself a day off. She describes how antsy she gets on vacation, to the point that she wants it to last only three days: "a day to get there, a day to be there, and a day to get home." Never mind the chronic migraines that seem to be the only thing that can slow her down—she's a worker bee and proud of it.

Not surprisingly, Joan rose through the managerial ranks of her company by overworking and demanding the same of her staff. After thirteen years with a Japanese-owned manufacturing company in Atlanta, Joan was packaged out. At the same time, a man she was dating was given a terminal medical diagnosis. Because Joan was receiving severance pay, she decided to delay job seeking to nurse him full time. He became her job.

When this man died a year later, Joan was bereft. Having never grieved the loss of her career, she now had two huge losses to process. But instead of doing the grief work, she ran out and got a job. A car accident a month into the new job finally stopped this Do-Bee in her tracks. In traction, immobilized for six weeks, the tears finally flowed.

Dutchboy Syndrome

Remember the story of the Little Dutch Boy, who held back the flood by sticking his thumb in the dike? Take your thumb out of that large dike holding back a sea of tears! Allow the grief, the tears, the short-term sadness to flow out of you. Avoid the urge to say or think, "If I start crying, I'll never stop." Disregard, for now, the advice of well-intentioned friends who tell you not to wallow in self-pity. Grief is not self-pity! Because "negative feelings" are so uncomfortable for us, we have a natural proclivity to avoid them. Ironically, they pass more quickly when you face them head-on, feel those feelings fully, and allow them to move through you. Eastern traditions consider emotions to be transient and the self to be spacious enough to simply allow those transient feelings to waft through, like butterflies moving through a wide open field. If you do the same, and simply allow the feelings without attaching interpretations to them, you will be far better off on the other side.

If you recognize the need to cry but feel blocked, consider a few sessions with a counselor or employee assistance provider, to which your company benefits may still entitle you. With support, you'll be able to pull the plug and let the tears heal you.

Waste Not—WPT Not

Don't waste time worrying about externals. From childhood report cards to job performance evaluations, we are programmed to seek approval. Progress in life and livelihood depends on making grades and numbers, according to external standards. No wonder we get caught up in "WPT," or "What People Think." Sometimes, depending on temperament and life experience, we develop chronic anxiety around these issues of measuring up to some standard that, upon deeper examination, is meaningless in the larger scheme. When losses come, especially something "defining," such as job loss, the WPTs can hit hard. We take too much personal responsibility for something over which we had no control and end up judging ourselves negatively.

Be careful to avoid this trap. Most layoffs have nothing whatsoever to do with one's work style or capabilities, so be sure to separate you as a person from the job you did. Remember that you are so much more than your job. Reinforce this sense of yourself by making a list of your *qualities* as a person. Look at all the nonwork activities you enjoy that allow those qualities to shine. Look at the validation and acknowledgment you get from all your relationships, particularly those outside of work. Separate who you are from what you do, and hold your head high. The WPTs are actually projections of your own negative self-judgments. If you hold onto your self-worth, those around you will do the same.

> **ASSERTIVE ANTIDOTES FOR THE WPTS**
>
> Assertiveness training is the best antidote to the WPTs. Try one of these seminal titles:
>
> • *Your Perfect Right: A Guide to Assertive Living* by Robert Alberti and Michael L. Emmons (Impact, 1995) gives you permission to set boundaries based on your core, emotional rights.
>
> • *When I Say No, I Feel Guilty* by Manuel Smith (Bantam, 1975). This landmark book on assertiveness and saying no has stood the test of time.

If you're plagued by worries of other people's judgments and can't see how these concerns are projections of your own self-blame, try this exercise: Write a paragraph about what other people are saying about you. Make it as long as your imagination will allow so it fills a page with worst-case-scenario judgments people could make about you. Go ahead—put this book down right now and write that statement.

Now take a different colored pencil or marker and strike out the name or pronoun of each person "making" these negative statements. Strike through every *he, she, they,* etc. Then go back and write "I" over each of those names or pronouns. Change the form of the verbs in those sentences as needed. Now reread that paragraph. How does this feel? Is it possible that the person making all these judgments is your own inner critic? Or does it represent someone else's voice you've carried all these years, like a parent, a teacher, a toxic boss? If so, write a rebuttal!

Use this exercise to see how these judgments are untrue and destructive. This is the time to build up your sense of self, not tear it down with fears of the WPTs.

Avoid Anesthetics

Remember Ted, valedictorian of his company-sponsored college degree program, whose sixteen years of service in telecommunications ended precipitously? He medicated his shock and despair with "a year of bad habits," including constant sitting in front of the television. Day after day he was morose, silent, isolated, and withdrawn, so much so that his wife and daughter lost patience with him. In response to their nagging, he e-mailed resumes, but since he never followed up, he got no responses. He got more depressed and resorted to numbing himself with alcohol. Pushed by his wife, Ted took the real estate licensing exam. He even tried selling property for a while. But this turned out to be a false start. Ted's a great technical guy and could design clever marketing material for real estate companies, but he fell apart trying to be a "people person." It wasn't a fit. Sadly, Ted had let himself become so anesthetized by his avoidance behaviors that he'd never stopped to explore what his options actually were.

Ted's advice, with the hindsight of "that horrible year of wasting myself away," is to get out of the house every day and go somewhere productive, as if you're going to work. "Even if it's to the library to read the morning newspaper, it'll keep your mind active rather than zing it straight to your misery and the lure of easy, mind-numbing drugs."

HUMOROUS VIDEO ANTIDOTES TO STATIC NEGATIVITY

•*Office Space:* **This 1999 comedy by writer-director Mike Judge depicts the plight of the Refugee by satirizing the consultants who were brought in to "cut the head count." The characters are clearly spoofs, yet their statements are so typical of what many Refugees hear that the double entendres can't help but make you giggle.**

•*Roger and Me:* **In this 1989 film, Michael Moore, the writer-director from Flint, Michigan, stalked General Motors' president Roger Smith to protest what the GM plant closing did to his hometown. GM laid off 40,000 workers due, Moore claims, to corporate greed. That theme is also at the core of *Downsize This*, a 1997 book and audiotape by Moore, and *The Awful Truth*, a series originally aired on Bravo Television in April 1999. Moore's work is couched in humor, but it touches on many of the excruciating aspects of corporate downsizing.**

Static Negativity

Stop collecting morbid statistics about people who *don't* work, such as "People die when they quit working," and watch out for people who ply you with similar negative warnings. Venting your frustration and commiserating with colleagues and friends who share your plight is healthy for a limited time, generally a few weeks. Thereafter, those you need most, your friends and family, will get annoyed with your sounding like a victim rather than hearing that you feel sad but that you also are taking action in new directions. This is the time to use Shakespeare's adage as your Letting Go mantra: "There is nothing either good or bad, but thinking makes it so." You have a choice in how you spin your Refugee story. If you keep telling yourself the victim version, it will become so ingrained that you'll be less inclined to see a way out.

Social Withdrawal

Be careful not to withdraw during this stage. In addition to your weekly support group (or counseling session), establish social get-togethers with family and friends. Sometimes current change will bring up memories of past losses, and being with good friends will allow you to share and heal more quickly. Also, the Refugee needs to battle withdrawal, shyness, and shame. You can avoid feeling responsible for your job loss and embarrassed by something over which you had no control by getting out and hearing other people's stories. Isolation only exacerbates fallacious thinking.

If you tend to avoid social contact because you fear that inevitable question, "So, what are you going to do next?" just remember that your friends, while well-intentioned, are possibly expressing their own fear of unemployment and may be ignorant of your inner state. Have a rejoinder that's innocuous or humorous. This might be something you can work out ahead of time in your journal or during a counseling or support group session. One possible rejoinder to, "Now what are you going to do?" is, "About what?" which may help the questioner wake up and recognize that you are more than your job or title.

AFTER HOURS

The following After Hours actions for Letting Go will help you shed your old shell and disengage from your prior identity. They might also help on those days when you feel restless, when you know you need to vent but you need a prop or exercise to help you do so.

RIP

A wonderful awareness exercise that's great for pulling you out of denial is to write a eulogy for your job. Please note: It's not *your* eulogy; it's for your former job. Personify it and pretend it has died. Pretend that it has reached the end of its useful life. Give it a date of birth, a chronological account of its accomplishments, and a description of its demise. Did it receive a terminal diagnosis? Did it die in its sleep? Or was its passing the result of a long, corrosive, but inexorable decline?

HUMOROUS ONLINE SITES TO LIGHTEN UP TOUGH TIMES

• www.jobhater.com, dubbed "the full-fledged site of hostility toward the workplace," is a link from Jobvertise, a straightforward job listing site. Enjoy "stupid boss quotes of the day," just for fun.

• www.Ishouldbeworking.com. Self-described as "your portal of slack," this site offers links to many other humor sites along with other distractions for disgruntled workers.

• www.i-resign.com. Here's a site for disgruntled workers in the UK. See in particular the page suggesting resignation letters, some serious, but most are tongue-in-cheek.

• www.dilbert.com contains Scott Adams's well-known Dilbert cartoons that boast, "I'm not antibusiness, I'm anti-idiot."

William

William, a twenty-four-year veteran of a large insurance conglomerate, provided sales and management training to agents in regional offices all over the country. He was on the road three weeks out of four. A traditional company man, he missed seeing his three children grow up during those years. His energy was spent helping his company grow, yet he was unceremoniously laid off during a recent downsizing. To add insult to injury, his stock options were manipulated in a way that cost him $30,000 when he went to cash them in. Here is his job's eulogy:

"I am the only person in attendance at this not-necessarily-somber occasion as we lay District Manager to rest. While alive, DM provided a high income, status, a title, and probably many unseen benefits. But there was a great toll in human sacrifice in the form of work addiction and exhaustion. Ah, yes, DM provided food, clothing, cars, houses, dinners, and recreation for a family of five during the good years. But near the end of DM's long life, career cancer set in. DM denied the sickness, living instead like a candle burning at both ends while signals all around were warning DM to change some things, any things, that would provide a survival strategy. Instead, DM died a long and painful death, clinging tenaciously to the only work it knew, while maintaining a parasitic hold over its human host.

"Do not grieve for District Manager, for there is always another unsuspecting, goal-oriented, status-seeking career climber willing to resurrect and honor the never-ending voracious needs this job requires. All that's necessary is that you forget who you are. Then you can mindlessly give your skill, creativity, energy, and most of your waking hours to fulfill the needs of District Manager. It's only fitting that I say a final good-bye to District Manager, for with this death, I get to LIVE. YESSS!!!"

William found some anger he'd been denying as he wrote his eulogy. Most important, he saw the price he'd paid while being on automatic pilot all those years.

Dis' Old House
If you find yourself—or others in your life—clinging to your prior work identity, actively DISconnect your self-definition by looking

at who you are apart from your former job. Write it down, or draw it with stick people and simple shapes.

•What talents, hobbies, aptitudes, and interests exist in you outside of career requirements?

•When was the last time you participated in any of them? How about resuming some of those interests now as you Let Go?

•Do people pigeonhole you, talking to you as if they are actually speaking to your work role or responsibilities?

•When you are introduced, does your career follow your name? Actively correct such assumptions. Ask people to avoid shoptalk. Bring up a recent movie you've both seen or an activity you might enjoy doing together. You must first disengage within your own mind; then you'll more easily be able to correct other people's automatic definitions of you.

> Freedom is what you do
> with what's been done
> to you.
> —JEAN-PAUL SARTRE

Catch the Spirit

Establish a spiritual practice. This might mean attending a church or synagogue, going on a spiritual retreat, stargazing, or lighting candles and listening to African drum music. Choose rituals of introspection that represent, to you, quiet beauty and the celebration of life. You don't have to overdo this. Even five minutes of such practice will help you step outside the stress of Letting Go and reconnect with the bigger picture of your spiritual life.

Bless Is More

As tough as it is to Let Go, all is not lost. To help you find meaning that's quality-based rather than quantity-based, take time to count your blessings—big ones and small ones. Most people begin this exercise by listing their material possessions—home, car, television, computer, and so forth. Our capitalistic culture has done much to reinforce the quantifying of success based on wealth, salaries, expensive possessions, and lifestyles. Surely you've met people who measure everything on the basis of money earned or lost. Maybe you got lost in that mode too. Break out by taking some time to look at your nonmaterial blessings:

- What about your health?

- What about the love of your family?

- What about the fact that you are the same person with or without that salary?

This does not minimize the fears that come with a loss of income. But when you do your accounting, be sure to look at everything in your life right now, not just the dollars. Recognize the freedom you have to enjoy the moment, to take full advantage of the growth this time-out affords you, and to get creative when the stress of Letting Go gradually lifts, beckoning you into the Wilderness between jobs.

BACKPACK FOR THE ROAD

1. To gather the lessons of Letting Go and detect any unfinished business as you move into the Wilderness, now is the time to write the story of your heroic journey—to the point of entering your personal Wilderness. This story begins back when you took the job you just lost. It's a story of disruption, and you are the mythic hero. To develop the content of your story, make the following notes:

How I landed the job:

_____

_____

_____

_____

My expectations when I took the job:

_____

_____

_____

_____

My experience on this job:

_____

_____

_____

_____

My On the Brink experiences:

_____

_____

_____

_____

How I lost this job:

_____

_____

_____

_____

How I expressed my grief and anger:

_____

_____

_____

_____

The door ahead of me, ushering me into my personal Wilderness, looks like:

_____

_____

_____

_____

These points are the outline for your story—so far. The rest of this story will be written later.

Now, in your journal, or below, write a title for your story. You might base the title and the story on the guiding metaphor you chose for Letting Go (page 92). Now begin to write this story.

[Title]

_____

One more instruction as you embark on this exercise:

Write your story *in the third person*. You can give the hero your name or a mythic name; it's up to you. Simply tell the story in the third person, blurt it out without editing, then set it aside. Remember, this is only the story of your disruption, so it may not have a happily-ever-after ending. It ends with the

mystery of the door ahead. It may feel like suspended
animation, but that's fine.

_____

_____

_____

_____

_____

_____

_____

_____

_____

_____

_____

_____

_____

_____

_____

_____

_____

_____

2. As you wrote your story, did any pockets of unfinished anger or sadness present themselves? If so, a new To Do List is in order:

List the feelings you had and the steps you need to take to release them.

_____

_____

_____

_____

List the resources you need to support you in this process.

_____

_____

_____

_____

Add a timeline to the items on these lists.

_____

_____

_____

_____

3. The grief work of Letting Go is typically more passive than active. When you surrendered into passively allowing your feelings to flow, what did you notice?

_____

_____

_____

_____

To what extent do you allow or disallow downtime for yourself, whether you're working or are between jobs?

_____

_____

_____

_____

In your journal, or below, park your inner critic and write as if you are an advocate of passive, yielding, meditative behaviors. If this is too foreign to embrace, write the name of your mate, your offspring, or a close friend at the top of the blank page. Then be an advocate for *that* person's need for occasional passivity. See what shows up.

_____

_____

_____

_____

_____

_____

_____

_____

_____

_____

_____

Forth to the wilderness, the chosen start.

—JOHN MASEFIELD

FOUR

Stage III:
In the Wilderness

Deep experience is never peaceful.

—HENRY JAMES

As you let go of your former job and work identity, you will find yourself entering the Wilderness. This stage is a *process* for everyone—a process of wandering. The old structures, rules, and habits are gone, leaving chaos, confusion, and crisis. We are between countries. Behind us is the Old Country with its known realities, a place to which we cannot return. And before us lies the unknown. There's a sometimes desperate desire to know the future so that we can move toward it and create a haven. But search as we might, all that's visible is bewilderment, almost like a thick fog that we intuitively sense we must traverse in order to discover a new identity on the other side.

A good nickname for this limbo is the DMZ, an acronym for Don't Move Zealously—because it won't work. Following a disruption, the Refugee must undergo a period of wandering before a sense of order returns. Included in this in-between experience is the feeling that you are not in sync with those around you. It's as if your identity and prior country have been amputated; you're no longer

whole. Just as amputated limbs remain "embodied" in one's awareness, it takes time to integrate the losses identified in Letting Go.
Like refugees who make it through a demilitarized zone to emerge
on the other side, the Refugee enters the Wilderness as one kind of
person and will, ideally, emerge altered in some essential way.

Jeannie

Jeannie, forty-one, had been a social worker for twenty years before
managed care transformed the social service department of her hospital into what she called a "mental health factory." Gone was her
right to see clients for the number of sessions *she* deemed appropriate;
she had to complete reams of paperwork to justify every additional
block of five sessions. Jeannie agonized over how to abbreviate treatment for seriously disturbed patients. She worked overtime for which
she couldn't bill. Eventually Jeannie experienced battle fatigue, having lost too many fights with supervisors over her beliefs versus their
bottom line. When her department was restructured and her position eliminated, she felt railroaded into the Wilderness.

During Jeannie's period of Letting Go, she clung to the old paradigm by applying for other social service positions. Her job-seeking
efforts finally collapsed when it became clear that every position
within an institution promised the same toxic regimen she'd experienced with her previous employer. Because her temperament and
training were geared toward being an employee, a member of a
treatment team and not an entrepreneur, Jeannie realized she had
no choice but to take time out, dip into her savings, and figure out
what other career options she could pursue.

As she lived with these unanswered questions and worked at
Letting Go, Jeannie found solace in nature. She had enough savings to take six months off to "find myself," as she put it. Because
colleagues and family members pressured her with "What's next?"
questions, Jeannie arranged to rent a cabin on the Oregon coast.
There, she could wander among redwoods and along deserted

beaches, terrain she described as matching her moods of desolation and soaring openness. Unable to identify with books on surviving organizational change, Jeannie took to reading obituaries and biographies, searching for personal resonance in others' stories. Gradually, Jeannie's process of soul-searching brought her to feelings of "union" with nature's elements. She found herself writing poems of identification with the tall trees, luxuriating in her communion with the larger realities of nature, and extricating herself from the assumption that she had to stay in social services in order to fulfill herself vocationally.

Herb

Herb, fifty, an attorney specializing in mergers and acquisitions, had his spirit broken after one too many exposures to corporate downsizing. He awoke one morning to the realization that he could no longer stomach his work, but rather than acting on this insight, he delayed and rationalized until he had no choice: a diagnosis of prostate cancer required immediate treatment and time away from the office. During the Wilderness experience of his recovery, Herb determined that stress had pushed him into cancer. Returning to his previous work seemed certain to metastasize his cancer into a real death; he felt this time-out was nature's way of giving him a death-and-rebirth opportunity. Herb used his disability insurance, along with savings, to take a one-year sabbatical. His wife was so overjoyed to have him around after years of his being out of town more than he was home that she offered to work part time to supplement their reduced income and provide the time and space for Herb to reinvent himself.

The gift of the Wilderness for Herb was that he became a writer. Under pressure and encouragement from his therapist, Herb began writing in a journal to express the pain and loss that he felt because of his cancer. The more he wandered in his writing, the deeper and more profound his insights became.

Before he knew it, Herb was publishing articles sharing his pain and the changes he saw occurring within his profession. Law school and the legal profession take one in the opposite direction of contemplation and philosophical musing, he felt; there is no time for such self-indulgence, not to mention how it might distort the critical (linear) skills needed to function as a high-powered legal eagle. Herb had been too driven and busy to ever ask the basic questions of life. Now he became an ombudsman through his writing, begging fellow lawyers to watch out, wake up, and see the wall they're heading for.

Everyone's methodology is uniquely their own, guided by temperament and individual style. Herb's wandering was internal, while Jeannie's need was for external physical exploration. The instinct to find resonance in nature is not coincidental. Put another way, the Wilderness is the *winter of our discontent*—a period in which the leaves have fallen, the earth is chilled, and there is no growth. During this wandering and wondering time, we must avoid trying to figure out what is next—because if we knew, we would act! Instead, we must turn inward, trust our instincts to provide guidance, and allow any creative impulses to move us through this period of wandering. In short, our work at this stage is simply to *BE* rather than to *DO*. Remember, Don't Move Zealously.

SIGNPOSTS

Once you are in the Wilderness, you will have released the job and its accoutrements. What's left is a gap, a loss of continuity, a boundless no-man's-land that alternately feels like an abyss or a wide-open sky. Signposts of this stage include:

•Feeling outside the mainstream, purposeless and useless.

•Feeling wide open, in a somewhat disoriented way, to a whole world of possibilities rather than limited by your prior job definition and environment.

• Waves of panic alternating with a willingness to take time to heal and regroup.

• Hypersensitivity to rejection, suggesting that active job interviewing may be premature.

• Impulses to create, make art, write memoirs, or launch projects.

• The sense that old assumptions about what holds meaning no longer apply, leaving feelings of emptiness, formlessness, and disorder.

The Wilderness experience can be both lonely and exhilarating. You may go to sleep feeling isolated by your outsider status, humiliated by feelings of rejection, and confused as to which way to turn, yet wake up the next morning to feelings of elation that the whole world is open to you. You may follow creative urges and launch new projects, only to feel, days later, that no one is paying you for this, so maybe it's a waste of your time.

Such a continuum of anxiety at one end and joyful openness at the other is characteristic of the Wilderness. This somewhat crazy-making mixture is the work of your mind and spirit releasing the old, digging down to reclaim your core energies, and recombining it all to find your future direction.

THE NOT-KNOWING

Uncertainty and ambiguity, hallmarks of the Wilderness, are extremely unsettling. You feel as if you are wandering in the dark, while also having compelling urges to initiate change in an effort to resolve the unrest. In spite of having done the work of Letting Go, this no-man's-land feels as if things are getting worse, not better. Welcome to "not-knowing." There's no way around this. You can only move through it by allowing its presence, no matter how long it takes. Though it doesn't feel like it right now, this lonely wandering is extremely productive. On the other side of its darkness is an

We collect data, things, people, ideas, "profound experiences," never penetrating any of them. But there are other times. There are times when we stop. We sit still. We lose ourselves in a pile of leaves or its memory. We listen and breezes from a whole other world begin to whisper. Then we begin our "going down."

—JAMES CARROLL

extraordinary depth of perception, one that can only be achieved by having lived through the angst of not-knowing.

Great literature offers considerable support and appreciation for this period of not-knowing. German poet Rainer Maria Rilke, in his *Letters to a Young Poet,* urged his protégé to "live the [unsolved] questions," with the promise that "gradually, without noticing it, you will live your way into the answers." Countless gifted storytellers and psychologists focusing on the concept of soulwork, such as James Hillman (*The Soul's Code*) and Clarissa Pinkola Estes (*Women Who Run with the Wolves*), likewise describe archetypal patterns in which the heroes must "go down," below our habits and attachments, to the roomy, undefined spaciousness from which new growth will inevitably evolve.

TIME TO THINK AND MOVE OUTSIDE THE BOX

Now is the time to force yourself to think outside the mental models to which you were captive before you became a Refugee. Doing so will allow you to see the misassumptions that perhaps you weren't aware you were making. Since the external validation derived from corporate feedback no longer exists, you have an opportunity to check your own internal compass, your emotional intelligence, to determine the direction of your days.

Above all, this stage prepares you for the intuitive hints that will multiply in the next stage, Seeing the Beacon. These hints of new direction are the gifts that come from the darkness of the Wilderness. To unearth this bounty, we must learn to love the murky limbo of the Wilderness. Just as seeds germinate invisibly underground before spring brings them out into the sunlight, so too will your Wilderness work mysteriously take root. And, like plants, your progress will be organic, not cognitive—you have no choice but to trust the process.

Whatever you do with your time and energy, make it thoughtful and temporary. Set small goals for each day, but don't worry if they

Compulsion is being trapped in a known psychic reality, a dead-end space. Freedom is in the unknown. If you believe there is an unknown everywhere, in your own body, in your relationships with other people, in political institutions, in the universe, then you have maximum freedom. If you can examine old beliefs and realize they are limits to be overcome and can also realize you don't have to have a belief about something you don't yet know anything about, you are free.

—JOHN C. LILLY

don't get done. Look for small resolutions, moment to moment, and take joy in their appearance. Experiment with new behaviors, new creative ventures, and new attitudes. Make these experiments lighthearted and as cost-free as possible. The idea is to "risk" doing things that don't smack of success or failure; they are automatically successful if you try them. Their outcomes may be confusing or surprising. It doesn't matter. It matters more that you use this time for catharsis, spiritual renewal, and growth.

During this stage, you are not in a good position to make healthy long-term decisions. If you were lucky enough to land a severance package or have savings that can support you through a self-imposed sabbatical, take advantage of it. Many Refugees wish they had made more creative use of their time in the Wilderness. We're so programmed to be busy and productive, we feel remiss if we take unofficial time off. Yet that's exactly what's best for you now, so Don't Move Zealously.

If finances are such that you have to pull in some income, try finding temp or contract work that is time-limited. It should, if possible, be a position that allows you to do low-level work almost robotically while making some money but that does not require you to learn new software or train for new roles.

If you choose to work during this time, be sure to keep reasonable hours—no more than 40-hour weeks and, preferably, less—so you can continue your Wilderness rituals and Interim Structure. If you don't stay open to your inner process now, you'll be doomed to do it later. You might jump into some new job prematurely, only to be cast out again or to realize that you jumped far too soon and lost precious personal recovery time in the process.

ARE YOU FEELING ANXIOUS ABOUT MONEY?

Barter exchanges act as "bankers," facilitating trades of property or services via "trade dollars" or credits instead of cold hard cash. Warning: Sometimes barter exchanges don't last, so do considerable research before joining one. To find a barter exchange near you, contact:

•International Reciprocal Trade Association, 175 W. Jackson Blvd., #625, Chicago, IL 60604, (312) 461-0236, or online at www.irta.net.

•National Association of Trade Exchanges, 27801 Euclid Ave., #610, Cleveland, OH 44132, (216) 732-7171, or online at www.nate.org.

Another online bartering resource is:

•www.loska.com/barter.

Charlie

Charlie, thirty-two, was forced out of an arts organization when its funding was not renewed. His first thought was to apply for grants to make a documentary film, but the Wilderness was taking its toll on his motivation. So Charlie decided to take time out and record oral histories of his parents' refugee experiences and those of his in-laws, who were also immigrants. Both sets of elders had protected their offspring from what they termed "their horror stories." Not only had they spent all their energies trying to assimilate into a Western culture, but they also feared that telling their stories would be too depressing. More significantly, they had determined that their histories were too upsetting to tell their children when they were young, so they never spoke about them. For Charlie and his wife, the offspring of these survivors, this was difficult because they were carrying their ancestral pain subliminally, not privy to the facts.

Gradually the oral history project became Charlie's obsession. He sat with them for hours, asking questions about their family trees, about their growing-up years, and, ultimately, about their tragic experiences as refugees. It was personally cathartic as Charlie unraveled some of his own childhood frustrations in learning about his parents' past. For the elders, it was the first time all of them felt it was truly important to recount their stories before they died without their children knowing them. They may have started their accounts with reticence, but they soon began sharing their stories in poetic detail.

It took Charlie weeks to complete the oral histories. He made copies of the audiotapes for his parents, his in-laws, and his in-laws' eight children. He created artwork, wrote poetry, and

DISCOVERING YOUR FAMILY TREE

Many people have discovered fulfillment and deepened identity through genealogy. These books will get you started:

•*How to Trace Your Family Tree: A Complete and Easy-to-Understand Guide for the Beginner* by American Genealogical Research Institute (Doubleday, 1975) is a beginner's guide to launching genealogical research.

•*Unpuzzling Your Past: A Basic Guide to Genealogy* by Emily Anne Croom (Betterway Publications, 1995). Ms. Croom has also published a workbook and sourcebook for beginning genealogists.

explored the music of the time of his parents' youth. Missing pieces to the puzzle of his origins were finally placed in their rightful slots. Thanks to the time afforded Charlie by the Wilderness, his entire family benefited.

Charlie's experience is not surprising. It is essential to see yourself against the larger context of your family and community during this time of restructuring your own life and character. Oral histories and genealogies are great tools for identifying threads of continuity, temperament, predisposition, and talent that have formed the tapestry of your total identity. To better understand where you will be going, this is the perfect time to see who you are in terms of where you came from. See Go Climb a Tree, page 146, for ideas about how to do such a project.

SYNCHRONICITY

Carl Jung, the famous Swiss psychiatrist, coined the term "synchronicity" to describe the coming together of inner and outer events in ways that are meaningful to the observer but cannot be explained by cause and effect. The Wilderness is a fertile time for synchronicities because, as Jung observed, periods of emotional intensity and upheaval open us to psychological breakthroughs. Sometimes the messages that come from synchronicities are not immediately clear, but gradually, we will find clarity. The key is to allow them to show up, to be open to anything.

A vivid instance of synchronicity happened to Brad, the animator we met in chapter one. After losing his teaching job, Brad indulged in his avocational passions for writing mysteries and playing music to stimulate his creativity during his Wilderness period. One day, Brad was in a studio session and mentioned his novel to a guitar player who excitedly said, "Oh, you've got to meet my sister Josie! She's a literary agent." In fact, Josie was a casting agent. But she liked Brad's book and agreed to show it to some New York friends who might have the right connections.

The next day, Josie was at a cafe on trendy Melrose Avenue in Los Angeles when she overheard a conversation. A woman introduced herself as an associate editor for a large New York publisher. Brazenly, Josie thrust Brad's book at the editor, who happened to be on the lookout for new authors. The book went with the editor to New York, and, *voilà*, Brad soon had a publisher, an advance, and a book destined for national exposure. That's synchronicity!

AGONY AND ECSTASY: DEALING WITH THE POLARITIES OF THE WILDERNESS

It is not because things are difficult that we do not dare; it is because we do not dare that things are difficult.
—SENECA

The Interim Structure that follows provides many healthy ways to manage this period of disorder and disaffection and make the most of its opportunities. Rather than wallowing in its frustrating aspects, look at the payoffs you'll receive for enduring the Wilderness: every Action you take, whether it's on the dark or light side of the Wilderness experience, will add insight to your new identity. And since moving through this stage requires creative exploration—the more the better—there's no limit to what you can try. Play out your dreams. Access your inner artist or musician. Knead dough or clay or new ideas to your heart's content. When periods of agony or disorientation hit, meet those rocky moments with the tools you learned during Letting Go, plus those you'll discover in the Actions for this stage. In short, every bit of your work through the Wilderness will have transformational impact—and that's a worthy payoff!

During Letting Go, a daily purpose was derived from your inner needs; now you are best served by listing lots of creative or expressive *outer*-directed behaviors that will give you fresh experiences and insights. Let your goals during the Wilderness include the following:

- Surrendering into formlessness

- Befriending not-knowing

- Active wandering and self-exploration

- Joyful creative play

AN OVERVIEW OF THE INTERIM STRUCTURE
FOR STAGE III: THE WILDERNESS

Goals During the Wilderness

- Surrendering into formlessness
- Befriending not-knowing
- Active wandering and self-exploration
- Joyful creative play

Daily Rituals

- Your Creative Journal
- Mindful Eating
- Exercise Ritual

Actions

I. *Navigate the Emotional Roller Coaster*

- Focused Breathing
- Talismans of Continuity
- Metaphors Be with You II
- Plant a Tree . . . or Cut One Way Back
- Tune Out
- Lighten Up
- Make Lemonade
- Ha-bit by Bit

II. *Fun-damentals—the Creative Side of the Wilderness*

- Collage Student
- Grow Down
- Scratch That Itch
- Bio-Morph
- Get Smart
- Shake Your Tail Feathers

III. *Become a Hunter-Gatherer of Deeper Personal Information*

- Review, Reduce, Recycle: Do a Life Review
- Go Climb a Tree
- Where There's a Will
- Get Clear

IV. *Integrate the Wisdom of Your Wanderings*

- Your Personal Altar
- Vision Quest
- Give Away
- Powwow
- The Long and Winding Road

INTERIM STRUCTURE FOR THE WILDERNESS

Your Interim Structure for the Wilderness begins with the continuation of the Daily Rituals you established during Letting Go. These behaviors were essential so that adequate processing of shock and loss could occur. They continue to be important now as your emotional experience becomes more complex. On the days that fear shows up, you may feel paralyzed and vegetative. On more comfortable days, you may lose your creative fire soon after launching a project. Similarly, it may feel as if nothing you try really works, at least not for long. If that's your experience, you're right on track. William Bridges, in his books about transition, dubbed this stage the Neutral Zone: it's as if you are "stuck in neutral," unable to drive forward or in reverse.

With time and practice, you'll become proficient at maneuvering between internal bouts of fear and outer expressions of creativity. You'll gradually become a kind of hunter-gatherer, collecting new insights, recognizing current needs, and following signals toward a new beginning. Once Refugees surrender to not-knowing, they typically report having had the most fun—and most profound insights—during the Wilderness stage of their journey.

> ### THE JOURNAL AS MEMOIR
>
> Over time, journaling can become so compelling that you find yourself excavating your history and discovering your personal story. A great resource for structuring such a memoir is Ira Progoff's book *At a Journal Workshop* (J. P. Tarcher, 1992). And if journaling awakens the storyteller in you, Sam Keen's book *Your Mythic Journey: Finding Meaning in Your Life Through Writing and Storytelling* (J. P. Tarcher, 1989) is a great tool. Originally published more than two decades ago, it still offers a unique method of helping you unearth and unite the experiences that make up the story of your life.

THE DAILY RITUALS

Your Creative Journal

Continue to write in your journal three pages daily, recording dream fragments, insights, ideas, and feelings. By now, your journal is your friend. Don't limit your writing to the morning ritual. Anything that comes up throughout the day should go into your journal as a means of externalizing and capturing your insights for later delectation.

Mindful Eating

As discussed earlier, your nutrition must be optimal to protect your immune system and facilitate the full, energetic use of your days. Use the Wilderness to creatively recondition your eating style: learn new menus; experiment with new fruits and vegetables; find a seasonal farmers' market to explore. Collect recipes you can whip up in a hurry, plus others that take so much time you feel you are creating a work of art. When you get back into full-time employment, you'll want these new habits of mindful nutrition to be so ingrained that you'll effortlessly continue to take lunch hours, choose your food for its nutritive value, and maintain a healthy body weight for your frame. What you learn now that you have time to focus will stay with you for life. Please don't squander this opportunity.

Exercise Ritual

Now is the time to vary your workouts to keep them interesting and to explore new avenues for movement and fitness:

- If you've been walking regularly, think about how you can use this style of exercise to wander different paths, hike new terrain, discover new areas in your community.

- Notice how you can project various mood states into creative routines and thereby externalize distress as you increase aerobic release. For example, you can use the agitation of anger in your body to run harder, or lift extra weights during a workout.

- Focus awareness of your body's state of well-being by taking physical inventory while walking or running. While deepening your

DANCE YOUR NOT-KNOWING

Dancer and author Gabrielle Roth inspires spontaneous movement to tap into the body's wisdom and connect with new ways of being and creating in her books, *Maps to Ecstasy: A Healing Journey for the Untamed Spirit* (New World Library, 1998) and *Sweat Your Prayers: Movement As Spiritual Practice* (J. P. Tarcher, 1999), and her recordings, *Totem* (Raven-Ladyslipper, 1995), *Initiation* (Raven-Ladyslipper, 1994), and *Ritual* (Raven-Ladyslipper, 1995).

breathing, scan your body for areas of tension; then use your workout to release that tension.

•Play music in the privacy of your living room and let your body move any way it wants—maybe crawling, rolling on the ground, standing on your head, or doing childlike antics. Turn up the volume, kick off your shoes, and move with abandon.

ACTIONS

Of all the Refugee stages, the agony and ecstasy of the Wilderness demand the greatest number of Actions. They are grouped into four categories that address the emotional and creative needs of this stage:

•Navigate the Emotional Roller Coaster

•Fun-damentals—the Creative Side of the Wilderness

•Become a Hunter-Gatherer of Deeper Personal Information

•Integrate the Wisdom of Your Wanderings

I. Navigate the Emotional Roller Coaster

The first set of Actions to take while wandering the Wilderness is designed to cope with the darker emotional experiences you'll encounter: periodic feelings of disorientation, panic, and confusion. The best antidote is focused breathing, which allows the feelings to move through you rather than grip you indefinitely. This Action will become your fail-safe strategy; the more you practice it, the more automatic it will become. Additional Actions in this section can then be implemented, even playfully, to stem the tides of fear and give you a sense of control.

Focused Breathing

Think of the moments of fear, foreboding, or not-knowing as pockets of energy that need emptying. Rather than avoiding them,

Everyone has a talent. What is rare is the courage to follow the talent to the dark place where it leads.
—ERICA JONG

simply acknowledge their presence and use focused breathing to ride out these emotional storms. Here's how:

When you sense anxiety building, stop whatever you are doing at that moment. Go sit in a comfortable chair, resting your head against its back and your arms on the armrests. This may feel counterintuitive, since most of us want to *do* something to ward off this inner agitation, or to distract ourselves from it. But avoidance will only *add* anxiety.

Close your eyes, allow yourself to focus on the inner agitation, and deepen your breathing. You'll notice that your breathing had become shallow while the anxious feelings gathered steam. What your body needs now is for you to deepen your breathing and thereby break up the knots of tension. As you inhale, deliberately expand your stomach as if you are taking each breath all the way down to your belly button. If this feels difficult because the anxiety is so uncomfortable, count each breath as you focus on deepening it. Count at least ten deep breaths.

> **Anxiety is the gap between the now and the later.**
> —FRITZ PERLS

Since the length of these cycles of anxiety is unpredictable, you might want to use imagery that sustains you during the focused breath work, such as riding a wild horse, or sailing through choppy waters, or maybe simply surviving a primitive wilderness adventure. Rather than bucking the storm (or the bronco), a kind of surrender that allows you to *join* or simply be with the turbulence will more gracefully get you through it while you breathe deeply and rhythmically.

With your eyes still closed, continue your deep, focused breathing until it feels easier to relax. After several minutes, gently tune in to your inner state. Is the anxiety still present, or has it subsided? If it's better, but still uncomfortable, count ten more deep, relaxed belly-breaths. You'll be amazed that, with practice, you'll need no more than the first ten focused deep breaths to clear those anxious moments. Again, remember that these periods of fear are cyclic and, above all, normal. Your inner nature is righting itself after the cleansing grief of Letting Go.

Talismans of Continuity

During a time of flux and change, it feels as if everything is fractured and confetti-like. Nothing feels stable because the future is unknown. Nevertheless, there are reliable ways to maintain continuity. In addition to your Daily Rituals, specific activities or symbolic objects can serve to keep you connected to what matters most in your life. Often these activities or objects are taken for granted when our lives are predictable. We appreciate their power more readily during times of disruption.

What are your unique ways of maintaining meaning? Regular involvement with loved ones? Fulfilling nonwork roles, such as grandparent, mentor, big brother/sister, or coach? Or do you use symbols, belongings, or activities such as sports or hobbies to feel connected? Identify something you can use as your talisman of continuity—an object or amulet that symbolizes the role or activity you do as naturally as breathing. Choose something that automatically centers your spirit and grounds you.

Kristi

Kristi, forty-four, who lost her managerial job during a merger, positioned a pair of her daughter's baby shoes beside several framed photos of ecstatic mother-daughter times. Though her daughter is now twenty-something and married, Kristi's angst is mitigated because these small tokens allow her to reconnect with memories of joyful times. Kristi says, "My body remembers those moments, and I feel instantly centered if I just sit beside those little shoes and look at the pictures."

Jon

For Jon, thirty-nine, a former bank executive, it's a baseball he caught at Dodger Stadium when he was ten. Jon's father barged into the dugout and got the ball signed by several of Jon's heroes. What a day that was! Now, when he forgets who he is, Jon holds that ball, feels the leather against his palm, and takes a deep breath.

Instead of, or in addition to, such solitary rituals, you may want interpersonal rituals to provide you with a sense of continuity. Most of us feel lonely when we're physically alone during this stage. There's no work team with whom to commiserate or celebrate, no water-cooler meetings, no figurative piñatas with which to criticize the boss or employees. It's important to find alternative groups with whom you can exchange ideas. Larry, for example, joined a group of retirees who gather at a corner donut shop because they provided the collegiality he so missed from his job as a sales manager. Even though Larry is twenty years younger than most of these guys, they've welcomed him into their fold and regaled him with Refugee stories of their own.

Metaphors Be with You II
Just as you developed a powerful metaphor within which you could release your grief during Letting Go, you need a parallel view of your Wilderness wandering time. Now, more than ever, you'll find metaphors that seem to perfectly depict your day-to-day experience. Read newspapers, fiction, or even obituaries in search of ways to define what you're experiencing.

Sharon

Sharon, forty-one, is a professor of English whose fifteen years of tenure were disregarded when her department was downsized and her job eliminated. She filed a grievance to fight for another position, but to no avail. During her Wilderness experience, she struggled mightily with the identity crisis that came from losing her prior "self." She felt so lost without her students, her colleagues, her sense of purpose. One day she stumbled on an article about the work of Ilya Prigogine, a Nobel Prize–winning scientist who studied thermodynamics and chaos theory. She was captivated by a discussion of what he called "dissipative structures." To sustain their shape, structures require a consistent amount of external energy. When that energy is reduced or changed, the structure gradually dissipates, or "destructures," into chaos. It is from that chaos that a new, more sophisticated structure evolves. Prigogine gave the analogy of the formation of stars in the universe: while they require tremendous energetic force to sustain them, new stars are born of the chaotic break-up or destructuring of stars that no longer receive the energy they need to survive.

Suddenly it made sense to Sharon. Her previous career identity had destructured into her current chaos. If she could just trust her own process, a new beginning would be forthcoming. The idea that a greater structure evolves from the dissipation of the old became her guiding metaphor, to which she returned repeatedly as confusion, disorientation, and feelings of no-self flooded her. Ultimately, Sharon moved to a new city and found greater career opportunities than she'd imagined while she clung to her prior job.

Plant a Tree . . . or Cut One Way Back
If the season is right, plant a rose bush or a small tree whose growth will mirror your own. Another strategy is to cut one way back and watch how that facilitates new, more dramatic growth in the future.

In California, coral trees become lush in the summer. Then, at what appears to be the peak of their growth, corals are drastically pruned, to the point of looking skeletal and consumptive. Following the tree's loss of lush foliage, this period of retrenchment seems barren—the tree, emaciated. The work of new growth is invisible, yet certain. The care and maintenance of a lovely coral tree serves as a great metaphor for cutting away the old to make way for the *greater* flowering that is to come. Is there a similar plant or tree that could represent this process for your Wilderness?

PLANTING YOUR GARDEN

To explore a cornucopia of ideas for planting those seeds and harvesting new life, go online to www.plantamerica.com. It's a gardener's delight, loaded with horticultural advice and software links to regional resources and associations.

Tune Out

Design and commit to undisturbed time during which you can be silent. Our culture is so stimulating, so demanding, so frenetic that we are not coached toward silence. It feels like a waste of time. But in the silence, all of our systems can unwind.

During the silence, you'll gradually lose your identification with limiting beliefs and corporate notions of fixity—a term that represents all of the quantifiable limits of your previous job. Your prior employer probably had a mission statement within which your job fit. Whether the goals were quantified or driven by customer satisfaction, for example, there was a fixed outcome you were expected to achieve. Unless you worked for an unusual company that encouraged thinking and working outside the limits of the company mission, you surely had to limit your work to the job description.

Now, however, you are free to roam far outside any such limited thinking. In fact, as you are realizing, that's the work of the stage you are in. It is essential so that you can reinvent yourself. Silence is the potting soil from which new seeds of identity can grow roots.

Here are some vehicles for achieving spacious silence:

Our language has wisely sensed the two sides of being alone. It has created the word "loneliness" to express the pain of being alone. And it has created the word "solitude" to express the glory of being alone.

—PAUL TILLICH

•Meditate. Sit quietly and practice deep breathing while your mind repeats a word or sound (like the "om" stereotype) that facilitates emptying it of thoughts and transporting you to a heightened state of relaxation.

• Relax quietly while listening to classical or New Age music and deepening your breathing. As you listen, focus on a single instrument, allowing it to pull you through the rest of the musical composition.

• Try a walking meditation. This consists of very deliberate, extremely slow walking while focusing first on your breath, then on the feeling of each muscle involved in each step while simultaneously noticing the terrain beneath your shoes.

• Visualization is another form of meditation that uses imagery rather than words to distract us from active thinking while allowing breathing to deepen, taking us into a highly relaxed state.

• Reading fiction, science fiction, or poetry can facilitate similar altered states for some people.

Experiment with the meditative processes that work best for you. You might discover that you relax best by engaging one of your senses more than the others. If you are more of a visual person, then imagery work might be the best vehicle for your relaxation pleasure. People who relax through physical expression are sometimes called kinesthetic; for you, a walking meditation might be ideal. No matter how you choose to do so, freeing your mind and spirit to soar into silence will release you from the past and open you to new possibilities.

TUNING IN

Emmett Miller and Jon Kabat-Zinn offer easy and enticing entry into meditative practice. Try these titles to get started:

• *Deep Healing: The Essence of Mind-Body Medicine* by Emmett Miller, M.D. (book version: Hay House, 1997; audio version: Hay House, 1999). Dr. Miller combines health education with guided visualizations to help you relax and tune inward.

• *Full Catastrophe Living* by Jon Kabat-Zinn (Delta, 1990). Dr. Zinn introduces meditation in an easy-to-learn manner.

• *Wherever You Go, There You Are: Mindfulness Meditation in Everyday Life* by Jon Kabat-Zinn (Hyperion, 1995). Offers a deep experience of mindfulness meditation, bringing one's consciousness into the present moment so one can "be" rather than "do."

Lighten Up

Humor is one of the most powerful ways to deal with stress and difficult life experiences. But first, a Refugee needs to establish some distance from the job loss before humor can be received as it's intended. During crisis or loss, we often merge emotionally with aspects of the loss. If humor is injected into your situation prematurely, it might be received as insensitive and harmful. That's another important reason for allowing the grief of Letting Go: the loss gradually becomes depersonalized until the Wilderness stage, when we finally feel the separation between ourselves and the prior job role. We are less vulnerable, so humor can be helpful in reinforcing our new perspective.

A heart that breaks open can contain the whole universe.
—JOANNA ROGERS MACY

Laughter is important to healing because it stimulates the same physiological changes and endorphin release as exercise: deeper breathing, lower heart rate, decreased blood pressure, and generalized feelings of relaxation. Suddenly there's release, followed by a systemic sense of joy, balance, and new perspective that can be extended with each foray into precious moments of laughter and play.

How do you prefer to nurture and develop your sense of humor? Do you enjoy stand-up comedy, Marx Brothers or Danny Kaye movies, current films, comic strips, or humor books? However you like to indulge your funny bone, take the time to do so during your journey through the Wilderness. Humor will be healing for you now.

LAUGHS FIVE DAYS A WEEK
See www.ditherati.com. This site delivers humor that Refugees will particularly appreciate, including quotes by executive types, framed with irony.

Make Lemonade

Develop "learned optimism" to reframe any pessimistic beliefs that might be attached to your recent job change. A variation on this idea is to be a Harold. *Harold and the Purple Crayon* is a children's story that has become a favorite business book. In it, a little bald-headed character with a big purple crayon draws himself in and out of various situations. If he's on a path that's too long, he draws a shortcut. If he gets hungry, he draws pies. If he finds himself in deep water, he draws a boat. Harold creates the solutions he needs as he proceeds through uncertain territory. Occasionally, during your Wilderness time, be a Harold. Sometimes you'll need surrender, not solutions. But as you tune in to your intuitive wisdom, there will be

Just remember, we're all in this alone.
—LILY TOMLIN

times when surrender has simply gone on too long, and it's again time to be a Harold.

Ha-bit by Bit

Benjamin Franklin defined freedom as "the ability to break a habit." Certain habits need to be maintained, such as getting to bed nightly at the same reasonable hour, brushing your teeth mornings and evenings, or exercising and eating in nourishing ways. Other habits may be sabotaging your movement through the Wilderness and your life in general, such as smoking or overeating. Addictive behaviors including overwork, excessive alcohol use, binge shopping, or gambling fit into this category as well. How about using your time in the Wilderness to free yourself of habit patterns that no longer serve you?

REFRAME THOSE PESSIMISTIC BELIEFS

"When pessimistic people run into obstacles, they give up; when optimistic people encounter obstacles, they try harder," says Martin Seligman, author of *Learned Optimism: How to Change Your Mind and Your Life* (Pocket Books, 1998).

Dylan

Dylan, thirty-five, is an architect in a solo practice. Unhappily single, he felt lonely as he approached his empty house each night after work. He'd walk in, go straight to his answering machine, then to his e-mail in-box in hopes of finding interpersonal opportunities to warm the stony silence. If there were messages, he could relax, feel loved, and be deliberate in creating a healthy dinner for himself. If there were none, he'd lapse into sadness, grab a few beers, and "go comatose until the night passed so I could get back to work and distract myself again." Clearly there were other options for Dylan's evenings, but his habit pattern precluded even contemplating them.

If you're willing to use your time in the Wilderness to replace negative behaviors with self-loving choices that you'll use when you're back in the saddle of a new career, here are two Actions you can try.

A Habit Fast

Identify a habit you want to explore and "fast" from it for a day or a week. If it's a long-standing behavior, even a day will be hard. A week would be great, but you decide where to begin. As you move through the day of your fast, notice how frequently you "reach" for your habit. This exercise sounds simple, but you'll be amazed at how readily you're willing to let go of such a fast when even slightly tempted. Write freely in your journal about what you discover about yourself *without* that habit. If you succeed in eliminating that habit for a full week, how about eliminating it for good?

The Delay Technique

The second way to break habits is by using the Delay Technique. First, make a list of self-nourishing behaviors you'd like to implement in lieu of negative habits. Use the strategies in this section for creative ideas, along with other behaviors you'd like to establish for the future, when you've healed from your Refugee experience and don't want to resume old habits. Have your list of preferred options written and available at a moment's notice. Attach it to your refrigerator, your bedroom mirror, the control panel of your television, or to your computer, if that's a place you'll need it for reference (or make copies and put them in several places). This way, whenever you are tempted to absentmindedly resort to self-defeating habits, you'll have immediate alternatives.

Suppose the habit you want to extinguish is numbing yourself through the use of junk food or overeating. People with this habit describe grabbing whatever's handy, usually food that doesn't require preparation. They'll eat standing at the refrigerator or kitchen sink, as if in a trance. They don't notice what they're eating, how much they've eaten, or even if they were hungry—until they've completed the habituated behavior. Often there's remorse or shame at having gorged, with renewed resolutions "to begin that diet tomorrow."

Applying the Delay Technique requires that you delay going to the refrigerator or cupboard, or turning on the television, or

Saying no can be the
ultimate self-care.
—CLAUDIA BLACK

engaging whatever device you're hooked on. Instead, go to a different area of your home—any area that does not trigger the negative habit. Sit or lie in a comfortable position, close your eyes, and breathe deeply until you're totally relaxed. Give this relaxation break a minimum of ten minutes. Set a timer if necessary so you don't get up from this repose too soon. During the relaxation, allow your body to rest, become aware of yourself in present time, and simply honor whatever is going on physically for you right now. Empty your mind by focusing on your breathing. Count belly-breaths. Release the tension you find within your body as you delay indulging the habit.

At the end of ten minutes, ask yourself what you truly need right this moment, based on how you feel right now:

• Are you tired? Then you need more rest.

• Are you frustrated from the trials or stresses of your day? Maybe you need a hot bath or a massage.

• Are you anxious or energetic in a way that your body wants to move? Think about exercise options.

• Are you feeling a bit claustrophobic from having been trapped indoors or in a car all day? Maybe a twilight walk outdoors is what your body is craving.

• Are you hungry? If it is hunger that suggests healthy eating, take time out to determine what to prepare that will support making good food choices.

The gift of this technique is that it brings your awareness into present time as opposed to worrying about the past (your day's events) or the future (what needs to be done next). Focused breathing makes you aware of what you're truly feeling and allows you to be fed what you truly need, rather than simply feeding your habit. If you become aware of needs that don't have self-evident alternatives, go to your list of preferred behaviors. It should be immediately obvious what to do next.

Habits are always tough to break and *trying* can create—or feel like—chaos. Why not use the natural chaos inherent in the Wilderness to repattern yourself in healthy, permanent ways?

II. Fun-damentals—the Creative Side of the Wilderness

As you move through the turbulence of the Wilderness with no clear direction in sight, your best work will come through creative self-expression. It's actually your only choice during this challenging stage of the Refugee journey: applying your analytic mind to the "problem" of what to do next will only produce options based on your past experience, which is what got you to Refugee status in the first place. What's called for now is to step outside your logical mind and return to childlike play.

Working with your hands is perfect at this time—ideally, in a way that starts with formlessness and allows any shape to occur, such as finger-painting, or playing with a mound of clay, or doodling. If you're musical, sit down with your instrument and play a variety of scales or tunes until you find one that seems to express this moment.

Create a studio space somewhere in your home that's not accessible to other family members. Fill it with craft supplies, toys, trinkets, found objects, and any other materials you can fashion into some form of self-expression. The idea is to encourage serendipity, to break out of habit patterns, and to vicariously release stress. Break into play in any ways that help you reclaim your "child's mind," the one with which you entered the physical world.

If you've spent years doing intellectual work that was analytic, linear, problem-solving, and deadline-driven, you might look at playful activity as a waste of time. It doesn't seem purposeful. You may feel foolish at first. That's okay. It's counterintuitive and may take repetition before you become fully engaged in this new way of thinking and acting, but don't dismiss it without several dedicated efforts. It will pay off. You'll be amazed at the insights and possibilities you'll produce. Besides, you don't have to tell anyone what you're up to. Just remember, as new feelings and ideas emerge, be careful not to spin them into full-fledged new businesses or career choices. Simply enjoy the pleasure you feel through creative play, write your impressions in your journal, and keep collecting objects for your fundamental-style fun.

Here are some specific Actions for you to undertake as you navigate the playful side of the Wilderness. The more of these creative adventures you explore, the likelier it is you'll experience release from fear, amazing synchronicities, and beacons of possibility that will serve you long past your Wilderness wandering.

Collage Student

Have you ever made a collage? It's fun, creative, and even nonartists can do it well. At first it will seem you've chosen random images, words, or objects for your collage, yet as you put it all together, you will find that the whole and its parts carry great meaning and, potentially, new insights. Try creating a collage that will contribute to the healing demanded by your Wilderness. Thereafter you can use any theme you want to explore for future collages.

Gather old magazines, newspapers, and personal photographs. You'll also need the following supplies:

- glue
- a piece of light wood or poster board (the base of your collage)
- a container for water
- a medium-size paintbrush with sturdy bristles
- any other papers or found objects you'd like to attach to your collage

Look for images that resonate with your Wilderness experience. Don't be analytical; just allow images that seem right to jump off the pages and call to your attention. Only cut out the parts that grab you: for example, images of

MAKING IT PERMANENT

If you want to attach objects to your collage, use a light wood such as ⅛-inch plywood for your base so those objects can be attached permanently. This is inexpensive and readily available at any home improvement or hardware store and many craft shops. Paint the wood with gesso to create the proper surface for gluing. After you've attached the images to your gessoed board, use Goop to affix the objects.

hands but not whole bodies, or landscapes, products, isolated words. Whatever suits you, cut it out and collect as many as you possibly can in a box.

Set up a work space, such as a card table, that allows you to move freely around the poster board. Spread out the cut images so that you can see all or most of them at once. Take several deep breaths; then simply begin. Spread glue on the back side of the image and then press it onto the board. Attach the pictures, one at a time, in as spontaneous and unplanned a way as possible. If you surrender to the process and try not to control it in any way, the pictures will seem to place themselves in a random configuration. This is what you want. Keep working until you've used all the images. In order to keep the poster from curling, place some heavy books on top of the finished collage while the glue dries. You can cover the collage first with a trash bag or other large sheet of plastic to keep any leaking glue from sticking to the books.

The following day, take a look at what you've made. Let the collage tell you a story. What do you see? How does your collage make you feel? Record your immediate responses in your journal. Revisit this project later, and see how your reactions change.

There are good classes and books on making collages that can render this process even more self-revealing. If you use gesso, Goop, found objects, and a variety of papers in addition to cut-out images, your collages can be prophetic. Or they can be amazing projections of what's going on inside of you. If you're quite pleased with your results, you can even shellac the final product as a keepsake reminder of a day the fog lifted in the Wilderness.

Sharon, the professor whom you met earlier, took a collage class during her Wilderness time. Never able to draw or paint, she figured this would be the closest she'd ever come to an artistic effort. The process was so simple that pretty soon she found herself combing beaches, garage sales, and flea markets looking for objects that called to her. They didn't necessarily suggest an outcome, but, once combined into a collage, they told her extraordinary stories. She saw a wandering minstrel in one collage, bedecked with small shells, foreign coins, and odd pieces of broken jewelry she'd found.

Two things come to mind that are euphoric for me. One is the universal euphoric: sex, that period of time when you are at an absolute peak of sexual feeling. The other is when I create something that moves me. When I am the audience to my own creation and I'm moved. If it were a drug and I could buy it, I'd spend all my money on it.
—PAUL SIMON

Over the course of several weeks, Sharon made three same-sized but entirely different collages, each with colored tissue papers and magazine cuttings. When she laid them side by side, that wandering minstrel suddenly followed a path of natural objects. Ironically, the three panels worked together. A year later, Sharon still felt haunted by them, so she had the collages framed in a triptych. They hang above her mantel as a treasured reminder of her Wilderness experience.

Grow Down

Children are gifted at teaching us what the present moment really offers. They have the ability—with which we are all born—to be naturally happy and playful. They don't hold on to pain once they've been soothed. Spending time with children while you are in the Wilderness can be extremely therapeutic and enlightening if you enter the world at their level. They hear stories and see reality on a more direct level than we adults do.

Jeremy

Jeremy, thirty-seven, a CPA who was downsized out of a large financial services firm, discovered the benefits of relaxation tapes while Letting Go. He ritualized a daily twenty-minute session with a favorite audiotape, and often his five-year-old daughter, Brittany, joined him. She'd stretch out alongside him on a chaise lounge on their patio and follow the guidance of the voice on the tape. During his Wilderness days, Jeremy had waves of restlessness and fear. When Brittany saw him raise his voice on the phone or curse at the computer, she'd gently put her arms around him and say, "Come on, Daddy, let's relax with the stress tape."

Children read us, love us unconditionally, and want us to be there for them and with them. It's incredibly therapeutic to spend time

> **When childhood dies, its corpses are called adults.**
> —BRIAN ALDISS

with little people when you're looking for inspiration. In addition, those of us who've become serious work addicts have literally forgotten how to play. There are no better teachers than young children whose "job" it is to see and maximize the joys presented by moment-to-moment opportunities for play. Even though you may not feel like it right now, almost any "growing down" opportunities will move you through your Wilderness.

Scratch That Itch

Build something from scratch. Apply your creative genius to a project on which you have total control, and through which you can move from a broken beginning to a unified outcome. There are few such gratifying projects in most intellectually driven work situations where most of us feel like cogs in a large machine.

Visit a hardware store or a builders' emporium. Wander the aisles and take note of improvements that you've always wanted to make in your home or office. Choose one and determine to do it! Talk with store clerks and brainstorm your project. Several large chain stores offer free classes for laying tile, building a deck, installing wallpaper, or redecorating kitchens and bathrooms.

If you prefer mechanical work, consider restoring a vehicle, upgrading parts on a mountain bike, or canvassing garage sales for discarded appliances you could update. Now is the time to live the entire rebuilding experience for yourself. Who knows what intuitive wisdom will find its way into your awareness while you're preoccupied with finding those missing parts.

CRAFTY OUTLETS

•If you don't have a hobby because you've been working too hard to discover one, log on to the Hobbies Industries Association Web site, www.i-craft.com, for ideas.

•If you already know how to sew, consider quilting, needlepoint, and other sewing projects for which local fabric shops could provide advice and resources.

•Community colleges offer programs on welding, woodworking, auto mechanics, and furniture restoration, along with facilities and equipment you can use for minimal fees.

•Visit your city's craft and folk arts museum for more ideas.

•If you get serious about the business of crafting, check out the *Crafts Fair Guide,* a listing of retail craft shows by community, at (415) 924-3259. Or subscribe to the *Crafts Report,* an industry newsletter for beginning or established crafts professionals, at (800) 777-7098.

Bio-Morph

Identify the people you most admire and then learn as much about them as possible. Read biographies, rent documentaries, write a "research paper," or just take really good notes in your journal. If possible, visit a historic home or museum dedicated to your heroes or their era. Identify what you admire about them and what qualities or aspects of their life you share or would like to share. If you could interview them or have them to dinner, what would you ask them? Record such questions. After you've done your research, answer the questions in your hero's voice, perhaps in a letter to yourself or as a "script" of your dinner or interview.

Get Smart

Learn something new. If your financial situation is such that you can take time off from the push for gainful work, learn something you've always wanted to try—like a foreign language. If it involves classes, you'll feel some comfort from the structure. It will free your mind from the bank of information required at your job and allow you to achieve mastery in a new area— one of *your* choice. In other words, you'll be thinking in new ways, and you won't feel as if you're "wasting your time doing nothing."

> ## MENTORS, MODELS, AND HEROES FOR ALL TIME
>
> Heroes tend to be creative, inspired, and inspiring throughout time. Try exploring some of these mythic and historic heroes and watch your own creativity take flight.
>
> •*Creating Minds: An Anatomy of Creativity Seen Through the Lives of Freud, Einstein, Picasso, Eliot, Graham and Gandhi* by MacArthur Fellow Howard Gardner (Basic Books, 1994).
>
> •*Sukhavati: Place of Bliss: A Mythic Journey with Joseph Cambell* is a video on which Campbell guides viewers through archetypal myths to help us identify our own possibilities. Available through Mystic Fire Video, (800) 292-9001.

Sally

For Sally, thirty-eight, it's sailing. A geneticist with her doctorate who lost her job during a downsizing at a university seven months ago, Sally got through the Letting Go stage by wandering the beaches, filling her journal, and lamenting the "lost" years of training and climbing the academic ladder. While contemplating the ocean on a glorious sunny day, Sally remembered that she'd always promised herself she'd take sailing lessons. Now she finally had the time.

"I've never had a life until now," she says today. "First grad school and the dissertation, then the job, and finally now I get to do what I want to do." Sally knows this is temporary. But she's having so much fun sailing and seeing nature at its best, she's in no hurry to "go back indoors and live in some dark cubicle or lab again." Sally says her intuition and checkbook will tell her when it's time to get back to work. Meanwhile, she is enjoying the moment.

Shake Your Tail Feathers

Throughout all the Interim Structures and stages in the Refugee journey, exercise is emphasized as an essential self-care ritual. It is equally important as a creative outlet, particularly during the Wilderness. You know that endorphin-like chemicals are secreted by the brain when we exercise aerobically, when we play, and when we laugh. Identify fun exercise that includes all three of these elements, such as dancing, yoga, drumming, wandering through forests, or even playing sports.

You probably already have your favorites. But now is the time to expand your repertoire and go for the exotic. How about a belly dancing class? Or tai chi or qi gong? Maybe driving golf balls at a local driving range would help you mobilize your endorphins, get you laughing at the wily ways of those balls, and give you something to whack. Kick boxing releases aggression as well as endorphins. Salsa, swing, or disco dancing will raise your pulse and get you out of the house. Many recreation centers and dance clubs offer free dance lessons.

GET SOME NEUROBIC EXERCISE

• Neurobiology professor Lawrence C. Katz, Ph.D., delineates simple yet profound brain stimulation he terms *neurobics* in his book *Keep Your Brain Alive* (Workman, 1999). Practice using all five of your senses in creative ways to expand your mental powers.

• A one-stop shop for creative play can be found online at www.learn2.com. Dubbed "the ability utility," this Web site offers step-by-step instructions ("2torials") on a range of hobbies, tasks, activities, and skills perfect for wandering the Wilderness. Its offerings range from how to change a flat tire to how to make stained glass.

Check your local listings for half-day or weekly classes in new exercise experiences that will take you into new inner territories as well. You'll be amazed at how these experiences inspire mental explorations you couldn't have invented by simply thinking or analyzing in traditional ways.

If you're uncomfortable spending money or being in public as you explore new physical options, go to your local video rental store and try some of these options in the privacy of your living room. It'll work just as well. Try buying new music and dancing (or dusting!) throughout your home. Other money-saving ideas include taking over the lawn-mowing, pool care, or dusting and vacuuming. This Action will help you feel productive and move you toward new outside-the-box adventures. Now get moving!

INSTANT, PERSONALIZED TRAINING REGIMEN

Ready to expand your physical repertoire? Go online to www.eFit.com and explore hundreds of ways to shake those tail feathers. Once you choose an activity, eFit will customize a training regimen just for you.

III. Become a Hunter-Gatherer of Deeper Personal Information

As the Wilderness stage progresses, your Daily Rituals and Actions are producing greater calm and clarity. Active exploration of Fun-damentals has similarly expanded you and produced insights that should be gathered, even if they don't make logical sense yet. Part of your "job" in the Wilderness is becoming a hunter-gatherer of what has worked in your life—and career—to date, what still needs weeding out and what is yet to be explored.

Toward that end, the following Actions are self-revealing exercises designed to deepen your sense of self and elicit your values and preferences. Once gathered, they will form a path out of the Wilderness and toward your New Land.

Review, Reduce, Recycle: Do a Life Review

When Veronica, the psychologist from chapter four, was laid off, she gathered thirty boxes of files, articles, and tidbits she'd collected during her fourteen years in the health care field. During that time, she'd also gone through a divorce. Her share of the marital memorabilia was in a storage locker she'd never had time to revisit. After three weeks of focused Letting Go, Veronica decided to organize her files before embarking on her next vocational push. She spent weeks weeding through research articles, workshop outlines, and memos.

As she dug deeper into the boxes, she remembered the long-neglected storage locker. "I flashed on my mother's death three years ago, and how unpleasant the experience of sorting through her disorganized closets was. I thought, 'I've been a packrat too. If I don't orga-nize them while I have this time, when will I ever do it?'"

From the storage unit, Veronica uncovered a forty-year-old stamp collection handed down to her from her dad, something she'd totally forgotten. She ran out to buy a new holder and thoroughly enjoyed designing the repackaging of the collection. Before obtaining her Ph.D. in psychology, Veronica had been a graphic designer. In the process of reorganizing the antiquated stamp collection, Veronica recaptured the joy she used to feel when immersed in artistic endeavors.

TIME TO DE-CLUTTER
The Wilderness stage is a perfect time to dig out by de-cluttering. *Lighten Up: Free Your-self from Clutter* by Michelle Passoff (HarperCollins, 1998) suggests that piles of stuff can drain your energy. This book in-spires you to see de-cluttering as a form of art and holistic release.

Next she discovered her thirty-two-year-old wedding gown. It had been stored in a long flat box under her bed, the very bed on which she'd conceived her thirty-year-old son. (So sentimental had she been about this marital bed that she'd ignored the backaches it gave her with each night's sleep.) This must be an heirloom by now too, she thought as she studied the dress. She took the gown to the cleaners, intending to box it more tenderly for some future grand-child. The $350 cleaning estimate was a wake-up call. "What am I saving all this for?" she asked herself. "I'll sell the dress, keep the veil, and write a story about it for my granddaughter."

Soon Veronica realized that she was doing a life review as she went through these boxes from her past. She found old costumes, beautiful baby blankets, and every card her son had given her since he was two. Revisiting her past brought Veronica deeply into the present. Gradually she released the urgency she'd felt to get a new

The moment one gives close attention to anything, even a blade of grass, it becomes a mysterious, awesome, indescribably magnificent world in itself.
—HENRY MILLER

job. She recognized that, somehow, this process was far more important. She surrendered to it, feeling "it had its own energy. The river of my life's journey will carry me into some future that I'm not supposed to know yet. All I feel right now is this compulsion to pick up where I left off yesterday until I've completed this process." Veronica is also thoroughly enjoying designing creative labels for the objects she's saving after sifting and sorting. She giggles to herself as snapshots of her past turn up. This is a very helpful action for the Wilderness stage. Do you have boxes or closets you haven't looked at in years? Now might be a good time to sort through them—who knows what insights and treasures you might turn up!

Go Climb a Tree

Most of our core values were taught or modeled for us in our original family. Similarly, many of the life and work choices we make are, consciously or unconsciously, based on the values and life choices we inherited from our ancestors. The perennial nature-versus-nurture debate over the origin of our temperaments and tendencies notwithstanding, we benefit from knowing as much as possible about our family tree. As you saw in Charlie's story early in this chapter, the Wilderness is a great time for doing oral histories of your elders. Now you can fill in the gaps of your history and at the same time be inspired by some of their choices and challenges.

THE NEED TO KNOW OUR ROOTS

Places Left Unfinished at the Time of Creation by John Phillip Santos (Viking, 1999) is a beautiful memoir about a Mexican-American family that expresses the drive in all of us to know our families, our pasts, and our roots.

To begin the process, write in your journal your thoughts in response to these questions:

• What do you already know about your ancestors?

• How is that information recorded so that your offspring or extended family can continue to know the facts and add their own lives to the saga?

•Which relatives have been particularly inspirational along your own life path?

•Do you have details of their lives?

Do the answers to these questions point to a lack of information about your family and a desire to know more about its past? If so, make appointments with the family elders you want to interview. Use a tape recorder so you can enjoy the dialogues without having to take notes. Facilitate their telling you their stories by asking what they remember of their own grand-parents, asking for as many anecdotes and origi-nal details as they can recall. Then move gently into their memories of their parents, their growth and development years, their experi-ences, their adolescent and adult choices, and so on. If you do an in-depth oral history, you'll want several two-hour (maximum) sessions with each elder in order to capture all of their information. You'll be amazed at both the depth of detail they can produce and their joy in sharing that information with you.

BACK TO THE FUTURE
Oral histories are powerful on many levels: the process of interviewing family members can be powerfully bonding and revelatory, not only in revealing your personal history but in predicting future family patterns. A tool for creating such memoirs is *Touching Tomorrow* by Mary LoVerde (Fireside Books, 2000).

Where There's a Will

Rarely do any of us sit down alone and list at least 100 things we'd like to do before we die. During the frenzy of our working days and evenings, we're too preoccupied or tired to even ask the question. Yet most of us hope there will be time for many pleasures before it's too late.

Many people think this is an easy exercise until they sit down to do it. They get to twenty-five, and they're dry. Then they get upset: "Surely there are more than twenty-five things I want to experience before I die!" But the necessary introspection takes time, and they've never had enough of that. Now you have the time. Take out your journal and write your list; be specific. Where do you want to take that French cooking class? Why not Provence? What wild and scenic rivers do you want to raft? Name them. If you want to start running competitively, name the race you want to finish. Are there relatives and friends you are out of touch with? List who they are and why you want to be in contact with them. List no fewer than 100 experiences, but the sky's the limit for this exercise. Big and small dreams. Keep your list and add to it as you think of more. Maybe you'll even treat yourself to doing some of these before this stage ends.

Get Clear

Without realizing it, most of us operate from values we've inherited or adopted from our family of origin, our education, our cultural biases, and our accumulated life and work experiences. Rarely do we stop long enough to assess what truly matters most to us. It generally takes crises to create such opportunities for self-reflection. Job loss is such a crisis. In fact, it can be a defining moment if used as an opportunity to ask the deeper questions. Here are three values-clarification exercises that, when used together, are powerful ways of identifying your highest values and choosing new directions based on who you are now.

The Five Years/Three Months Exercise

For this exercise, you'll need three sheets of paper, or you can use the space provided here. At the top of the first page, write what will be the exact date five years from now. If today is November 22, 2000, write "November 22, 2005." Then, as quickly as you can, write a list of what you want to be doing, having, and enjoying on that future day. Don't think too hard. Just write everything that comes to your mind and be as specific as possible. Rather than writing global wishes, like, "I want the world to be at peace," write very personal preferences, including what you want to be earning, experiencing, owning, disowning, and so forth. Just write until you feel empty.

Date Five Years from Today: _____

What I want to be doing, having, enjoying: _____

_____

_____

_____

_____

_____

_____

_____

_____

_____

_____

_____

_____

_____

_____

_____

_____

_____

_____

Put that sheet aside, and, at the top of a second sheet, or in the space provided here, write the exact date it will be three months from today. In our example, that would be February 22, 2001. Before you write anything further, close your eyes and imagine this: Your life is busy, happy, and full. You decide it's time for one of those well-body physicals, just to be sure you are maintaining good health. You go to the doctor feeling certain you'll receive a glowing report, only to be told that you have a terminal illness. None of the symptoms are visible, nor will they be as the disease progresses. But you have only three months left to live. During those three months, you will feel just as healthy and energetic as you do today. But on the stroke of midnight three months from today, you will peacefully die in your sleep. What do you want to do in these last three months of your life? Write whatever occurs to you as quickly as you can, being as specific as possible. Rather than writing, "I want to spend time with my family," write their names and specific amounts of time you want to give each. Specifics appropriate for this list might include, for example, "Teach my daughter to throw a curve ball"; "See the pyramids at Giza with Mom"; "Eat scallops at Le Cirque at sunset"; and so forth. Read no further until you complete this question.

Date Three Months from Today: _____

How I will spend the next (last) three months of my life:

_____

_____

_____

_____

_____

_____

_____

_____

_____

_____

_____

_____

_____

_____

_____

_____

_____

Now, put the "Five Years" and "Three Months" pages side by side. Circle the items that occurred on both lists. On a third sheet, or on the lines here, list the circled items.

_____

_____

_____

_____

_____

_____

———————————————————

———————————————————

———————————————————

———————————————————

———————————————————

———————————————————

———————————————————

———————————————————

———————————————————

These items are your highest priorities at this time in your life.

What this exercise accomplishes, quickly, is a top-of-your-head list of your long-term (the Five-Year List) and short-term (the Three-Months List) goals. When you contemplate the combined list, you'll likely agree that these items are very important to you at this moment in your life. Keep in mind that if you did this exercise a few years ago, or when you do it a few months or years from now, the items might be very different. It's a useful exercise for pivotal times in your life.

The second exercise for values clarification will deepen the results you achieved in your Five Years/Three Months experience. Ideally, this exercise should be done with six colored marking pens or crayons.

The following is a list of values or qualities that is by no means complete. Read over the list and, at the bottom, add any that occur to you for the purposes of this exercise. Then, take one colored pen and circle your ten highest values. Only ten.

Values Checklist

Spiritual growth	Understanding	Community
Ecological integrity	Knowledge	Helping society
Impressing people	Challenge	Power, authority
High earnings	Love	Friendships
Creativity	Influencing people	Aesthetics
Variety	Independence	Recognition
Opportunity for growth	Time freedom	Publicity
Affiliation	Excitement	Applause
Artistic achievement	Pleasure	Self-expression
Competition	Public acclaim	Stability
Moral fulfillment	Tranquility	Decision making
Intellectual status	Routine	Travel
Precision	Fast pace	Belonging
Health maintenance	Pressure	Investments
Political effectiveness	Long vacations	Initiating change
Personal effectiveness	Generating ideas	Teamwork
Ethics	Status	Adventure
Admiration	Advancement	Bliss
Arts	Balance	Leadership
Calm	Challenging problems	Money
Market position	Nature	Communication
Mindfulness	Collaboration	Humor
Job tranquility	Honesty	Generosity
Integrity	Inner harmony	Mindfulness
Sharing	Gratitude	Excellence
Simplicity	Wonder	Will
Ethical practice	Order	Serenity
Compassion	Right livelihood	Accountability
Purity	Vitality	Privacy
Trust	Resonance	Decisiveness
Renewal	Patience	Fame
Public service	Wholeness	Emotion
Efficiency	Wisdom	Self-respect
Expertise	Involvement	Loyalty
Detachment	Competence	Others

After you've marked your ten highest priorities in one color, take a second color. If you could select only the top five of those ten, which would you choose? Circle them in the second color.

With another color, choose the top four.

With a fourth color, choose the top three.

Now, the top two.

Finally, cross off one that would leave you with your single most important value. What is it? _____

Are you living that value right now? _____

If so, how? If not, how could you use this time of self-exploration to do so? _____

_____

_____

_____

How about the rest of your top three, five, ten values—are you living them actively right now? _____

Were they compromised in the job you just left? _____

_____

If they were part of your recent work experience, is the loss of that daily experience contributing to your grief? _____

What could you do to increase the top ten values in your life right now?

_____

_____

_____

_____

_____

_____

Now combine the list of your ten highest values with the third list from your Five Years/Three Months exercise. Looking at both lists, what patterns do you see? _____

_____

_____

_____

In those patterns, what clues suggest a livelihood to which you would be suited? What clues suggest you desire a more values-based lifestyle or work style than you've had?

_____

_____

_____

_____

What activities do the lists suggest your spirit is craving and that you could include in your life during this wandering time?

_____

_____

_____

_____

To complete your work on Getting Clear, make a list of goals for yourself based on your highest values. It might include a studio for expressive, creative arts; telephoning lost friends; taking a cost-free excursion into a particular nature preserve or ethnic neighborhood; or brainstorming with friends or significant others about how to make your top three values more a part of your daily life.

_____

_____

_____

_____

_____

_____

_____

_____

_____

_____

_____

_____

_____

_____

_____

As you continue the process of wandering in the Wilderness, refer to this list whenever you feel at a loss for Actions. Implement as many as you can during the Wilderness—and beyond.

IV. Integrate the Wisdom of Your Wanderings

You've produced a considerable body of creative work during this stage, both inner process work and outer creative expression. Now is the time to gather the wisdom of all of that work and ground it with a final set of Actions that will move you toward Seeing the Beacon of renewal. The following strategies will help you organize your wandering and bring closure to the Wilderness experience. Toward this end, Native American traditions are particularly powerful. Beginning with the building of a personal altar, try several of the following Actions and see what additional wisdom you can bring to this stage of your journey.

ANCIENT WISDOM FOR MODERN TIMES

Explore these resources for traditional rituals and remedies as you gather the wisdom of your Refugee journey:

• *The Power of Ritual* by Rachel Pollack, (Dell Paperback, 2000). Suggests rituals for daily balance and inspiration.

• *Everyday Magic: Spells and Rituals for Modern Living* by Dorothy Morrison (Llewellyn Publications, 1998). Creative rituals and remedies combining ancient wisdom with modern technology.

Your Personal Altar

If you used your Wilderness wanderings to produce art, crafts, poems, or any other tangible creations, gather them in one place and create an altar to your work. Use the altar as a centering place for contemplation, meditation, or ongoing questing in your search for meaning and direction. Sit near your altar when you do your daily journaling, invoking the spirit of your creative core. By so doing, you are tapping into a deep archetypal ritual that may lead you, effortlessly, to even more new insights. As they come, add those insights to your journal. Again, simply collect these treasures and trust this process.

Vision Quest

One of the most important Native American traditions is the rite of passage known as a vision quest. Traditionally, it was a moment of passage from the protection of the parental home into one's adulthood. For many non–Native American people, this experience is only incidentally encountered; it is not intentionally created. But it's a very appropriate exploration to undertake as you leave the Wilderness. The general approach to a modern-day vision quest involves taking oneself away from the routines of daily life for three days and three nights. If you want to be completely in keeping with the Native American tradition, you would sit alone in nature without food, books, electronics, or companionship. You would simply allow the impact of silence and solitude to guide a spiritual search for meaning and direction.

You can modify the Native American tradition by taking just a day or two to go on your own version of a vision quest—to the ocean, to a forest, to a comfortable campground, or anywhere you choose, as long as it's a natural environment and you go alone—with a journal and walking shoes. Allow the nature of your surroundings, in combination with your internal nature, to be guided toward a vision for your future or for a unique contribution you can make to your family or community.

Whether you actually take yourself away or just visualize such a vision quest, imagine some of the outcomes Native Americans describe:

WITNESS AN AUTHENTIC VISION QUEST

•**Photographer Don Doll, S.J., takes viewers on an authentic vision quest via portraits and stories of real Lakota men and women on his CD-ROM titled *Vision Quest: Men, Women and Sacred Sites of the Sioux Nation.* Further information and inspiration from Native American wisdom can be found in:**

•***Secret Native American Pathways: A Guide to Inner Peace* by Thomas E. Mails (Council Oak Distribution, 1988). A treasury of ceremonies by medicine men with instruction for applying them to modern life.**

•***The Sacred Pipe: Black Elk's Account of Seven Rites of the Oglala Sioux* edited by J. E. Brown (University of Oklahoma Press, 1989).**

•Identifying one's gift (in the form of a unique talent, mission, skill) that can benefit the community. Thus defined, the seeker can return from his or her wandering and put that gift to work. As a Refugee, you can apply this concept by using the gathered insights of your Wilderness Actions to write a mission statement that defines your gift and depicts the work you want to contribute in the New Land.

•Seeing the world through different eyes. Just as every culture has key assumptions that are only questioned when they come into conflict with a contrasting culture, so does the "culture" of your prior work environment differ from that of your wide-ranging Wilderness experience. Expand your vision quest so you can "see" the fruits of your wandering from different vantage points, such as your inner artist, the eyes of a child, the voice of a mentor.

> **I'm looking for the face I had before the world was made.**
> —WILLIAM BUTLER YEATS

Give Away

Another tradition in Native American practice is called a "Give Away." This exercise was often performed by the tribal chief, who was also the poorest man in the village. He gave away food, horses, blankets, trinkets, and staples that his people needed. Hold your own Give Away by gathering clothes or household items that are in good condition but are no longer important to you. Even if you have only a couple of items, the energy released by such "gifting" is powerful. Simultaneously, you are creating the space, in yet another way, for new life to come in to you.

Powwow

This Native American ritual can help you to celebrate your coming out of the Wilderness. Typically held in the spring, a powwow celebrates the seasonal renewal of life. For you, a powwow in the form of a party with close friends could be your coming-out-of-the-Wilderness event, celebrating your inner renewal and excitement about the rebirth that's clearly on the horizon.

EXPLORING NATIVE AMERICAN HEALING ARTS

Some traditional rituals and remedies for healing can be found in these wonderful compendiums:

•*American Indian Healing Arts: Herbs, Rituals and Remedies for Every Season of Life* by E. Barrie Kavasch and Karen Baar (Bantam Doubleday Dell, 1999).

•*The Native American Almanac* by Martha Kreipe DeMontano and Arlene B. Hirschfelder (IDG Books Worldwide, 1999).

The Long and Winding Road

The following Road of My Career exercise is an art therapy process that gathers the wisdom of your work experience and fuels the next stage of your Refugee journey. Looking at the big picture of your career trajectory adds one last link to the chain of insights you've gleaned so far.

Gather colored felt-tip pens and a large, rectangular piece of drawing paper, ideally butcher paper, that can cover a desktop. Draw a road or path that represents the course of your working life. Draw your road across the upper half of the paper, leaving room beneath the road to write later on in the exercise. Use your imagination in creating the shape of this road: Do you want it to look like a game board, with squares representing each job to date? Or is it a zigzag, crooked path? Would a winding road with lots of switchbacks better represent the overall image of your job history? Or, when you take this big-picture view, does it look as if your career has traveled a straight road, with only an occasional switchback for bad or disappointing jobs? Draw whatever feels like an appropriate design for your road.

At the beginning of your road, draw a symbol for your first gainful employment, and note your age at the time or the year(s) of employment next to the symbol. Move forward and depict the next job you held with its dates, and so forth, until you get to the present. Again, let your roadway take whatever twists and turns it wants to give you the picture of what your career has looked like to date. If you've worked for many years at the same company, use this exercise to look at the various jobs or roles you experienced within that company. After you've completed your work history, leave some roadway open for the future.

Underneath *each* job symbol or depiction, write your initial responses to this set of questions. If there is not enough room, use large Post-Its for this purpose.

• What was your goal or expectation when you took this job?

• How were those goals met (or not met)?

• What did you learn from this job (occupationally as well as emotionally)?

• What decisions did you make as the result of your experience on this job?

• When you contemplate your time at this job, what images stand out for you?

• Were there any special mentors, training, or advancement opportunities you took or wish you had taken?

• How did this particular job enrich you? How did it move you along your career path?

When you've completed your notations for each of the jobs along your career path map, step back and look at the map as a whole. Having thus placed yourself and your career in historical perspective, what are your feelings regarding the course of your career to date? Jot them down in your journal, along with responses to the following questions:

• What hints of talent, aptitude, passion, or special skills seem to run through the entire picture of your life's work to date?

• Which stops along your journey would you not repeat if you had it to do again?

• Which would you be happy to revisit?

• What destinations suggest themselves when you look at the big picture you've drawn?

Even if your work history is more of a mosaic than a straight trajectory, you are likely to notice an underlying motif of interests, talents, and inclinations that have always been part of your identity, your passions, and your favorite jobs. Stand back and look at those themes. See those themes combining to form a leitmotif, or Beacon, that has always shone through your preferred activities and will likely be with you regardless of what your next job entails.

If you begin to understand what you are without trying to change it, then what you are undergoes a transformation.

—J. KRISHNAMURTI

Ask yourself these questions, jotting your responses in your journal:

•If you had to name the overarching themes that best express your nature throughout your life and your career path to date, what words would you choose?

•As you articulate these ideas, do you feel that you've ever truly claimed this core pattern as a necessary ingredient in your chosen career? If so, when? If not, why not? Are you ready to do so now? If you're not ready, is this because you haven't yet identified your pattern? If so, go back to the beginning of this book and find the Actions that will help you identify them. Without identifying these core themes, you'll be unable to find your right livelihood.

•During job interviews, have you told your interviewer how important these attributes are to you, how essential to any job you undertake? If not, now is the time to start doing so. Now is the time to reinforce these essential qualities, reclaim them, and go forward with the determination to include them in any job you contemplate. They are nonnegotiable because, without these ingredients, you won't be happy.

Jorge

Jorge never stopped long enough to determine where his passions lay. An offspring of Cuban refugees who fled Castro in the 1960s in a hail of bullets, Jorge, at age thirty-six, was his family's greatest source of pride: He was the only relative in the extended family to go all the way through graduate school and become an attorney. He landed a good position in a large Chicago firm and was soon being groomed for partnership. Five years later, and seemingly out of the blue, Jorge was given his walking papers after a senior partner determined that Jorge's "outspokenness was a liability with the high-end clients the partners had to deal with." At first heartbroken, Jorge discovered during Letting Go that he was more troubled about his family's shame at the loss of "their son the lawyer" than he himself was about being turned out of the firm.

Jorge used his severance for a much-needed vacation, but the pall of his job loss marred his ability to have fun. Upon their return home, Jorge's wife talked him into using the employee assistance counseling that was offered as part of his outplacement package. As Jorge vented his pain and made room in his heart to explore values and preferences, he uncovered his core passions of advocacy and animal rights. Much as he lamented the loss of his $90,000 annual salary and the prestige that came with his prior position, Jorge admitted that he dreaded going back into traditional law practice and "continuing not to have a life." His greatest difficulty was letting go of the programming and attachment his family had to his professional status.

Finally Jorge dove into the work of the Wilderness, venting copiously in his journal, wandering among volunteer opportunities in animal-rights organizations, and doing *pro bono* legal work. One day in the shower, it came to him: Why not use the balance of the severance he'd received to buy a business related to animals and do advocacy work on the side? The same day, during his final session with his counselor, Jorge spoke excitedly about all the possibilities his passions offered. En route home from the counselor's office, Jorge bumped into an old friend and told him about his newfound direction. A week later, this acquaintance connected Jorge to a person who had a pet store for sale.

> The only important thing is to follow nature. A tiger should be a tiger; a tree, a good tree. So man should be man. But to know what man is, one must follow nature and go alone, admitting the importance of the unexpected.
>
> —CARL JUNG

PULLING IT ALL TOGETHER

As you worked through the many Actions offered in the Wilderness, you identified the essential values, preferences, talents, and themes of your career—and life—to this point in time. Take charge of these insights by developing some intention statements for yourself.

The word *intention*, from the Latin *intendere*, means to stretch toward, to aim at. It's an act of will for the attainment of a specific end. Based on all that you've discovered during your Wilderness wanderings—your Gathered Wisdom, the insights provided by Getting Clear and the Long and Winding Road, the joy you reclaimed doing Fun-damentals—what ends do you *intend* for yourself? Remember, intentions are not wishful thinking; they are aims upon which you plan to take action. As you move toward Seeing the Beacon, the next stage of your Refugee journey, list below the intentions that occur to you as you pull together all that you've learned in the Wilderness.

> Man is made by his belief. As he believes, so he is.
> —THE BHAGAVAD GITA

_____

_____

_____

_____

_____

_____

_____

BACKPACK FOR THE ROAD

1. Having released the trappings of your old job and plumbed the depths of your personal Wilderness, you've got a new chapter to add to the saga of your heroic journey—the story begun after Letting Go. Begin by creating the following notes that will inform your writing:

Verbal snapshots of the beginning, middle, and end of your Wilderness wanderings, with particular focus on your emotional awarenesses:

_____

_____

_____

_____

_____

_____

_____

_____

_____

_____

_____

_____

_____

A list of the exercises and artistic and interpersonal experiences that gave you the most insight. Across from each action, write whatever insights came to you through that particular exercise:

_____

_____

_____

_____

_____

_____

_____

_____

_____

_____

_____

_____

_____

Indications or hints that you are moving toward the light of a new beginning:

_____

_____

_____

_____

_____

_____

2. Now write the next chapter—in the third person—of your hero's journey, this time through the Wilderness. Tell the story as if the snapshots described above are the outline. Set up no particular ending to this chapter; just make it the next episode and include the gathered insights your hero has achieved. End with his/her seeing the beacon, as if from a lighthouse shining out in the distance—a beacon guiding our hero to a new home.

_____

_____

_____

_____

_____

_____

_____

_____

_____

_____

_____

_____

_____

_____

3. What does the gathered wisdom of the Wilderness stage, plus any insights derived from the new chapter of your heroic journey, imply about what your next job must contain? Write out a hypothetical job description that would encompass what you've identified. Make this an Intention Statement as you move toward Seeing the Beacon:

My Intention for My Next Career Move:

_____

_____

_____

_____

_____

_____

_____

_____

_____

_____

SEEING THE LIGHT: THE END OF THE WILDERNESS

The Wilderness is a halfway point in your Refugee journey. As you explore your recovery process at this stage, do you see any resistance toward moving forward? Is there still any festering resentment toward your ex-employer? Any reluctance to seize the opportunity for new directions? Use your journal to write about any such resistance. If it continues, it's important to share your feelings with someone you trust—your outplacement or career coach, a significant other, a close friend, or a psychotherapist. Ideally, the work of Letting Go and foraging through the Wilderness will have dissipated much of the grief and cleared the way for Seeing the Beacon.

*When we walk to the edge of all the light we have and take the
step into the darkness of the unknown, we must believe that one of
two things will happen: There will be something solid for
us to stand on, or we will be taught to fly.*

—PATRICK OVERTON

FIVE

Stage IV:
Seeing the Beacon

*If one advances confidently in the direction of his dreams, and
endeavors to live the life he has imagined, he will meet with a
success unexpected in common hours.*

—HENRY DAVID THOREAU

Like a ship that's been lost at sea, the Refugee eventually spots
a beacon shining through the fog, signaling the way to safe
harbor. A new home. At first it's a mere twinkle in the dark.
It requires an act of faith to move in its direction. With a steady
stroke, we wend our way toward the light and realize there is guidance when the time is right. When the Wilderness of the DMZ has
been truly lived, the healing strategies explored and life lessons
gleaned, we realize that in fact the Beacon is internal and has always been with us.

Christopher

Christopher's engineering jobs with three computer-chip manufac-
turers each ended after two years when his divisions were either
sold or closed. After the third layoff, Christopher got listless,

disheartened, and, by his description, "lazy." His buddies had referrals to programming jobs, but Christopher decided to spend some downtime on unemployment and "play as much volleyball as possible until I'm ready to get back in the game of business again."

Yet Christopher avoided working the recovery stages. He was getting depressed, sleeping a lot, withdrawing socially, and feeling like a failure when two of his former colleagues—both twenty-nine, the same age as Christopher—bragged to him at a party that their stock options were worth more than $200,000. They told Christopher that the latest buzzwords over happy-hour beers were, "Do you have your second comma yet?" referring to the second set of triple zeros representing $1 million. The fact that the same company that laid off Christopher was paying such high dividends in other divisions was too much. He burrowed deeper into sadness.

The turning point for Christopher was precipitated by a series of additional losses. His grandmother and both great-grandparents died within three months of each other during his unemployment. This cluster of losses compounded Christopher's depression and drove him to counseling, where he finally began the Refugee journey.

He started with a life review (page 144). The only child of three generations of scientists and engineers, Christopher recognized he'd never been encouraged to "think differently." When he did his list of "100 Things to Do Before I Die" (page 147), it became clear that what he really wanted was to use his athletic gifts in semiprofessional competitive sports and, possibly, to coach underprivileged, at-risk boys.

Once he uncovered this direction, Christopher went into high gear. He used his analytic engineering skills to map steps and a timetable through which he could parlay his athleticism into a coaching position. He took temporary engineering work to support himself. Knowing the work was short-lived made it more tolerable. He volunteered to coach a high school volleyball team and signed up for several tournaments that offered money prizes. Now Christopher is well on his way to achieving his vocational goals *away* from engineering—a field that had been Christopher's dad's idea, not his own.

For each Refugee, the outer experience en route to a revitalized sense of self is different. For some, like Christopher, successive job losses become the vehicle for breakdown and eventual breakthrough. For those who receive generous severance packages, deliberate time out, with the help of outplacement counseling, may become the path toward self-exploration and renewal. For others, the work of Letting Go and wandering the Wilderness occurs underground while they work in temp jobs, consult, or take new jobs but are nevertheless forced to experience the Refugee stages because they feel emotionally compromised by their losses.

However you get there, a truly new beginning occurs only as the result of difficult soul-searching. Such deep work can seem futile and meaningless when no clear outcomes are immediately visible. But at this point in your Refugee journey, the insights you've gathered during the Wilderness align to show you the thread or theme of your core competencies against the light of new possibilities. Treasure the lessons of the Wilderness. Now is the time of their resolution.

The experience of Seeing the Beacon is one of strengthened self-esteem, periods of learned optimism, and moments of pure inspiration that suggest avenues worth pursuing. There is a palpable knowing that you are near the end of your journey. The New Land is just over the horizon. You can taste it now.

> A cover of darkness, separation, and confusion are necessary prerequisites for the eventual rebirth of a lost and wandering soul.
> —NOR HALL

IS THIS THE NEW YOU?
In an effort to take control of their careers, one out of four—a total of 36 million—American workers have become free agents or independent professionals.

SIGNPOSTS

There are no clear signposts that mark the transition from the Wilderness to Seeing the Beacon. It's really something you just know. You gradually feel the inner fog lift. Confusion is replaced by optimism; inner work segues into external results; thoughts become actions. Synchronicities seem to multiply.

Brian

Brian's career-change options hit him in totally unpredictable ways after a long period of disillusionment and wandering. A thirty-nine-year-old physician specializing in preventive medicine, Brian spent ten years working for an HMO, where he saw twenty or more patients a day. On his own time, Brian developed innovative flu-prevention programs for the elderly, as well as early-detection strategies for people with cancer and AIDS. Each time he presented his well-developed proposals to his colleagues, Brian was encouraged to shepherd them through the ranks of his managed-care corporation to the top decision makers. Yet, each time, the administrators wielding the money shot him down, deeming such programs too expensive. Never mind that the mandate of the HMO is prevention, and never mind that Brian could prove millions of dollars in treatment costs would be saved with early-prevention programs. The head honchos were bottom-line driven, fixated on "cutting the head count" to save money rather than using the tenets of good medicine for that purpose.

When the last rejection came, Brian knew that he had to quit his job. Aside from the likelihood of being caught in a looming downsizing effort by the hospital, he felt so ethically compromised that he simply couldn't continue working in a managed-care environment. After a period of grief over what seemed to him wasted years of medical training at Harvard and Yale, Brian agreed with his wife that he needed a self-imposed sabbatical. She was making good money as a CPA, so he could afford to slip into his Wilderness period and wander intellectually, emotionally, and spiritually.

The Wilderness was torturous for Brian. He'd been so intellectually driven for so long, he'd forgotten how to play. Creative wandering seemed like a waste of time. Yet, a one-day welding class at a local community college finally captivated Brian and allowed him to surrender to something new and different. Bending steel to create art became, for him, the perfect metaphor for reversing the unbending nature of the managed-care environment.

After a few months in the Wilderness, yet still not clear about where to go professionally, Brian accepted an invitation to speak to a local Kiwanis Club about preventive medicine. The group asked Brian to tell his story about leaving the HMO. As he spoke extemporaneously about the increasingly reduced periods of time doctors were allowed with each patient, coupled with the patients' specialists never getting together to brainstorm and share notes about each case, Brian got an idea. Why not create a health care program that included the very attributes missing in the managed-care world? He envisioned a team of health care providers covering many modalities, all located in one setting that allowed the providers to meet regularly as a team to process the best treatment options for each patient. Brian hurried out of that meeting, ran to his computer, and dove into a creative binge that resulted in a program that is already being implemented.

Brian's disenchantment with his working environment is shared by countless workers whose industries are driven more by Wall Street than Main Street. Sometimes these professionals don't realize how marginalized they feel until they are removed from the day-to-day corporate mentality. After a period of wandering and soul-searching, most Refugees recognize that authority, flexibility, and growth opportunities are at least as important, if not more so, than pay increases. And holding on to something that doesn't fulfill those core values is clearly not as gratifying as holding out for what will.

RECLAIMING YOUR "DAIMON"

Everyone has a unique calling, a concept brilliantly detailed in James Hillman's book *The Soul's Code* (Warner Books, 1996), in which he calls that inner direction our "daimon"—a core gift or talent with which we are born. Joseph Campbell, whose lifelong work was the encyclopedic collection and interpretation of the world's myths, likewise spoke passionately about the personal mythology we each carry as a means through which we express ourselves. Campbell described how "inspiration breeds aspiration." If we identify and "follow our bliss," as he put it, we aspire to fulfill its most cherished notions. Careers, particularly if they are our right livelihood (the Buddha's term for meaningful work), provide the opportunity to combine our innate talents and bliss with a company's mission. The synergistic result gives us a strong sense of meaning and purpose. It's no wonder, then, that we feel so lost and disconnected if the job that fulfills our "daimon" is yanked out from under us, pushing us from the Brink to Letting Go.

Hence, the work of the Beacon stage has several facets: First and foremost, you must hold fast to your highest values and ideals for what you want from your New Land—the insights and preferences gathered during your time in the Wilderness. Second, you must create opportunities for serendipitous insights. The conjunction of these two aims will lead to synchronicities that will, eventually and unquestionably, guide you to a new homeland.

A CAVEAT: THE FALSE START

Be careful during this exciting stage to differentiate between what is a real island of opportunity and what is a mirage. Fears of running out of money, compounded by the continued discomfort of not knowing, can set us up to rush the process, take easy solutions, or follow other people's advice rather than honoring our own deeper wisdom. The result will be a false start—jumping into a position that isn't a fit with the preferences you've defined for yourself, like Jessica, who rebounded into a job, then quit one week later. When people experience such false starts, they look back, after the fact, and usually recognize the blatant signals that suggested they not take that path. Inevitably, they are forced to Let Go of yet another job, and, worse still, their fragile self-esteem is shaken as feelings of doubt and regression kick them back to the Wilderness.

So be careful! You've worked too hard and come too far to make mistakes that can be avoided by taking a bit more time for careful deliberation. Revisit the gathered wisdom you recorded in your Backpacks from the prior Refugee stages. Check in with your family, support group, and counselors to troubleshoot anything that might prove to be an impulsive false start.

A word about the difference between the concepts of false start and synchronicity. Typically, a false start is characterized by an intellectual decision based on fear—fear of having been wandering too long, fear that nothing is ever going to come along and here is this opportunity—maybe you should just do it. Refugees who leap into false starts later recognize that they had to rationalize to talk themselves into this path. Synchronicity, on the other hand, is completely nonlinear, nonrational: It's a coincidental convergence of outer and inner events that seem to appear out of nowhere. Our rational minds have nothing to do with synchronicities. To differentiate between a false start and a synchronicity, look at your participation in the circumstances: Were you driving toward this start or were you not even part of its formation, yet here it is?

THE MAGNIFICENCE OF SYNCHRONICITY

The stars seem to align when synchronicities occur. For more on this phenomenon, here are two great resources:

• *Soul Moments: Marvelous Stories of Synchronicity—Meaningful Coincidences from a Seemingly Random World* by Phil Cousineau (Conari Press, 1997). Introduced by well-known Jungian scholar (and expert on synchronicity) Robert Johnson, this book will assure you that staying the course of your recovery journey brings surprising benefits.

• *The Power of Flow: Practical Ways to Transform Your Life with Meaningful Coincidence* by Charlene Belitz and Meg Lundstrom (Three Rivers Press, 1998). Teaches sixteen techniques for fostering synchronicity in your life.

Julia

Julia, forty-four, has always worked in financial services, rising from stockbroker to director of training for institutional sales and investment bankers. She loved training and development and thought her position was indispensable—until a reorganization of her firm reduced her role. Disillusioned by the firm but still high on her training abilities, Julia decided to quit and open a private coaching and consulting business.

Julia packed up her three-year-old daughter, sold her New Jersey home, and moved to Colorado, fulfilling a lifelong dream. She worked long hours and networked constantly, eventually developing a consulting business that allowed her to do the best of what she used to do, though at an admittedly lower income. Simultaneously, Julia worked the Refugee stages, feeling the grief and confusion of the Refugee experience in spite of having left her job voluntarily. She'd always been "corporate," so becoming an entrepreneur was not easy for her.

After a year in Colorado, Julia got a call from her old supervisor. He offered her a position as director of international training at a salary nearly twice what she was bringing home in Colorado. Julia's first reaction was negative. Having bought a new home in her dream state and established great new friendships, her heart told her to stay put. She also distrusted the company's stability, having experienced four reorganizations in eight years. But the financial enticement drowned out her doubts. At Julia's behest, the company bought her Colorado house, packed Julia and her daughter up, and moved them back to the East Coast. A real estate agent was provided to help Julia purchase a new home in a beautiful area of her choice, and she returned to the company two years after leaving it.

For about nine months, all went well. Then—*déjà vu*. The summer markets had been volatile, requiring (so the company said) a 5 percent downsizing: 3500 people, including Julia, were laid off during a worldwide reorganization. Julia was given a small severance package, but it wasn't enough to support a return to her beloved Colorado. Plus, she now owned a house in New Jersey. There was no choice but to ramp up her coaching and consulting work and relive all the Refugee stages—again.

In retrospect, Julia's first move to Colorado was inspired. She'd always wanted to live there, and her short sojourn West validated her fondest dreams. Although the international aspect of the new offer intrigued her, as did the promise that she would not have to commute into New York City each day, Julia says, "I should have known not to trust them. This firm lops off what they term 'the bottom 10 percent' whenever the bottom line demands saving money. It doesn't matter if people perform above expectations. If they fit into that 10 percent, they're gone."

Now Julia's revamped consulting practice is doing well. She specializes in outplacement coaching for executives and urges them to do their homework on any and all offers. "People who reach out and grab the first job out of fear usually end up downsized again," she says. "Above all, it takes time to move consciously and mindfully through the recovery stages before a Refugee has reconnected her lifestyle needs with her career options. They are both important, and they need to be congruent for a new beginning to really work." As for Julia's dream of moving back to Colorado, she's all but given it up. Her practice is established in New Jersey, she fears uprooting her daughter yet again, and she hopes one day to retire in Colorado.

In the midst of winter, I found there was within me, an invincible summer.
—ALBERT CAMUS

The work of Seeing the Beacon is about remaining patient and maximizing the potential of every opportunity to foster new insights and new connections before making any decisions. Brian's revelations occurred during a life review he shared while giving a speech. Julia had to crisscross the country before she settled into gratifying self-employment. Similarly, your moments of personal genius will occur when you're least expecting them.

Having come this far, trust that you've planted the seeds and nourished them well. What's necessary now is a healthy Interim Structure and Actions geared toward finding and recognizing new opportunities, both internal, in the form of insights, and external, via instrumental people or resources that will appear as if out of the blue and bring fresh possibilities.

INTERIM STRUCTURE FOR SEEING THE BEACON

The grief of Letting Go is behind you. The confusion of the Wilderness, mixed with its creative binges, has led to many explorations that might have seemed tangential but ultimately allowed you to break up old attachments and see the first shoots of new possibilities. What you need to support you now is faith in your own nature as you open yourself to new possibilities. This is a time to take your clearly defined values and preferences into meetings with career counselors, recruiters, and human resource contacts. Explore on-line resources and have a resume perfected that, at a moment's notice, you can send to anyone with a lead. Go on job interviews that allow you to perfect your interviewing skills while assessing the fit of the jobs with the calling you've identified as your core passion.

FOLLOWING YOUR CALLS

For a passionate illumination of the reliability of those intuitive messages from within, read Gregg Levoy's powerful book *Callings* (Three Rivers Press, 1998). It's also available on audiotape (Random House, 1997).

It's as if you now have a fresh mound of clay in front of you, and you get to mold it into any form you want your career to take. Begin with the attributes you've already defined and, as each new insight comes along, add a piece to your sculpture, crafting it deliberately and joyfully as you go. Above all, don't settle! Veto job offers that don't include *most* of the elements you require. Those vetoes will be part of your sculpture too. They add depth to your sense of choice.

The finished work of art—your next career—will be textured by all the lessons along your career path, combined with the positive and negative experiences of working through the Refugee stages. This can be great fun. You're out of the woods and into the light of day. It's only a matter of time before you're in your New Land. Your goals now focus on:

• reinforcing your core strengths, talents, and preferences;

• defining new directions—your calling—based on all the Refugee work to date;

• solidifying centering strategies during your job search.

AN OVERVIEW OF THE INTERIM STRUCTURE
FOR STAGE IV: SEEING THE BEACON

Goals During Seeing the Beacon

- Reinforce core strengths, talents, and preferences

- Define new directions based on all the Refugee work to date

- Solidify centering strategies for stress management during job search

Daily Rituals

- Your Journal as Beacon Collector

- Mindful Eating

- Exercise Ritual

After Hours

- Burn, Baby, Burn

- A Watched Pot . . .

- Mentors and Models

Actions

I. Psychological Self-Management Strategies

- Good Day, Sunshine

- Your Emotional Plumb Line

- Hold On and Hold Out

- Common Grounds

II. Reflections of the True You

- Interior Redecoration

- Test the Waters

- "Brand" New You

III. Job's a-Coming

- Continuing Ed

- Due Diligence

- Stay in Control of Your Resume

- The "Hidden" Job Market

- Your Personal Board of Directors

- Mind Your Own Business

THE JOURNAL AS TRAVELING COMPANION

Oscar Wilde's play *The Importance of Being Earnest* has a great line to reinforce your journal ritual: "I never travel without my diary. One should always have something sensational to read on the train."

THE DAILY RITUALS

The Daily Rituals of Letting Go and the Wilderness are surely ingrained in your life by now. While Seeing the Beacon, a few variations on your core rituals can optimize your progress toward the New Land.

Your Journal as Beacon Collector

In addition to centering and stabilizing you, your journal during this stage is your forum for inner dialogues about options coming your way. You can try them on for size, get feedback from your inner muse, play with counteroffers, or take joy in refusing to become a citizen in a country that clearly doesn't fit you.

Mindful Eating

You know how to take care of your diet now, having been deliberate during the previous stages. If your appetite was reduced during Letting Go and the Wilderness, it might feel robust again as you proceed through the Beacon. Maintain healthy eating patterns and get all your essential nutrients.

On the other hand, overeating is a coping mechanism some Refugees use to tranquilize the pain of Letting Go and the disorientation of the Wilderness. If that's been an issue for you, now is the time to use the gradual return to inner comfort during the Beacon stage to reformulate your diet. Increase fiber, decrease fats, eat only at mealtimes and when you're hungry. All the behaviors you establish during this stage will become the ground from which you'll nourish yourself in your New Land.

Exercise Ritual

As before, your daily workouts need to be cardiovascular as well as strength-building. During this stage, your improved self-esteem and clarified self-definition can extend to your fitness regimen. Challenge yourself as follows:

•Once each week, choose a different workout, class, or instructor to try for the fun of it or for stretching your abilities in new directions.

•Use visualization to reinforce a vision of your idealized career path. By visualizing what you want, even during body movement sessions, you'll anchor the template you're creating rather than revert to old patterns of fear and unworthiness.

•Sense yourself unfolding new wings like a baby bird. Careful stretching during your workouts should focus on upper back extension, chest and shoulder openings, arm swings leading with the chest, arching movements while gazing upward—up and out into new places.

•Find a yoga teacher who understands what you're going through emotionally and can help you express your feelings through movement.

Because you're contemplating serious vocational options during the Beacon stage, exercise is essential. It aids the mind-body-spirit connection that's critical for healthy decision making. If you feel as if you are about to jump for a job offer, perhaps too quickly, call a timeout for a workout. This delay, in combination with aerobic activity, will get you back in balance and possibly save you from a false start. Similarly, punctuating an offer-counteroffer process with timeouts for exercise will help you look at the big picture—what will your life be like if you do or don't follow this career path?

ACTIONS

The Actions that follow are divided among four skills you'll need as you wend your way through this stage:

• Self-management strategies to support your psychological transition from the inner world of the Wilderness to the outer world of Seeing the Beacon.

• Actions that validate your passions, talents, and preferences—reflections of the true you.

• Methods through which you can assess the fit of potential job situations with the true you—because during the Beacon, a job's a-coming. No doubt!

• After Hours strategies for further self-care and decompression, especially designed for this stage but also useful as tools for the New Land soon to come.

I. Psychological Self-Management Strategies

Good Day, Sunshine

Determine to see each day as a creative act. Think of beginning your morning by harnessing the power of the sunrise to help you stay focused on the "big picture" of your new life ahead. If you're an early riser, greet the first light of day and be deliberate about what you want to do before getting out of bed. Remember how, during your corporate days, you used to *spend* your time in a variety of ways to get the job done or just to get through tedious days? Now think in terms of *investing* your precious time in ways that will advance you along your path. With mindful attention first to your self-nourishing daily rituals and then to the choices you are making for each day, you'll reach sunset with a feeling of purpose and contentment. After a good night's rest, when you greet a new morning, you'll have a delightful feeling of a fresh beginning and a world of *possibilities*.

If you are, by nature, a nocturnal person, your mornings may feel less invigorating than

PAMPERING YOURSELF WITH LOTIONS AND POTIONS

Aromatherapy and essential oils can be amazingly soothing and centering. These books suggest many ideas on their many uses, supported by scientific explanations.

• *375 Essential Oils and Hydrosols* by Jeanne Rose (Frog Ltd, 1999)

• *Medical Aromatherapy: Healing with Essential Oils* by organic chemist Kurt Schnault (Frog Ltd, 1999).

your powerful evening hours. Nevertheless, upon waking to the beginning of each new day, you will have a choice about what this day can contain. The key is seeing each day as a new beginning, replete with opportunities for creative self-expression.

Your Emotional Plumb Line

All of us handle stress differently. Some people thrive on a great deal of stress and enjoy the challenge of constantly putting out fires. Others are sensitive to the slightest overstimulation and suffer physical, mental, and emotional symptoms that can become chronic. Determine your stress personality, based on your temperament and past work experience. Are you thick-skinned, relatively impervious to stressful environments? Or do you fear disapproval, often operating with an edge of discomfort and anxiety, suggesting that your work environment needs to be peaceful and noncompetitive? In most cases, we are born with these temperaments; they are neither good nor bad. All that matters is that you recognize your tendencies. Do not enter (or reenter) an occupation that, by its nature, is not a fit with your stress personality.

Once you determine your stress temperament, develop an emotional plumb line to monitor your stress level. Daily centering strategies will keep you balanced and gauge your body's needs. These strategies should be specific to what you know works best for you, such as:

- taking frequent breaks away from your job-hunting station to stretch;

- scheduling a daily half-hour meditation or exercise break;

- putting up your feet while sipping a cup of herb tea.

The behaviors themselves are for you to design. The point is that you use this stage of your recovery to habituate relaxation and

TREAT STRESS WITH JOY

Dr. Paul Pearsall, author of *The Pleasure Prescription* (Hunter House, 1996), compares the low-stress, high-health Polynesian culture with our stressful Western way of life and concludes, "It's not too much stress, it's too little joy" that causes our distress. This book will inspire you to live more joyfully.

Until one is committed, there is hesitancy, the chance to draw back, always ineffectiveness. The moment one definitely commits oneself, then Providence moves too. All sorts of things occur to help one that would never otherwise have occurred. . . . Boldness has genius, power, and magic in it. Begin it now.
—JOHANN WOLFGANG VON GOETHE

centering breaks, begun during the Brink, that you'll take with you to the next job situation and beyond. By conditioning your emotional plumb line, you will be aware of what you need before you are in crisis. And once you recognize your body's distress signals, you'll intuitively steer clear of work environments that are likely to cause too much stress and deprivation.

Hold On and Hold Out

As you patiently move through this stage, one of the best psychological self-management strategies is to regularly affirm the intention statements you developed at the end of your Wilderness wanderings. Restate them below to remind yourself what's *nonnegotiable*. If your highest values include knowledge, authority, autonomy, and flexibility, hold the intention that those attributes will be key ingredients of your next job.

_____

_____

_____

_____

_____

_____

Affirm, daily and in your journal, your intention to find a job that contains the *challenges* you need. *Do not accept anything less* or all the work you've accomplished throughout these recovery stages will be for naught. The wrong job will soon become so toxic that you'll probably have to leave it and resume your wandering until the right one does come along.

DISCOVER THE CAREER THAT BEST EXPRESSES *YOU*

For many people, traditional career advice books work well, particularly the venerable *What Color Is Your Parachute?* by Richard Bolles (Ten Speed Press, 1999). If you want deeper self-discovery, try these excellent resources:

•*Do What You Are* by Paul Tieger and Barbara Barron-Tieger (Little, Brown, 1995) introduces personality types based on the Myers-Briggs Type Indicator and suggests careers aligned with your specific personality.

•*Zen and the Art of Making a Living: A Practical Guide to Creative Career Design* by Laurence G. Boldt (Penguin, 1999) offers inspirational, imaginative guidance to determine your right livelihood.

•*Doing Work You Love: Discovering Your Purpose and Realizing Your Dreams* by Cheryl Gilman (NTC/Contemporary, 1997) provides exercises to guide you toward your right livelihood with equal emphasis on physical health and intellectually driven ambition.

Marty

Marty knew he needed a new job because he was no longer growing in his present position with a sporting equipment company. Without leaving his administrative assistant job, he aggressively marketed himself within the company. Marty's boss was sad at the prospect of losing an assistant so capable and versatile, but she saw Marty languishing and gave her blessing to an internal job search. After doing the necessary work to clarify his values, Marty realized his needs for his next job: authority, autonomy, and the opportunity to create and expand a project he could call his own. Above all, he wanted his job to contribute to the lives of the less fortunate. It was unclear how his charitable needs could be met within a sports and fitness company that produces products and requires bottom-line results. But that value was so important to Marty that he determined to make it a part of his next job description. Because he had seniority, he held on to the belief that he could achieve such a position within the company, rather than go to work for a nonprofit agency where his values would be more likely to be found than in a corporate culture.

Once Marty had clarified these components, he never looked back. He knew it might take months to land in new territory. Meanwhile, another corporate change was afoot, a reorganization of administrative assistants on the executive floor. Several people were packaged out, while those remaining had to work for two senior managers. The idea of assisting more than one manager was out of the question for Marty, who worked too much overtime as it was. He told his boss he would complete a three-month project he'd been assigned, but thereafter would leave the company rather than accept the reorganized job. Marty put all his energy into the project, letting go of his internal job search. He figured he'd simply deal with a total job change when this project was completed.

Unknown to Marty, part of the reorganization included the creation of a new job in community relations—one of the departments

Marty had explored previously. The new title was global employee involvement manager, a role made in heaven for Marty. In fact, several key executives nominated Marty for the post without his knowledge. Marty was shocked and honored when the director of community relations offered him the job. They sought an insider with a deep grasp of the organization. Marty fit the bill. And the job itself fit *his* bill: Responsibilities included empowering employees to do volunteer work with charities of their choice in ways that the company could implement, plus developing a speakers bureau, expanding philanthropic activities for the company as a whole, and coordinating these efforts globally.

When he read the job description, Marty burst into tears of joy. It included every one of the core values he'd declared in his intention statement, plus one more. It would be a brand new department, a stretch for the company but more important, a creative stretch for Marty, one that was "scary enough to be a true challenge!" He's convinced it only came about because he held fast to his intention.

Just imagine what clearly defined goals—plus the courage of your convictions—can do for you when you set your mind to it.

Common Grounds

There is a self-supporting career search agency called 40+ for executives over forty who seek new careers. Part of the group's structure for members is that they get up every morning as if going to work, dress in professional attire, and show up at the local 40+ office to do their "job" of job searching. In the executive suite, they use office computers to compose and send resumes, attend frequent, interesting workshops, search job banks, and—above all—network with one another. The boosts in self-esteem and feelings of solidarity with fellow seekers are immeasurable. Volunteer positions within 40+ rotate among current members; they are mandatory, so everyone is forced to assume responsibilities for making the agency run efficiently. In the process, each person feels valued while getting to display his or her administrative talents. When members go out on interviews that may not be right for them, they nevertheless bring back to the group at large referrals for other members who might be the perfect fit for that particular opportunity.

If you can find a group like 40+ that is specific either to your age or your industry, go for it. If not, maybe you'll want to start one. The sense of community and common ground will reward you daily. In either case, use the group's structure to construct a day that demands getting out of bed and getting down to the business of job hunting, because that's what it is—a business.

II. Reflections of the True You

Interior Redecoration

Look around your home. Do the colors, the lighting, the garden, and overall decor reflect what you want in your life right now? Do they reflect the conclusions of your Wilderness wandering? If not, redesign or rearrange your nest to reflect your newfound sense of self. Ask yourself:

- How does your environment need to be changed to reflect those changes?

- What free or inexpensive changes could you make right away?

- What symbols or images could you use to remind you to hold fast to your intentions for yourself?

REFLECTIONS OF A NEW YOU

Redesign your home environment to reflect your new inner and outer directions. Some interesting resources include:

• *Use What You Have Interior Decorating* by Lauri Ward (Perigee, 1999). Inspires using material you already have, but in new, innovative ways.

• *The Feng Shui Anthology* by Jami Lin (Earth Design, 1997). A beginner's sourcebook for understanding and experimenting with feng shui.

• *Complete Illustrated Guide to Feng Shui* by Lillian Too (Element Books, 1996). Too has several texts on the art of feng shui as well as a kit that makes a game of redesigning your environment.

Gabe

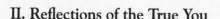

A twenty-seven-year-old medical exercise specialist, Gabe lost his job at a medical startup when the company ran out of money. Before that, he'd worked for two years at a psychiatric hospital, where his innovative ideas for managing a difficult adolescent population were ignored. He had been elated when the startup company *courted* his cutting-edge programs for functional fitness. The salary was low, but he got shares of the company in exchange for his dedication in the form of sixty-hour workweeks. Friends in high tech who'd given two or three years of such overwork had been handsomely rewarded when their companies were acquired. Gabe figured he couldn't lose. At the very least, he would learn a lot, plus he was given a managerial title that would set him up for the future no matter what happened in this company.

It all looked promising until the seed money ran out and venture capital could not be found. Patients were paying for services out-of-pocket, because insurance wouldn't cover much of the exceptional physical therapy Gabe could offer. Patients achieved dramatic reversals in their deteriorating medical conditions, yet, programmed to expect insurance reimbursement, they dropped out when it was denied. Marketing to attract a new customer base was beyond the company's limited budget. Word-of-mouth referrals were not enough to support existing staff, so Gabe was among several cut back to independent-contractor status. Good-bye to dreams of "handsome rewards."

Gabe was able to recapture some old clients and revamp his fitness-training practice enough to get by while he worked his way through Letting Go. During the Wilderness, Gabe reactivated some of his favorite extracurricular activities: He joined a city soccer league and an outrigger racing team. He called old friends with whom he'd lost touch during the hectic days of being chained to his computer writing protocols for the startup. He started networking to give public talks on topics related to his passion of creative rehabilitation strategies for physical handicaps. Gradually, Gabe's original fire returned, but Letting Go of his disillusionment seemed the hardest part of his recovery. It made applying for work difficult because he didn't trust most companies. Either they were too institutional to suit him now, or they were startups with the same potential problems he'd just experienced.

When the idea of interior redecoration was presented, Gabe

recognized a missing link. For three years, he had lived in a studio within a large family house. Gabe enjoyed the camaraderie of roommates, but he worked in the same room that he slept, ate, socialized, and hung out on the phone in. Over time, his room became a jail cell. Gabe determined to find a new home environment, even though he was not making enough money to be frivolous.

A month into his search, a roommate situation in a beachfront duplex popped up. Fifty people applied for the rental, but Gabe determined it would be his. He approached it as if it were a highly desirable job. Not only did he present letters of stellar recommendation and good credit history, he also provided the decision maker with a couple of deep-tissue massages free of charge—giving his future landlord a hands-on sampling of Gabe's passion and integrity. A week later, Gabe got the apartment. A tiny bedroom became his new cocoon, but he had the use of the rest of the unit, which included breathtaking ocean views.

"Now I can expand the rest of my horizons as I gaze out at these," Gabe resolved. He sifted through his belongings, paring his environment down so he'd see no clutter. A strong sense of closure about his prior job came simultaneously with returning the key to his former landlord.

> If one changes internally, one should not continue to live with the same objects. They reflect one's mind and psyche of yesterday. I throw away what has no dynamic, living use. I keep nothing to remind me of the passage of time, deterioration, loss, shriveling.
>
> —ANAÏS NIN

How about *your* home environment? When you look around, does what you see reflect how you feel inside? Is the space light, bright, open, simple? If your "job" right now is applying for a new job, do you have a designated work area away from your living space? Please don't place your desk, computer, and work accoutrements in the areas where you sleep or eat. Or if space is at a premium and you have no choice, create a portable desktop and filing system so you can contain the work area and close the doors to it, figuratively if not literally, when it's time for nonwork activities.

Remember Veronica, whose life review consisted of letting go of thirty boxes of files? Just as that invisible but pivotal Wilderness experience was formative for her, so will redecorating your external environment provide a reorganization of your priorities during the

Beacon stage. Visible change on the outside will empower your continuing feelings of renewal. Ultimately, the seeds that are germinating underground will burst forth in all their glory as you set the stage for your new beginnings.

Test the Waters

After prolonged time in Letting Go and the Wilderness, the Beacon beckons us back to the world of the working. There may not be a career opportunity yet, but getting out in a purposeful way is what this stage calls for. Find some kind of work assignment, even minimal-wage or temp work, as long as it is in a *meaningful setting*.

Lorraine

Lorraine, fifty-two, was a dental hygienist. Over time her work felt more and more impersonal as the schedule became increasingly demanding. When the large practice in which she worked was sold to another health care company, Lorraine took a small severance package and determined to find a new career. Having recently gone through a difficult divorce, she knew all about stages of grief and clicked right into the Refugee journey. Lorraine knew firsthand the necessity of allowing wandering time and the need for support during this very scary period. She reconfigured her women's support group to include other Refugees with whom she could commiserate and stay on track through her recovery.

Lorraine calculated that her severance and savings would give her up to a year of Wilderness time as long as she could take some kind of supplemental job to cover food and car expenses. Because reading was her first love, it was provident that one day, while perusing books in her favorite bookstore, Lorraine noticed a Help Wanted sign propped against the cash register. She spontaneously applied and landed that part-time job in an environment that represented bliss to her.

Excited to meet interesting people, Lorraine threw herself into the job. The owner saw Lorraine's ability, her intellectual curiosity, and the fact that she was in transition. He offered to teach her the software that bookstores use to track inventory. Shortly thereafter, the owner groomed her to become his store manager.

Two states away, Lorraine's daughter Brooke knew a man who wanted to sell his small-town bookstore. Brooke proposed to her mother that they invest as partners and own the store together. For Lorraine, it would mean moving from her marital home and the town in which she'd raised her four offspring, but it was an opportunity to physically and symbolically put the divorce and the old life behind her.

"Why not?" Lorraine thought. "This is like manna from heaven. Nothing's ever simply 'come' to me this way. I've gotta go for it!"

Had Lorraine not clarified and committed to her preferences, her needs and values; had she not validated her new sense of self with her support group; and finally, had she not trusted her instinct during a spontaneous evening of shopping for books, her life might never have entered this vibrant New Land of entrepreneurial book selling.

In less providential cases, doing temp work through an agency, for example, might bring you to less inspiring environments yet provide supplemental income. At the very least, such jobs might remind you of what you *don't* want.

It took me fifteen years to discover that I had no talent for writing, but I couldn't give it up because by that time, I was too famous.
—ROBERT CHARLES BENCHLEY

"Brand" New You

Set out to create a really good product (you) and, over time, you'll become your own brand. There are three legs to the stool that is Brand You. The first is product superiority, based on your experience, training, and temperament. The second leg is integrity—how you treat people and how you treat the environment. The third is how you connect with your clients or customers—the words you choose, your passion, and your talent. Once you identify your

Brand superiority, your confidence in selling yourself will naturally follow.

A second step for this strategy is to think of yourself as having been a passenger on the bus or train that was your previous company, but now you're driving your own vehicle—solo:

• What kind of vehicle are you driving? _____

• On what kind of terrain are you driving? _____

_____

• What are the qualities of the view—the surroundings?

_____

_____

_____

• Imagine a logo representing Brand You. See it beautifully etched on the sides of your vehicle. Describe it. _____

_____

_____

_____

CREATING YOUR OWN BRAND
For an in-depth approach to identifying Brand You, see William Bridges's *Creating You & Co.* (Addison-Wesley, 1997). Bridges provides a model through which you can identify your strengths and bring them to the unmet needs of any company.

• Feel yourself contained in this dream car as it transports you into a New Land, a work environment that fits you as perfectly as this vehicle reflects your core energies. What is this like for you? _____

_____

_____

_____

III. Jobs a-Coming

Continuing Ed

Now is the time to develop work skills that will boost your value in the eyes of employers. Read books by futurists to determine what's ahead in your industry. Make a commitment to learn something new, a skill that constantly changing workplaces will require, such as new software or operating systems. Be aware that your technical skills must be maintained at a rather sophisticated level if you are looking for a good income, job growth potential, and a wide field of opportunity. Even if you return to your previous industry and you haven't been gone too long, job responsibilities are changing so quickly that you may feel you're scurrying to catch up. And, since you're not likely to land a job for life, skill building must become an ongoing process.

Due Diligence

When you approach job opportunities, think of yourself as a venture capitalist considering an investment. No successful investor would jump into anything even fabulously promising without doing "due diligence," which is research and homework on every aspect of the company and the industry as a whole. Every career move that presents itself deserves a feasibility study:

- What is the history of this company?

- What do the people already working there have to say about the culture of the workplace?

- How family-friendly is this workplace? (Even if you don't have children, these policies are indicative of an ethical culture.)

A LIBRARY TO THE FUTURE

Technology has sped the rate of corporate growth such that, in addition to staying current within our industry, it's important to have a sense of where business is heading. The following books are excellent resources:

- *Who's Running Your Career? Creating Stable Work in Unstable Times* by Caela Farren (Bard Press, 1997). Using forty Leading Career Indicators, the author teaches you how to anticipate the impact of technological advances and maintain career resilience.

- *The Age of Spiritual Machines* by Raymond Kurzweil (Penguin, 2000). Kurzweil offers futuristic predictions based on today's technological realities.

- *New Rules for the New Economy* by Kevin Kelly (Penguin, 1999). Kelly encapsulates our economic future within a framework of ten rules for how the wired world works.

DID YOU KNOW . . . ?

There are "gripe sites" online where you can listen in on employee gripes before you take a job at that company!

• www.VaultReports.com has uncensored, company-specific bulletin boards dubbed electronic water coolers.

• www.industryinsite.com is an online networking site that allows you to read what more than 60,000 fellow members have shared about hundreds of companies, jobs, industries, and cities. The site allows for anonymous exchanges so anything you post or receive is protected.

• Laid-off employees from Intel and MCI vent at www.FACEIntel.com and www.xmci.com respectively.

• What kinds of challenges and incentives will you be offered?

• Is the company committed to training and development?

• How will your potential boss offer you healthy mentoring?

• Does this company offer a generous retirement package?

• Does this employer value play as much as goal-setting and linear strategizing?

• What does your gut say both during and after your interview process?

Don't let an attractive salary override the messages your intuition is sending you. You've been through the grinder as a Refugee. Having worked through the recovery stages, you are much richer in wisdom and experience than when you left your last job. Capitalize on what you know, and don't settle for any job that doesn't pass your most stringent feasibility study. If you get an offer that doesn't contain what you want, realize that you'll probably get other offers as well. Hold out for the right one!

FINDING THAT HIDDEN JOB MARKET

Called Recruiters Online Network, www.ipa.com describes itself as "your gateway to the hidden job market," through which companies and job seekers are connected via international headhunters.

Stay in Control of Your Resume

Karen Battoe, a longtime outplacement counselor in Florida, reports that only 15 percent of employers even read resumes. They say that their employment needs are *now*, so they call recruiters and let them do the work. The current job market is flooded with resumes, especially when you consider the rise in the number of online resumes and executive coaches, on top of traditional sources such as recruiters, career counselors, and outplacement agencies. Battoe suggests, "Don't allow that piece of paper that represents you to just float out there in the mail, online, or to just anyone who arbitrarily requests it. It's okay to send a certain amount of them out there, but hold on to several and push through to get an interview. . . . *Present your resume in person whenever possible.* Or let a recruiter present your resume. Then you'll be a live resume when you go to the interview."

The "Hidden" Job Market

Read your daily newspaper to learn about massive expansions expected from mergers and acquisitions. Typically such corporate machinations begin with a melding of workforces that results in some downsizing. Yet, ironically, once that dust settles, it also often involves hiring many new employees. A newly reorganized company will try to develop new hires who cost less, fulfill newly created positions, and bring fresh energy. When you see this formula playing out in the business pages, you've discovered one of the "hidden" job markets. Send your resume right off to the human resources person or recruiter for the reconfigured company. Get it in before the new jobs have even been posted. (One caveat regarding this strategy: It's not wise to hang on until such expansion happens with your *prior* employer. In many cases, laid-off workers are not rehired after a reorganization.)

Another such hidden market is one that venture capitalists fund. If you read the business section of the daily newspaper and "follow the money," you might see a high-potential startup that will be recruiting soon. Again, get your resume in before the formal recruitment begins!

RELEARNING THE JOB MARKETPLACE

Here are some resources to help you assess any job offers that may come your way during this stage:

• *Are You Paid What You're Worth?* (Broadway Books, 1998) by Michael O'Malley, a corporate compensation consultant, helps you compute the overall market value of any job and increase the total compensation package you might be offered.

• These three Web sites provide information about publicly traded, privately held, and international companies, along with suggested books, message boards, and e-mailed newsletters: www.companysleuth.com; www.corporateinformation.com; and www.hoovers.com.

• For research and analysis sites on many companies, see www.gartner.com.

Your Personal Board of Directors

If you have made a false start or two during this Beacon stage, assess any future job offers by buying some time in negotiations to consult your personal board of directors. Here's how:

GETTING THE SCOOP

For free, easy, and instant business, economic, and global business news 24 hours a day, see www.businesswire.com; www.wired.com; and www.techweb.com.

Using your journal or a large piece of blank paper, draw a conference table. Who would sit on your ideal board of directors to advise you about your next career role, the environment in which you'll perform that role, the career track offered? Draw some stick figures—or more developed images if you're so inclined—detailing whether these people are male or female, real or imagined.

Whom do you know whose advice you would treasure? A current or past mentor? A teacher or coach from childhood? A business owner or manager whose work you've studied in books? Your board might include an entrepreneur, an artist, an athlete, a philosopher, experts in your field, a time-management guru, a financial planner. The point is to choose people, real or imagined, who represent the key aspects of yourself, the subpersonalities within you that will want to be fulfilled along your new career path. Place them around the table and visualize them working well together so that when you present your current job offer to them as a group, they'll appear practiced at responding to you. They'll know your history, your work through the Refugee stages, and your clearly defined goals for your immediate future.

ARCHETYPAL GUIDANCE

To access and explore some of the archetypal subpersonalities we all embody, read Carol Pearson's *Awakening the Heroes Within: 12 Archetypes to Help Us Find Ourselves and Transform Our World* (HarperSan Francisco, 1991). Pearson teaches a dozen classical patterns that can become paths to wholeness.

Next, present your job offer, its salary and benefits, its job description, its physical environment, growth opportunities, and anything else you feel is important in assessing the offer. Ask your board questions such as:

• Is this an ethical company?

• What is the culture like—the internal politics?

•What kinds of teams exist at this company, and how are they formed?

•Do I have the right team in place for me personally?

•Who would my peers be?

•Knowing my passions, can I operate from passion in this job?

•How available are mentors?

•What kind of training will I need, and how available is it on this job?

•What kinds of international or travel opportunities come with this job?

•What stresses might come with this assignment that I'm not seeing?

Add any additional questions that occur to you. Then write the answers from each character in dialogue form or in a list. When you feel dry, set aside your writing and take a break, ideally out in nature. Several hours later, sit down with a cup of tea and read the "feedback" from your personal board of directors. If you discover that you don't have enough information, you may want to go back to your prospective employer and ask for the information you need. After you have all the feedback and information you need, sort through it and use your personal board of directors to make your decision.

Mind Your Own Business

Many displaced workers long for the freedom and creativity of self-employment. How about you? Do your passions and expertise combine to suggest a profitable business idea? There are many resources to help you assess such a possibility.

SMALL BUSINESS ADVICE

To explore general small business postings, go to some of the online aggregate sites for small business advice, including:

•Quicken: www.quicken.com/small_business

•Small Business Administration: www.sba.org

•MSNBC's aggregate site: www.msnbc.com/news/280213.asp

The Internet is an ideal place to begin. Each mainstream portal, such as Yahoo!, Excite, AltaVista, and Infoseek, provides myriad small business postings.

Most major newspapers also have postings both on- and offline. Also, if you know the industry you'd like to be part of, look for a local trade association or trade journal for competitive intelligence as well as local resources.

Before you take too many steps toward self-employment, be certain that you have the personality and fortitude for this work style. Ask yourself:

- Can you delay gratification, waiting three to five years for financial success?

- Can you tolerate working long hours, wearing several hats, and not seeing much of your family during the startup years?

- Can you live without a steady paycheck and company-paid benefits?

- Are you computer-literate enough to do your own billing, tax filing, recordkeeping, and inventory control?

- Can you afford to invest in and keep up with technology specific to your industry?

- Are you a highly motivated, take-charge person with enough tenacity and perseverance to weather the unforeseen?

- Do you have a strong support network of colleagues, friends, and professionals (e.g., accountant, attorney) to assist you and refer business your way?

FINDING YOUR INDUSTRY

If you know what kind of business you want to launch, these sites advise you on the nuts and bolts of getting started:

- **www.garage.com** offers Bootcamps for Startups, a twice-yearly intensive to teach would-be entrepreneurs how to start up and to hook them up with venture capitalists. This site also offers a bank of resources for the high-tech Netrepreneur including banking, insurance, research, and instructive "stories from hell" that teach what *not* to do.

- **www.forecastpro.com** offers "MBA-ware," which includes people management software, programs to help you forecast demand for your product or service, guides to negotiating with suppliers or clients, and help with strategic planning.

- *Inc* magazine and its Web site **www.inc.com** offer books and free software (shareware) for writing your business plan, plus a library of articles on the pros and cons of self-employment. They also provide a searchable database called "Virtual Consultant" where you can find forms, surveys, software, credit reports, business associations, and businesses for sale as well as Web site development for the online business.

Continued

AFTER HOURS

Burn, Baby, Burn

Now that you're looking forward to life in the New Land, let's create a transformational ritual. It is designed to "cleanse" you of any leftover issues from the old paradigm of your lost job in exchange for new challenges and goals.

Begin by choosing a tangible container: a box, a vase, an empty can, an old briefcase, even an old sock or file folder. On a large sheet of paper, draw words, symbols, or pictures of what was "contained" in your past job. Include your title, your duties, the people, environment, unique equipment—everything you can think of that your mind and spirit associate with that position. Also include lifestyle accoutrements (special vehicle, calendars, clothing, or software) that came along with this job. Finally, throw in any internal compromises or sacrifices in your personal life, such as excess overtime or inadequate salary or benefits. Don't forget the lack of time for children, friends or mate, hobbies, sports, or adventures, or the extra costs for day care and laundry/dry cleaning. Take lots of time to do this thoughtfully and thoroughly.

Once you've completed your drawings, fold them up and stick them into your container. Now design a ceremony to dispose of this container and, in doing so, to officially end the previous vocational phase of your life. You'll be ending that phase and initiating passage into the New Land. You might want to burn the container (of past sacrifices) and spread the cooled ashes in a grassy area or a garden to symbolize new life.

You may want to create a ceremony in which you exchange the old for a new way of working. For example, you might work with

• At SCORE (Service Corps of Retired Executives, www.score.com), retired experts in a variety of industries will review your idea or business plan, at no charge, and advise you on its viability. Most large cities also offer nonprofit Small Business Development Centers that consult on strategic planning for your business idea. To find the SBDC or SCORE office closest to you, call (877) 726-7356.

• You can get free advice from business schools' MBA programs, such as those at Columbia, Duke, Stanford, and Harvard, all of which offer MBA candidates as consultants to local businesses. Contact your local schools to find out how to get help. Expect to be asked for a short proposal outlining your project.

two containers, one representing the old way of working, as out-
lined above, and the other representing your New Land. Load all
the attributes of the old job into the old container. Then decide
which of those might be important enough to bring with you into
the New Land, to provide continuity or to be revamped into a
healthier work style or lifestyle. Take those particular drawings out
of the old and save them in the new container before you burn the
old to "release" it. Another variation on this exercise is to do two
collages, one representing what it's time to let go of, the second representing what you want to hold on to.

Later, record your insights about your choice of containers in
your journal. What does that particular box or vase or Tupperware
symbolize for you, in and of itself? Why did you gravitate toward
that container? Write about the container versus the big picture of
your life as a whole. Often we get so caught up in our careers that
we forget there is life outside that particular "container." Now you
have the opportunity to break out of the container of your past life,
releasing any limited identities and exchanging those for new possibilities.

A Watched Pot . . .

You know that cliché: A hotly pursued job search can be futile and
incredibly frustrating, while an ideal opportunity lurks where you
least expect it. Look what happened when John followed a suggestion that he take a day off from his intense job search to apply fun-
damentals.

John

John is a forty-nine-year-old, award-winning architect and real estate developer. Not only did he design and build the home his family has occupied for twenty years, but he was also the chief architect
of a subdivision that later became an incorporated city. When the
real estate market crashed in the early '90s, John lost his lucrative

post with a large developer and had his own crash into despondency. Instead of moving consciously through Letting Go and a meaningful Wilderness experience, John jumped at the opportunity to perform due diligence work for a local bank that was making its money by foreclosing on large developments that couldn't weather the market's crash.

Imagine this creative designer whose passion was based on *building* communities having to make his living by taking them apart. It crushed John's spirit, caused serious clinical depression, and nearly destroyed his twenty-five-year marriage. John was operating from fear, insisting he had to be making money rather than "doing his stages." Better this job than no job, he thought.

John eventually had to go on antidepressants in order to maintain his commitment to making money. Rather than taking the suggested time out, which he could afford, his only concession to the Refugee journey was to join a support group for fellow displaced professionals. When John offhandedly shared his passion for photography with his support group, they assigned him the task of photographing an event coming to town. Some itinerant artists were traveling the West Coast, using indigenous rocks to create Stonehenge-type structures on beaches. Their constructions cast unique shadows with each shift of sunlight and shadow, creating a paradise for amateur photographers.

John procrastinated until the last day these artists were in town. He went only because the support group assigned it. "I really don't have time for this," he protested. To his surprise, he delighted in photographing the scene and returned several times to capture different effects of light and shadow. He also befriended the traveling "sculptors," got invited on a photography expedition to Arizona, and actually gave himself another afternoon off to have tea and chat with these free-spirited visitors.

As John was leaving the cafe with his newfound friends, someone called out his name. It was a long-ago colleague from John's days in architecture, now one of two principals in a new firm searching for a third principal with exactly John's skills! On the spot John was offered a job that made his heart sing. It was again about building communities, but this time in the sky—negotiating land deals for telecommunication satellite installations all over the world.

Just think what might have happened (or not happened!) had John not taken that afternoon off. After a long period of resisting the Wilderness, it took clinical depression and pressure from peers to allow himself a day of passionate play. Only during a moment when he stopped looking did John serendipitously bump into his new beginning.

> Genuine beginnings begin within us, even when they are brought to our attention by external opportunities. It is out of the formlessness of the [wilderness] zone that new form emerges and out of the barrenness of the fallow time that new life springs.
> —WILLIAM BRIDGES, *TRANSITIONS: MAKING THE MOST OF PERSONAL CHANGE*

Mentors and Models

Whether you decide to launch your own business or restart your career in service to someone else's business, you are the entrepreneur of your own career, selling Brand You. As you progress through the preparation and development stages of the Beacon and New Land, stories of how others have accomplished similar goals become invaluable. Toward that end, read books about business leaders or biographies of men and women you admire. *How to Succeed in Business Without Being White* by Earl Graves, publisher and CEO of *Black Enterprise* magazine (HarperBusiness, 1997), is particularly useful. Against great odds, including his family's refugee experience and the racism he battled throughout his amazing career, Graves has become a gifted and inspiring business coach for all of us. His ingenuity, tenacity, networking skills, integrity, and ethical approach to business life are applicable, no matter what our career choices might be. Put this book in your backpack as a Beacon companion en route to the New Land.

Sometimes we can see and pursue the Beacon and land exciting interviews, yet nothing seems to gel. This can be discouraging, particularly given the intensive soul-searching work that got you this far in your Refugee journey. If this is your experience, don't lose heart. Dip into the Backpack that follows and celebrate your Beacon. Then work through any setbacks in the Pit Stop chapter that follows.

BACKPACK FOR THE ROAD

1. If you are using outplacement or career counseling, how could you get more benefit from it, having seen your Beacon?

_____

_____

_____

_____

_____

_____

2. In spite of your work to this point in your Refugee journey, what limitations or roadblocks do you see that may still be blocking your path to the New Land—a job based on your preferences and Beacon?

_____

_____

_____

_____

_____

_____

3. Since the Beacon is clearly directing you to a New Land of meaningful work that you can almost touch, imagine a scenario in which you have gotten that perfect opportunity. Describe a hypothetical day in your life on this job:

_____

_____

_____

_____

_____

_____

Beacons of hope, ye appear!
Languor is not in your heart,
Weakness is not in your word,
Weariness not on your brow.

—MATTHEW ARNOLD

Overcoming Roadblocks

It has done me good to be somewhat parched by
the heat and drenched by the rain of life.
—HENRY WADSWORTH LONGFELLOW

Remember Christopher, the volleyball player we met in the previous chapter, who had to hit the wall of depression before he could surrender into his Refugee journey? Many of us operate like Christopher, especially if we've never had to reinvent ourselves prior to a Refugee experience. Out of anger or fragility, we might resist the process, ignore the signposts, or refuse to take action during critical stages of the Refugee journey.

During a crisis of confidence, it is essential that you practice the Actions of each stage and trust the process that will lead to your right livelihood, the New Land. Even though there will be false starts—ideas that seem amazingly exciting but turn out not to be your path, or interviews in which you're sure you'll be offered the job only to come in second—hold on to all that you've learned, especially to your well-defined Beacon. If you get temporarily immobilized by self-doubt or disappointment, try some of these strategies to break through those roadblocks:

Think Small

Small changes add up to big transformation. Dream big, but don't get overwhelmed. Think of your career goal as a jigsaw puzzle. When disappointment comes your way, regroup quickly and remember that all you have to focus on is the piece that is the next step in your puzzle. However small this piece might seem, it is nevertheless part of your big dream, your intention for yourself. You are a work in progress, and each small step brings you closer to your imagined destination.

GETTING OUT OF OUR OWN WAY

Stepping back often feels counterintuitive when nothing seems to be working. But creativity studies suggest breakthroughs occur most often when we get out of our own way. For more on this, see this inspiring book by the author of the original concept of "flow," Mihaly Csikszentmihalyi, *Creativity: Flow and the Psychology of Discovery and Invention* (HarperCollins, 1997).

Take a Hike

If something that looked like a sure thing falls through and you feel "back at square one," take a break from your job search. This break is a time for catharsis, to cleanse your body-mind-spirit of disappointment and negative thinking. Negative self-talk, such as "I'll never find a job," or "I'd better take the next thing that comes along," or "I'm a dinosaur" . . . or "too old" . . . or "too slow," will only set you back further. Rather than continuing to obsess over your fears and losses, spend a day hiking in a forest. Or try an outdoor workout, followed by a movie you've wanted to see. Have lunch or dinner with supportive friends, as long as you don't discuss your "setback." Plan to spend at least twenty-four hours not thinking. Then, take out your trusty journal.

In your journal, list the *actions* you have learned on your journey that will help you prevent this setback from tainting your job search. You already know these, so you're just reinforcing the lessons you have under your belt. In fact, these are Actions that you've probably already practiced throughout your Wilderness and Beacon work, such as informational interviewing, expanded networking, or online job searching.

After you complete your list, draw the actions as steps within a road map you could implement right now. Add target dates for accomplishing these steps. For example, if there are people to phone or meet with for greater networking, list their names and the exact times

DID YOU KNOW . . . ?

Informational interviewing is a way of learning about a particular company, industry, or position by setting up an appointment and actually interviewing a key executive. Often job offers result from informational interviews. Target a company in which you'd like to work, bring carefully planned questions, and stay no longer than 20 minutes to leave a good impression.

you intend to talk with each. Or list how many targeted cold calls you will make on what days. If there are online job sites you have not yet researched, on what days will you do so?

It may not have been very long ago that you began your journey as a Refugee, but you are no longer the person you were On the Brink, Letting Go, or In the Wilderness. At this point, what at first appears to be a setback becomes an opportunity to remind yourself how far you have come and how much stronger and better equipped you are to deal with whatever comes your way. Now you can see a false start as not a setback.

VIRTUAL INFORMATIONAL INTERVIEWING

The Web can also be a source for informational interviewing. Go to www.wetfeet.com where you can actually interview real people at the site's "Real People Profile" section. Also check out the site's "CompanyQuicks" and "Company Q&A" sections for performance data, information on companies' strategies, job opportunities, and literally all the information a live insider in each company would tell you during an informational interview.

Reaction, Re-Action

Sometimes disappointments block us from seeing more options. If this happens and your action steps get roadblocked by fear and worry, do some journal work about the questions that plague you. Write one question at the top of each blank page; then write everything that comes to mind. Or convene your personal board of directors and pose your questions to them. Your questions might include:

- How long is this going to take?

- Where will I land?

- What shall I do?

- How shall I repackage myself?

- What am I not seeing that might be standing in my way?

Knowing how disconcerting setbacks are during this period of ambiguity, be assured that your feelings are normal. Once vented and processed, they will shift into renewed commitment to hold your intentions and stay the course.

> **Life must be lived forwards, but can only be understood backwards.**
> —SØREN KIERKEGAARD

Give

When setbacks or roadblocks appear, finding meaningful volunteer work can do much to restore your self-worth and flagging self-esteem. It might even lead to a job! Volunteer work in and of itself has great power to heal. With money removed from the equation, you can experience a pure sense of contribution and, as a result, heightened self-worth. It's also a great opportunity to test-drive an aspiration. It doesn't require a full-time commitment—a few hours or days per week are ample for a restoration of spirit. So rewarding are the benefits that you may want to continue volunteering even after you have a new job.

A great role model for this strategy is former president Jimmy Carter, who was only fifty-six years old in January 1981 when he was "involuntarily retired from my position in the White House." "What was I going to do with the next twenty-five years?" he writes in his book *The Virtues of Aging* (Ballantine Books, 1998). Although he called that event a "watershed" in his and his wife's lives, he lost little time before his volunteer work gave him—and the world—his next career. In the nearly twenty years since his "retirement," Jimmy Carter has worked tirelessly all over the world to champion social justice, improve the lot of Third World citizens, and provide conflict resolution where sitting presidents hit roadblocks. He's a living testament to the empowerment brought by simply giving and its potential for a new career or business—in Carter's case, the Carter Center in Atlanta and the Carter-Menil Human Rights Foundation.

Give and Take

If you have discovered your Beacon and spent time forming it into vocational goals, find a mentor who is a master at the very career you are targeting. Propose a way to apprentice yourself with him or her. It will get you into that industry, give you free training, and create the potential for good networking. You might also find this career isn't quite what you had in mind and will thereby get the chance to refine the definition of your Beacon.

Friendly Reflection

Sometimes defensive patterns that were modeled in our original families show up and sabotage our best efforts during periods of disruption. Have friends, support-group colleagues, and significant family members "mirror" you. Allow them to tell you if they hear you getting stuck in blaming your ex-employer, your outplacement counselor, or the human resources people that aren't beating down your door to hire you. Ask yourself: Are there payoffs to staying unemployed, or to maintaining feelings of hurt and betrayal?

Watch out for self-defeating traps such as victimhood ("It's not fair. . . . Why me?") and martyrdom ("I gave my life blood for that company. . . ." or "No one cares about me; I might as well give up.") Beware of surrounding yourself with people who offer you these rationalizations or allow you to wallow in self-pity, like other displaced workers with their own misery-loves-company attitude. At some point, with healthy grief work and creative self-exploration, there's no alternative but to take charge and move your life forward. If negative feelings persist, consider getting counseling for support in moving forward. This is also a great topic for journaling but it will only be fruitful if you are brutally honest.

BREAKING OUT OF OLD PATTERNS

Sometimes we have to use creative tricks to break ourselves out of old belief systems that might be sabotaging present progress. *The New Diary* by Tristine Rainer (J. P. Tarcher, 1978) is a good tool for developing healthier, more productive patterns.

Get Personal

Don't hide out—create frequent interpersonal opportunities. The Refugee journey can be isolating. Watch out for computer and TV addictions. Better to play a board game than a computer game. Assign yourself the task of getting social, in some way, *every other day*. You can do this more frequently, but commit to this minimum of social outreach, *separate* from your job-seeking activities.

Just as you needed to get out of the house and involved during Letting Go and the Wilderness, social interaction is critical now. It can also be a pivotal networking opportunity; many people get job leads from their social network. Arrange lunch or dinner dates with friends. Attend interesting lectures or poetry readings, theater or concert events, or free dance classes. Plan outings, hikes, or bird-watching treks. Do anything that promises social interaction, intellectual stimulation, and the requirement that you "show up" fully as a participant. In addition to the opportunity to meet new friends, your social skills, participation in community, and sense of connection will all be enhanced by these forays and will keep you grounded, during your job search, to the hard-won idea that you are more than a job title.

Become a Temp Explorer

Whereas temping was suggested during the Wilderness to get you out of the house and give you some purpose, now is the time to use temp agencies as an entrée to companies in which you might like to work. The salary will be lower than it would be for permanent work at that company, but temping provides an immediate opportunity to show this employer (and yourself) what you can do. It's like a live-action resume. At the end of the temp assignment, you may have a job offer. On the other hand, having gotten an inside look at the company, you may choose to reject any offer. The job or the company may not be what you thought, and you can cross it off your list, no harm done. A caveat: In some industries, they give the most problematic, boring, or frustrating work to the temp.

DID YOU KNOW . . . ?

Temporary workers are classified in three categories:

• Temp workers are typically employed by agencies and work no more than six months at a given location.

• Independent contractors work for many different clients, set their own fees, and comply with IRS guidelines as to payment of payroll taxes.

• Contract workers are also independent but basically work full-time for one firm at a time under a limited but well-defined contract.

The U.S. Bureau of Labor Statistics reports that the number of temporary employees rose 43 percent between 1989 and 1994. As of 1999, there were 12.5 million such alternative workers in the U.S.

Kevin

One Refugee, Kevin, fifty-seven, a seasoned architect, described a four-month temp assignment in which he was given a serious design flaw to "fix" and "sell" to exasperated building officials who had rejected several other plans. The task required enormous overtime because he had no support staff, but it introduced Kevin to the world of consulting and independent contracting as a career option.

Use temping to broaden your base of experience or to try things you've dreaded in the past but know you must face as you reenter the marketplace. Do you dread public speaking? Does working in cubicles rather than enclosed offices make you uncomfortable? Do you need to polish your negotiating skills or learn to set better boundaries? Find temporary assignments that will help you develop such skills. In fact, some temp agencies now offer health benefits for people who want to be permanent temp workers. Such an option might be appealing if you find you like constantly changing tasks and meeting new people—or if you quickly tire of the same people!

Contracting

Outplacement professionals suggest that an assignment such as Kevin's be done on a contract basis rather than by temping. As a temp, the bulk of the fee goes to the temp agency, not the worker. Further, when the short-term assignment is complete, it's far less likely that someone like Kevin would be offered a job at the salary he deserves. Whenever possible, it's better to contract directly with the hiring company.

Many companies now "outsource" work that used to be done in-house, so independent contracting can itself become a full-time job with

FOR HELP FINDING TEMP WORK

The following Web sites are your shortcut for finding temp work and advice:

•The biggest is Manpower at www.manpower.com, with half a million temp workers worldwide.

•Another giant is Kelly Services at www.kellyservices.com.

•For temporary tech work, Manpower and Kelly are still the largest, but medium-sized companies are also helpful. Mac-Temps at www.mactemps.com has offices in thirteen metropolitan areas nationwide and provides Windows and Unix temps as well as Macintosh specialists.

•Hookup! at www.hookupjobs.com places mostly full-time workers in interactive media positions, but the firm also offers temps who are skilled at creating graphics content for print media and the Web.

•The National Association of Temporary and Staffing Services (www.natss.org), with chapters in forty-five states, can refer you to member companies that agree to abide by the NATSS Code of Ethics and Good Practices.

considerable variety. The downside includes having to make new adjustments to work content and cultures with each change, the absence of a benefits package, and the need to constantly find new assignments.

Use Your Guides

Are you using all the outplacement help you can get? If you don't have the luxury of company-appointed job coaches, how about enlisting your own? See page 54 for how to find a coach. You've accomplished a rugged, lonely journey through recovery stages that required a lot of internal work. No one could really do it for you. Now comes the task of landing a new job, which is external work requiring all the experts you can find; asking for help is no sign of weakness.

GURUS UNITE!

A great resource both for offering and for finding contract work is www.guru.com. The site is also loaded with constantly updated links of value to self-employed "gurus."

Refugees describe this part of the process as a "numbers game." It's about contacting as many recruiters as you can find to target the industry you want, getting as many resumes in the right hands as you possibly can, and networking with every appropriate resource imaginable. If this is unfamiliar terrain for you, consider hiring a personal career coach with expertise in your industry. Now is not the time to go it alone. Use your guides, enlarge your network, and follow every lead.

Career coaches and outplacement professionals are usually eager to support their clients' job search *unless* Refugees refuse to do their part of the bargain. Because their caseloads are large, counselors tend to give more of their attention to clients who do their homework and demonstrate tireless pursuit of their vocational dreams. Be that driver. Don't settle. Be persistent, and you will arrive in the New Land you so richly deserve.

To laugh often and much; to win the respect of intelligent people and the affection of children; to earn the appreciation of honest criticism and endure the betrayal of false friends; to appreciate beauty and find the best in others; to leave the world a bit better whether by a healthy child, a garden patch, a redeemed social condition; to know even one life has breathed easier because you have lived—this is to have succeeded.

—RALPH WALDO EMERSON

SIX

Stage V:
In the New Land:
The New Reality

Success is never final.

—WINSTON CHURCHILL

At last the Refugee comes out of exile and enters a new land. For the Corporate Refugee, this New Land is a new work environment that will become the next occupational "home." In spite of the loss, grief, potholes, and dead ends that punctuate the dark side of each refugee journey, most Corporate Refugees report transformational outcomes at journey's end. All of your conscientious work through the recovery stages is rewarded. It truly feels as if you have come in from the cold, come back to a sense of belonging with a new tribe. A new life is offered, and a new cycle begins.

There is—and should be—great celebration when the new job finally comes along. At the same time, keep in mind the realities of the marketplace, which is fickle at best. The idea of continuity—on this job or any other—is an illusion. Disruption and unpredictability are the constants in careers from this day forward. Hence, the guiding metaphor to your survival in the New Land may be that of a change artist. Having learned all the nuances of the Refugee experience, along with the Interim Structures that best supported you along your journey, you are fully equipped to survive masterfully, even if the ground of this New Land should someday shift beneath your feet.

Colin

Colin's Refugee experience forever changed his approach to his career. After twelve years at a large furniture manufacturing organization, Colin had worked his way up to human resources manager. In the early years, Colin was challenged by his boss's mentoring and the opportunity to obtain a master's degree through a company-sponsored program. Over time, however, losses began mounting: Colin's boss retired, his father died, and the company went through several reorganizations that left Colin with less staff and more responsibilities. Additionally, Colin had to be the hatchet man, giving out pink slips and feeling the heartbreak for each recipient. Ultimately, Colin was laid off too. In many ways, he was relieved to be out of this toxic environment. But he took only a month for Letting Go, fearing financial destitution if he waited too long to get back to work. He called recruiters to start looking for his new job, even though he still felt "depressed, gloomy, guilty, and angry—all at the same time."

Colin had no trouble garnering job offers and soon took a position as head of human resources in a new city, uprooting his wife and two-year-old daughter—more change, more loss, and more complications along his Refugee journey. Colin and his young family were welcomed into the new company and new city, but, no

DID YOU KNOW . . . ?

The number of women-owned businesses in the U.S. has doubled during the past twelve years to a total of 9.1 million, or 38 percent of all businesses, according to the National Foundation for Women Business Owners. Greatest growth occurred in nontraditional industries, including construction, wholesale trade, transportation/communications, agriculture, and manufacturing. Since women-owned businesses employ 27.5 million people, workers would be wise to learn about gender differences in management styles.

matter how much time he was allowed to ramp up in his new position, Colin continued to feel listless and sad. When he explored his feelings, Colin decided that he'd sold out by taking another corporate job. What he really wanted for himself was a private career-counseling practice—something that seemed financially impossible since he was the sole wage earner for a young family.

Finally Colin could no longer ignore his pervasive sadness. He feared getting stuck in clinical depression in spite of his outer success. Ultimately, Colin went through the Refugee stages, even though he continued to work in his new job. As he did the necessary emotional processing, Colin gradually reorganized his new job. He created alliances in the company that would give him permission to do some of what he would do if he had a private practice, such as getting certified to provide specialized training and one-on-one coaching of disgruntled employees. He developed support and outplacement groups for people who got "right-sized" out of the new company. He redesigned the human resources role to match his personality, away from the policies-and-procedures function human resources has typically become. Each change Colin implemented was the outcome of his own soul-searching and movement through Letting Go, the Wilderness (of not knowing if he could stay "corporate"), and Seeing the Beacon of possibilities in this new company.

Now Colin is blissfully happy in his New Land. Having completed his Refugee work and reorganized his job, he says, "For the first time in my corporate career, I feel my job actually matches the lofty mission statement of the company at large." In addition, he works no weekends, gets semiannual bonuses and stock options, and takes time to write articles for trade publications, illustrating how human resources functions can be innovative while meeting bottom-line needs.

> ### DID YOU KNOW . . . ?
> According to the Bureau of Labor Statistics, the unemployment rate remained between 4.1 and 4.5 percent throughout 1998 and 1999, a thirty-year low. 45 percent of workers who left or lost their jobs were unemployed for less than five weeks before finding a new job. Yet salaries haven't increased—in spite of this tight labor market. Matching or surpassing one's prior salary often comes in the form of extra benefits, such as gym membership, four-week vacations, and other perks.

Colin did his Refugee work the hard way. Had he felt financially secure enough to take off several months between jobs, he could have moved through the stages more restfully. But Colin's case demonstrates how working the stages can still be done, indeed *must be done*, even if a new job comes along right after a layoff.

It's unlikely that anyone can be spared the grief of job loss, the wondering and wandering of that limbo between jobs, and the adjustment challenges in the new environment. Even young high-tech workers—"cowboys" who pride themselves on riding from one high-paying job to the next in mere eighteen-month spurts—experience unsettling disruption. They may deny the feelings, but at some point, burnout, disillusionment, or further disruption will hit them.

Remember Jessica, the Kevorkian Club member in chapter three? Her fear of surrender detoured her into an unhappy false start with her previous company, catapulting her into necessary Refugee work. Later, she found meaning as a college instructor but was still dipping into savings to make ends meet. After two years, Jessica decided to throw her hat back into the corporate ring, this time with a clear vision of what she would and wouldn't accept. No sooner had she sent off her resume to a couple of recruiters than she received a call from an old friend at her original company, asking Jessica to refer a good candidate for a new internal consulting position. It was an extension of the quality-control function Jessica had managed before, but this time it involved interfacing with outside suppliers rather than focusing on the internal issues that had so frustrated her before. Jessica thought it over, then suggested herself for the position. Two interviews later, the job was hers. Not only did the company promote her to a VP level, but they also continued her benefits right where they'd left off two years earlier.

Jessica asked why the company hadn't offered her this position two years ago. She was told that her years as an external consultant were necessary for them to view her as a candidate for this exciting new job. They wanted someone who not only knew the inner workings of the company but also had relationships with their vendors and competitors. Ironically, Jessica had to do those two years in the

> **There are no true beginnings but in pain. When you understand that and can withstand pain, then you're almost ready to start.**
> —LESLIE WOOLF HEDLEY

> **Just because everything is different doesn't mean anything has changed.**
> —IRENE POTER

trenches, both for her own internal growth as a Refugee and for her future growth with the very same company she had left.

SIGNPOSTS

The outer marker of the New Land is your new job, complete with a clearly defined role and job description. In place to support you are staff, training, a comfortable office or work environment, a benefits package, and a written company policy that includes scheduled evaluations and financial incentives. Having done your due diligence (page 193), you have landed in a culture of like-minded professionals with whom you anticipate healthy collaboration. Your boss includes you in important meetings and has time to get you up to speed in your new position. You see opportunities for growth and innovation. The job is challenging, but you're confident you'll be able to maintain reasonable working hours and have a life outside.

Internally, there may be a mixture of joy at having found a New Land that feels like a fit with your values and talent, mixed with trepidation from having so recently experienced the Refugee journey. Apprehension that the ax may fall yet again is normal for Refugees. So too are occasional doubts and confusion as you adjust to new coworkers, new software, new ways of working, and new surroundings.

At best, arrival in the New Land is an event, while true adjustment and assimilation are a process that takes time. The key word, again, is *process*. Be gentle with yourself. If you diligently worked the stages and strategies of your Refugee experience, you know that each stage had a kind of momentum that moved in accordance with

YOU MAY HAVE MORE BARGAINING POWER THAN YOU REALIZE

Before you settle on a salary for your new job, visit www.JobSmart.com where salary surveys for a wide range of professions will tell you what your skills should bring. Similarly, at www.jobstar.org, a site that focuses mainly on salaries in the California job market, you'll find a treasure trove of links and data on making money, listed by industry, by region, and by profession.

A BOON TO WORKING WOMEN

For a cornucopia of business-related information from managing work-family balance to all kinds of how-to tools for launching a company, managing finances, interviewing effectively, and dealing with age or gender bias, visit www.womenconnect.com.

your readiness. It may not have been measurable while you lived those stages, but now, in retrospect, you can see how organic the movement actually was. Similarly, there is a gestation period during your transition into the New Land.

Just as Letting Go involved destructuring your old identity so the fallow time of your Wilderness wandering could clear the space for a new identity to form, so too does acculturation in the New Land require a restructuring of your sense of self so you can gradually fit into your new job. Psychologically and physically, this phase is about adaptation to the new ways of being and doing. It takes both focused awareness and a kind of yielding, the yin and yang of learning new behaviors in combination with confidence in your core strengths and talents. Everyone's adjustment process is unique to his or her temperament and life experience, but, for all of us, it takes time.

STRUCTURE FOR THE NEW LAND—AND BEYOND

As you settle into a healthy engagement with the new reality, the following Interim Structure will support your transition from newly arrived Refugee to citizen of the New Land. It contains three essential ingredients:

- First—*and this is vitally important*—establish a structure for your days that incorporates the self-nourishing rituals you developed during your journey. Now is not the time to sacrifice self-care because "I have a job and I don't have time." That's probably how you got sucked into an overidentification with your previous job to begin with.

- Second, stay alert for any signals of potential future disruptions so you can prevent regression back to the Brink. This includes holding on to your newfound identity and not giving it over to your job.

- Finally, all of the wisdom you gathered during the previous stages must be codified so it remains available to you. Think of it as your Refugee Survival Kit. By embracing these goals, you'll not only assimilate quickly in the New Land, you'll also become steady on your feet for future change. Here are the goals for the New Land:

• Hold on to your whole-person identity (don't give it to the job!).

• Maintain self-care rituals and actions.

• Codify the lessons of your Refugee journey for future reference.

DAILY RITUALS

As you journey forward, use the following template of four basic self-nourishing behaviors to keep yourself balanced and prevent burnout. Within these basic rituals, you can add getting plenty of rest, drinking lots of water, injecting laughter and play into as many days as possible, and exploring the spiritual path of your choice. If you maintain your commitment to these healthy basics, your workdays and interpersonal time will be more gratifying, and you'll remain steady on your feet regardless of what the future brings.

TIME STRETCHERS

Healthy boundaries require good time management. Two resources to help you stretch time are:

• *First Things First: To Live, to Love, to Learn, to Leave a Legacy* by Stephen Covey, A. Roger Merrill, and Rebecca R. Merrill (Fireside, 1996). Learn to apportion your limited time based on your highest values.

• A great time-saver when you go online is www.ceoexpress.com—a well-organized aggregate site that provides every imaginable meta-link for news, business resources—even humor, sports, and health.

Your Morning—or As-Needed—Journal

By now you've established a daily journal practice, and you know its worth as a repository for your thoughts, feelings, dreams, insights, and problem-solving processes. As you adjust to the realities of your New Land, your journal continues to be extremely important as a way to ground you during those often chaotic days. It allows you to remember your values, priorities, and intentions as you reiterate them consciously or unconsciously in your writing. It provides a safe place to vent any confusion, disorientation, or impatience with this new beginning. It's also a place to celebrate your success, put

AN OVERVIEW OF THE INTERIM STRUCTURE FOR STAGE V: IN THE NEW LAND—AND BEYOND

Goals for the New Land

• Hold on to your whole-person identity (don't give it to the job!).

• Maintain self-care rituals and actions.

• Be clear about how you got here and maintain your personal survival kit.

Daily Rituals

• Your Morning—or As-Needed—Journal

• Mindful Eating

• Regular Exercise

After Hours

• Board Meetings

• Schedule Fun

Actions

I. *Assimilating in the New Land*

• Baby Steps

• Your Power Object

• Rubber Band

II. *Steady on Your Feet*

• Assure Your Financial Stability

• Health Insurance

• Base Camp

• Create Centering Strategies

• Passive Job Searching

closure to your wandering time, and record lessons you want to remember for future reference. Continue your journaling as you assimilate in the New Land. Thereafter, use it on an as-needed basis for instant venting and centering.

Mindful Eating

You've established an increasingly healthy pattern of eating during the stages of your Refugee journey. This includes a low-fat diet, regular meals, and focus on the sensual aspects of the foods you choose. In the New Land, there will be old triggers including deadlines, meetings, excess work, and demanding managers—any of which might tempt you toward self-defeating behaviors such as skipping meals or eating at your desk or in your car. Determine, as you enter this New Land, to maintain the mindful eating pattern you ritualized. Establish boundaries from the first day on the new job so those around you don't expect you to be available during lunch hours. Some days you may have business lunches, but on your "free" days use the time to take a break to nourish your body and mind with healthy eating.

Regular Exercise

You know the benefits of daily cardiovascular workouts plus regular strength, flexibility, and balance training. You also know how essential exercise is for managing stress, getting good sleep, and maintaining general health and fitness. No matter how demanding your new work schedule may be, it's critical that you book in time for regular workouts. Plan these before your new responsibilities, not around them. Ideally, there should be thirty minutes of daily cardiovascular exercise, plus longer workouts three times a week to target strength, flexibility, and balance

HEALING FOODS

If you find yourself experiencing fatigue or other physical symptoms as work pressures resume, here are two great alternative medical reference books that provide nutritional solutions to many symptoms and medical conditions:

•*Prescription for Nutritional Healing* by James Balch, M.D., and Phyllis Balch, C.N.C. (Avery, 1997). This is a thoroughly researched resource book for alternative medical health presenting nutritional, herbal, and complementary medical solutions organized by symptom or disorder for easy access.

•*Healing with Whole Foods: Oriental Traditions and Modern Nutrition* by Paul Pitchford (North Atlantic Books, 1996). Suggests ways of getting nutrients exclusively through food rather than seeking supplements for that purpose.

training. The most time-efficient way to accomplish the longer workouts may be with a trainer or in a fitness center. If you established a routine during the earlier Refugee stages, now is the time to solidify and ritualize it so you have a location and fixed schedule you know you can maintain. Use a personal organizer to schedule workouts right alongside the rest of your appointments. You are worth it!

IN CASE YOU FORGET

If you can't afford a personal trainer but would like the benefits, including structured training programs and reminders to get out there and *sweat*, here's an online resource for you: www.asimba.com. This motivational fitness site acts as a personal trainer, helping you keep track of your fitness regimen and e-mailing you reminders once you've designed a workout program.

Decompression

You started this ritual during the Brink—a time-out to decompress between the stress of the workday and the activities awaiting you at home. Now is the time to reestablish such a demarcation. An easy way to establish this behavior is to make a list of decompression options, remembering that it is meant to be body-based, not intellectual. You might include these on your list:

- Participating in some form of exercise after work and before returning home.

DECOMPRESS AT YOUR WORKSTATION

Movement and posture are key ingredients for decompression. *Work'ercise* by Jacquie Ogg and Sherry Ogg-Kabatoff (Top-to-Toe Inc. and Workplace Workout Inc., Edmonton, Alberta, Canada, 2000; (780) 435-1691 to order) is a CD-ROM presenting a Feldenkrais-based "workstation workout" of body-balancing stretches. It's great for use away from your workstation as well. (Also available on video.)

- Claiming the first twenty minutes of your time at home for meditation, relaxation, a hot bath, or a cup of herb tea taken in your garden.

- Stopping at a park or beach en route home, getting out of your car, and contemplating nature while you focus on deepening your breathing and bringing your attention into the present moment.

- Using aromas, lotions, or homemade potions during your peaceful relaxation time, fragrances that reliably work to bring you into your body and foster instant relaxation.

Once you have a list of your options, commit the time for decompression at the end of *each* workday and decide in advance which action from the list you will do. Ideally, decompression rituals are to be done solo. If you include your mate or children, in no time you'll be serving their needs rather than tuning into your own. Arrange with your mate to manage your children during your decompression time. If you are a single parent, establish your child's own ritual to be done in his or her room or play area. Explain your actions so your children understand the importance of this ritual. They will respect it and even help you enforce it.

ACTIONS

The Actions for the New Land and beyond are divided into three categories: assimilation strategies to ease your adjustment to the New Land; suggestions for a healthy infrastructure to keep you steady on your feet in the New Land and beyond; and after-hours reminders to keep you balanced.

The underpinning to your ultimate health and well-being as a Refugee is all the wisdom you gathered from each stage of your challenging journey. Your Refugee Survival Kit at the end of this chapter will help you remember—and celebrate—how you achieved passage into this New Land.

I. Assimilating in the New Land

Baby Steps
The enthusiasm and celebration of being in a new cycle can ebb into feeling overwhelmed by the realities of "the new normal"—a workplace loaded with demands for your time plus ever-increasing technological skills, flexibility, and far more responsibility than ever before. Establish a series of small steps to facilitate your adjustment and help you stay in the present moment. You aren't expected to get up to speed all at once. Prioritize your steps on the learning curve demanded by your new job. Be assertive if coworkers or managers expect too much too soon. Hold your boundaries, and

use the centering strategies you learned throughout your Refugee journey.

Your Power Object

Choose an object (or several) to represent the wisdom gathered during your arduous Refugee journey. It might be something from nature—a rock or shell. It might be a religious symbol that holds great meaning for you. It might be an object from the altar or the vision quest (page 157) you underwent during the Wilderness stage. It could even be a toy, like a bionic superhero, whose visible strength symbolizes the physical and emotional power you developed for yourself. Lucy, for example, paired her "bionic supergirl" doll with a toy shield and created a little scene that became an altar to her core strength. She placed these objects on top of a corner bookcase in her office, out of view of visitors but easily visible to herself. The shield is her protection against those (including herself sometimes!) who would pull her toward feelings of inadequacy or fear. The supergirl inspires her to hold her boundaries when dealing with difficult people. You too can derive great strength from visible reminders of all you've come through and want to bring forward through the rest of your working life.

Rubber Band

Don't stick your head in the sand now that you have a new job. If trouble looms, the On the Brink signals will be there, and you will recognize them—as long as you don't say to yourself things such as, "It can't happen to me again," or, "I have technical skills that will always be in demand."

LEARNING TO STAND YOUR GROUND

To help establish and hold your boundaries in your new work situation—without losing your temper or your poise—here are some invaluable books:

• *Difficult Conversations* by Douglas Stone, Bruce Patton, and Sheila Heen (Penguin Books, 2000). Members of the Harvard Negotiation Project tell you what to say when you have to say no to an assignment or confront a difficult colleague.

• *Bargaining for Advantage* by G. Richard Shell (Overlook Press, 2000). Use your personal style to negotiate or fight for what you want and need.

• *The Tao of Negotiation* by Joel Edelman and Mary Beth Crain (HarperBusiness, 1993). A primer for compassionate conflict resolution, whether at the breakfast table or in the boardroom.

• *The Magic of Conflict* by Thomas F. Crum (Touchstone Press, 1987). Aikido master Crum teaches simple breathing techniques and movements to transform stress and conflict.

Instead, keep a list of your skills, the changes you see happening in your industry, and any intuitive inklings that occur to you in your journal (or desk drawer). Save an updated resume on your computer. Be ready to move, if necessary, rather than becoming complacent just because you're back in the saddle at this moment.

II. Steady on Your Feet

Assure Your Financial Stability

Once you have a steady income, it's time to put your financial house in order. If your time away from work required dipping into savings, let that be a closed chapter and begin a new financial paradigm. Here are a few suggestions, culled from general financial planning resources. Consult with your accountant or financial advisor to determine the best steps for your fiscal fitness.

• Establish a budget that you and your family develop together. Beware of living above your means. In addition to covering fixed living expenses, detail each family member's extra needs so you can replenish savings and plan for the future. Make copies of the budget for each family member, relative to their level of understanding.

• Set up a savings plan whereby you'll have enough savings to support your overhead for at least six, ideally twelve, months in the event of a loss of income. Protect this fund by keeping it in an insured, interest-bearing account that is hard to dip into. You can use this money in case of disaster (including job loss) or toward the realization of a lifetime goal, such as opening that coffee shop in Puerto Vallarta you always wanted.

• Consult a financial planner to create a retirement plan. Even if you have a 401(k)

Along with any broadening positive growth comes a broadening realization that we all stand on cracking ice.
—ST. LUENZA

DUMP THAT DEBT
The Consumer Credit Counseling Service is a nonprofit organization that provides free advice on eliminating credit card and installment debt. The CCCS will plot a payment plan toward debt freedom, help you with creditors if you need lowered monthly payments, and work with you to develop a new budget. Call (800) 388-2227 to find the nearest CCCS office.

or pension benefit, it may not be there when you retire. Take charge of your future needs. How much will you need for a healthy retirement? In what ways will you accomplish this?

• Devise a methodical plan and timeline to become debt free. Once debt free, determine to operate on a cash basis or within a budget that allows you to pay off your credit card charges at each billing cycle.

Health Insurance

Make sure you have it. Whether you find a reasonably priced health insurance plan that you fund yourself, or a managed-care policy or program in which your new employer splits the premiums with you, do it! It would be disastrous to be caught in a catastrophic health situation without coverage. Health insurance is not a place to cut costs.

> In spite of everything, I still believe that people are really good at heart.
> —ANNE FRANK

Base Camp

Identify the continuities in your life, such as family members, good friends, objects with history and meaning. Create a collection of images, scrapbooks, and mementos that have personal resonance so that just contemplating them brings you feelings of comfort and connection. They might include the objects that you gathered for your altar during the Wilderness combined with new symbols to reflect the newly defined you in this New Land and beyond. These are the DNA of your life experience, impervious to the vicissitudes of corporate or business life. In addition to spending quality time with the important people and pastimes you've identified, it's also important to surround yourself with images and symbols that remind you of them, thereby reinforcing the sense of meaning and connection that is essential to health and well-being.

DID YOU KNOW . . . ?

A June 1999 article in *Fast Company* discussing leadership suggested that the best leaders carry "a mental map of their industry, of opportunities, and of discontinuities [and] they check that map constantly." When warning flags go up on one's mental map, "leaders have to hit the undo key without flinching."

Carry Self-Protective Mental Maps

Certain teams are hired with the knowledge that their jobs are time-limited. Thus, they hold that expectation or mental map and are prepared for the project to end. Compare that with the banking industry wherein workers are not hired with the understanding that mergers are likely. Hence, workers feel they've launched a long-term career path and end up shocked and angry when the unforeseen ax falls. Create your own mental map of what to expect on your new job. Chase down any disruption points every day; don't deny them. If things change on your original mental map, recalibrate and set it again . . . and again . . . and again. Stay awake!

Create Centering Strategies

Our cultural programming is performance-oriented, with hurdles, long-jump, and long-distance goals to be accomplished in order for success to be acknowledged. Such a linear approach is fraught with anxiety and takes us out of the present moment. Instead of joining that mentality, think in terms of *contribution*: What can I give to this project? . . . This day? . . . This stage? . . . This task? When you start with this attitude, you'll notice a subtle shift from a strictly mental, analytic focus toward a more balanced, mind-body awareness. You're then able to breathe into your core self with all its capabilities, and the task is no longer loaded with performance anxiety. You become more relaxed, and each task becomes an opportunity.

Throughout your recovery as a Refugee, you've learned the value of conscious, deep breathing as a vehicle for bringing you into the present moment and into your body. That is the only way to tune in to your moment-to-moment needs and respond to them. Centering simply means taking a few moments out to close your eyes, take a few deep breaths, and check in, so to speak. Then you can look upon the task at hand from a fresh point of view. If, as you take those deep breaths, you discover fatigue, frustration,

CENTERING STRATEGIES

It's a good idea to have an arsenal of centering techniques that instantly help you relax and feel "connected" during stressful times. Aikido master Tom Crum has produced a wonderful workbook of strategies in *Journey to Center* (Fireside, 1997). Lessons for unifying body, mind, and spirit are spiced with humorous, memorable anecdotes.

stress, or agitation that doesn't easily dissipate, it's time to stop whatever you're doing and resolve your distress.

Here is a list of options for balancing your body, mind, and spirit to avoid the devastation likely from unmanaged stress. Many of these suggestions recapitulate Actions you learned along your Refugee journey. Feel free to add to the list any additional strategies that occur to you. Keep the list in a visible place so that, when you overdo or forget to take breaks or blank out any ready ideas, you can refer to your list and choose an item that works for you right at this moment.

• Relax, with yoga, meditation, breathing.

• Look at your self-talk. Restate negative thoughts based on the maxim, "There is nothing either good or bad, but thinking makes it so." Stress often comes from our perception of things, not the things themselves.

• Engage in laughter and play.

• Use assertive self-expression in lieu of bottling up your negative feelings.

• Practice self-assessment to determine if anger, frustration, or resentment are causing your stress. If so, write a letter in your journal to the person or situation at the center of your stress, thereby releasing the pent-up emotion.

• Call a friend to vent. Or use a support group or therapist for this purpose.

• Move: exercise, dance, stretch, take a movement class.

• Create new time management strategies realistic to the tasks at hand.

• Delegate tasks if there's too much on your plate.

The political campaign won't tire me, for I have an advantage. I can be myself.
—JOHN F. KENNEDY

Passive Job Searching

Given the ongoing turbulence of the job market and the likelihood that, in certain industries such as high tech, job change occurs every two years for many people, it is wise to keep your resume updated and float it passively.

AFTER HOURS

Board Meetings

Convene your personal board of directors (page 196) monthly. Regular meetings with your "advisors" will do much to prevent your feeling lost or confused. Just as you used your hand-picked board to assess your job offers, once in the New Land, it's important to set aside time for these monthly meetings. Remember, this board reports to Brand You (page 191). It's their job to keep you on track, to be available to reorder your priorities as needed, and to provide feedback. Determine that, say, the first Sunday evening of the month will be your meeting with the board. Bring your journal to the meeting. Visualize the conference table and note who is present. You may retain the advisors you visualized during the Beacon, or you may need to replace some.

BE PASSIVELY ACTIVE

At www.headhunter.com there is a specific area for passive job searching—a sad statement as to loyalty and retention issues, but a self-protective strategy for someone who's made the Refugee journey at least once. Also, check out www.resumezapper.com, a site that "zaps" your resume, based on keywords you select, to literally hundreds of employers in your industry.

Formulate questions specifically about where you are in your job and your life. The following questions may serve as a good template for those meetings, in addition to any topical issues you face from month to month.

- Am I setting and maintaining healthy boundaries, both at work and between work time and nonwork time? If not, how can I start?

- Is my support network of family, friends, colleagues, and mentors adequate and effective? If not, what do I need to change? How can I effect this change?

- Am I taking time to be alone on a daily basis? If not, how can I do so?

•Am I prioritizing my time and energy in ways that are consistent with my highest values? If not, where have I strayed and how can I get back on track?

•Do I have a balance of exercise, nutrition, rest, and playfulness in my lifestyle? If not, what action can I take immediately to rectify this?

•Do I have a strong sense of personal identity separate from my job? Or am I sliding into overidentification with the job? If it's the latter, what can I do to recover my sense of self?

As you consider these questions and issues, use your journal to record your thoughts, feelings, and, most important, your list of actions.

Schedule Fun

Use a personal organizer to plan refreshing events, giving them the same importance as any other appointment. If you have a mate, schedule a date night at least once a week. Do the same with your children, who treasure their "alone time" with Mom or Dad. Are you involved in sports or group activities? Be sure to continue them. They represent elements of your core self that transcend the New Land. They also offer great opportunities for decompression, allowing feelings of competence and pleasure to mitigate the early—temporary—instability of the New Land. Are there lectures or classes in the weekly calendar section of your local newspaper? Book them into your schedule and get yourself there. If you value your nonwork time and determine to treat yourself to hobbies, entertainment, and

MAINTAIN A HUNGRY MIND

Although long-distance learning via online courses can be frustrating if you have to add downloads and plug-ins, it can also save a lot of time by providing creative courses you might not find elsewhere and allowing you to work at your own pace. Here are several on-line resources to explore for educational offerings both online and offline:

•www.hungryminds.com. In addition to online and offline course offerings on a huge number of topics, this site provides interesting study tools.

•www.edupoint.com. More than 500,000 real-world classes offered by brick-and-mortar institutions, saving you countless hours of thumbing through catalogs.

•www.youachieve.com. Nearly 2000 "gurus" have created 326 online courses offered in three formats: 60-minute workshops, 20-minute clinics, and 5-minute articles, for a fee of $399 for a one-year subscription.

•www.geteducated.com. This site offers long-distance learning as well as consulting for product development.

social events by scheduling them, you'll maintain a healthy work-life balance and prevent overidentification with your new job or role.

Lessons of the Journey: Your Corporate Refugee Survival Kit

Your responses to the following questions will define your arrival in the New Land and, more important, they will comprise your Refugee Survival Kit for the future. If you answer these questions in enough detail, they will become your new *intention* for your new life. They will infuse and inform each decision you make, both at work and away from it. When your spirit flags, rereading your answers to these questions will revive your high standards and keep you on track. Your employment will be about *earning a life*, not just earning a living.

• How did this new reality come about?   _____

_____

_____

_____

_____

• Did you design it proactively? How?   _____

_____

_____

• Were you hired away from a prior job or did the new job come about when you were not actively looking? (Describe.)

_____

_____

_____

_____

•How did your inner work of values-clarification influence your choice of this New Land? _____

_____

_____

•How long was your Wilderness wandering? _____

_____

_____

•Looking back, do you feel you made full use of your "down" time? _____

•What was left undone or incomplete? _____

_____

_____

_____

_____

•Can you finish that work now, or schedule time for its completion soon? _____

•What values and priorities surfaced for you during each of the Letting Go, the Wilderness, and Seeing the Beacon stages?

_____

_____

_____

_____

•Among those core values, which ones do you see manifesting themselves in this new job?   _____

_____

_____

_____

_____

•How can you maximize these core values, as well as your talents and passions, in your new work environment?

_____

_____

_____

•How will you use your work time and energy in ways that truly matter to you?   _____

_____

_____

_____

•If you had the Refugee journey to do again, what would you do differently?   _____

_____

_____

_____

•Were you impatient with any of the Daily Rituals or Actions in ways that prolonged your pain? Describe.   _____

_____

_____

_____

_____

•Are you willing to take better care of your health, both on and off the job, than you did in your last job? If so, how?

_____

_____

•Do you see the value of grieving your losses and healing old resentments so none of this old baggage enters your new beginning? Explain. _____

_____

_____

_____

•What have you learned about the value of playfulness? Of laughter? Of daily exercise? Of "failure"? Of good time management? Of taking time out? _____

_____

_____

_____

_____

_____

_____

_____

_____

•What issues did you discover during your Refugee journey that you choose never again to suppress? Examples might include:

—Overidentification with work as a source of self-definition. If you worked through this one and don't want to return to the old paradigm, what will you do to define yourself anew? _____

_____

_____

_____

_____

—Allowing overwork to spill over into your marriage or family life so much that you feel resentful and guilt-ridden. In the past, did you feel you had two full-time jobs, with family life feeling like a burden rather than a joy because you were always too fatigued to relax? How will you balance these commitments differently now? _____

_____

_____

_____

_____

—If you are single, working such long, hard hours that you never stopped to find a mate or explore avocational interests. How will you avoid this in the future? _____

_____

_____

—Losing yourself to the job such that any intimacy in your life came from your "task companions" at work rather than friends unrelated to your job. How will you handle this now? _____

_____

_____

_____

_____

—Unable to give the support and attention you'd like to your immediate family, your children, mate, or elders, due to overwork and fatigue. Have you righted that balance during the Refugee journey such that your values have realigned? _____

_____

_____

_____

_____

_____

CONCLUSION

An Amazing Comeback Story— to Mirror Your Own

He's a revenant [somebody who has made a comeback] with all the symbols that carries—courage, tenacity and the rest . . .

LOS ANGELES TIMES, JULY 17, 1999

These words apply to virtually every Refugee who's been to hell and back as the result of job loss. In this case, they were applied to someone whose heroic journey should stand as an inspiration to us all: Lance Armstrong.

Armstrong's career is professional bicycle racing. At age twenty-seven, he was diagnosed with cancer—which had manifested itself in multiple tumors throughout his lungs, brain, and testicles. In spite of surgery, debilitating chemotherapy, and a year of depression, Armstrong said, "I've always been a fighter, always. You spend a year so scared and terrified that you feel like you deserve the rest of your life to be a vacation. But you can't. They don't give you those. You have to return to your life."

And return he did. After painstaking training and meticulous preparation, in 1999 he entered—and won—the most grueling bicycle race in the world, the Tour de France, a three-week endurance test for any athlete, let alone one who so recently faced a life-threatening disease. Armstrong's attitude was even more

239

winning: He declared himself changed by his recovery experience, saying that the qualities of his life and his relationships are far more important to him now than his winnings.

Most Refugees don't have to deal with recovery from terminal illness at the same time as that of job loss. And certainly there is life after job loss, though it might not have felt that way as you endured the stages from On the Brink to the New Land. Yet the overall experience unquestionably changes us. We become more realistic about corporate economics, less identified with our jobs, and, ideally, more motivated toward quality of life itself.

Refugees who have truly lived the stages report that it "woke up" dormant aspects of themselves, including vocational roads not taken; gifts and talents long suppressed that, once defined, could actually be expressed in the very work they already do; values clarification they never stopped long enough to do; and the recognition that we are living a new economic paradigm that will only intensify. Strategic job-hopping is the new norm. Downsizing is an acceptable option for corporate belt-tightening. As a result, your loyalties need to be aligned to include your own and your family's best interests before that of the company.

The Refugee template will undoubtedly be something you'll return to again and again throughout your career. Having worked your way through it the first time, you have demystified its pathways. The fear and foreboding that came with your first job shift will never be quite as intimidating because you know there is a positive end to it all. Many Corporate Refugees have said they were so paralyzed by loss and fear the first time around that they regret having not enjoyed their time between jobs.

Should there be another Refugee journey in your future, you will not only be prepared with Daily Rituals and Actions for the stages, but you'll also be able to seize the days and deepen your experience along the way. Consider all the lessons that have come from this first experience. Now multiply them and you'll almost welcome future opportunities to practice the Actions of a successful *revenant*.

Fortune and love favor the brave.

—ANONYMOUS

RESOURCES

I. Resources to Support Your Daily Rituals

JOURNALING

The Artist's Way, by Julia Cameron. J. P. Tarcher, 1992. Provides in-depth explanation of the benefits of daily journaling.

At a Journal Workshop: Writing to Access the Power of the Unconscious and Evoke Creative Ability, by Ira Progoff. J. P. Tarcher, 1992. This revised edition of Progoff's original, published in 1975, offers a challenging process for excavating your personal history and turning your journal into a memoir.

The New Diary, by Tristine Rainer. J. P. Tarcher, 1978. Includes tons of great ideas to keep you inspired and break through when you feel "empty."

Your Mythic Journey: Finding Meaning in Your Life Through Writing and Storytelling, by Sam Keen and Anne Valley Fox. J. P. Tarcher, 1989. Helps you uncover your personal myth and unite life experiences to view the big story of your life.

WATCHING YOUR DIET

Age-Proof Your Body: Your Complete Guide to Lifelong Vitality by E. Somer. Quill, 1999.

Healing with Whole Foods: Oriental Traditions and Modern Nutrition, by Paul Pitchford. North Atlantic Books, 1996. Suggests ways of getting nutrients exclusively through food rather than seeking supplements for that purpose.

Healthy Homestyle Cooking, by Evelyn Tribole. St. Martin's Press, 1994. Offers healthy, low-fat recipes for "comfort foods."

Jane Brody's Nutrition Book: A Lifetime Guide to Good Eating for Better Health and Weight Control, by Jane Brody. Bantam, 1989. Easy-to-understand reference book on American-style nutrition.

Moosewood Restaurant Low-fat Favorites, by the Moosewood Collective. Clarkson Potter, 1996. Borrows from the famous (fat-heavy) Moosewood Cookbook to offer us delicious low-fat versions.

The New Whole Foods Encyclopedia: A Comprehensive Resource for Healthy Living, by Rebecca Wood. Arkana, 1999. Shows you how to eat right and feel better.

Prescription for Nutritional Healing, by James Balch, M.D., and Phyllis Balch, C.N.C. Avery, 1997. Thoroughly researched resource book of alternative medical health; presents nutritional, herbal, and complementary medical solutions and is organized by symptom or disorder for easy access.

Steven Raichlen's High-Flavor, Low-Fat Cooking, by Steven Raichlen. Penguin, 1992. Low-fat cooking advice and recipes from an expert who has made a career of teaching people how to cook delicious and healthy food, and who also has books on Italian, vegetarian, and Mexican cooking available.

www.eatright.com. Web site of the American Dietetic Association. Provides menus, books, and newsletters.

www.food.com. For healthy take-out food, this Web site partners with 12,000 restaurants nationwide to bring your e-mailed order to your door.

www.mealsforyou.com. Presents recipes, menus, and shopping lists for designated categories, such as vegetarian and gourmet.

MAINTAINING PHYSICAL FITNESS

Maps to Ecstasy: A Healing Journey for the Untamed Spirit by Gabrielle Roth. New World Library, 1998. Using her own history as background, the author inspires self-discovery through movement.

Sweat Your Prayers: Movement as Spiritual Practice, by Gabrielle Roth. J. P. Tarcher, 1999. Teaches the use of free dance for stress release and creative self-expression.

The following audiotape programs provide guided, expressive movements based on the above books: *Initiation,* CD by Gabrielle Roth, Raven-Ladyslipper, 1994. *Ritual,* CD by Gabrielle Roth, Raven-Ladyslipper, 1995. *Totem,* CD by Gabrielle Roth, Raven-Ladyslipper, 1995.

Work'ercise, by Jacquie Ogg and Sherry Ogg-Kabatoff. Top-to-Toe Inc. and Workplace Workout Inc., Edmonton, Alberta, Canada, 2000. (780) 435-1691. A CD-ROM (also available on video) offering a Feldenkrais-based "workstation workout" of body-balancing stretches. Great for use away from your workstation as well.

www.asimba.com. A motivational fitness site that acts as a personal trainer, helps you log your fitness, and e-mails you reminders once you've designed a workout program.

www.eFit.com. Offers basic and customized fitness education, inspiration, and video clips to get you started with fitness.

GETTING ENOUGH SLEEP

Easing into Sleep, by Emmett Miller, M.D. Hay House, 1996 (audio). Dr. Miller, a physician and poet, focuses on sleep in such an effective, gentle way that you won't be awake by the end of the tape.

The Promise of Sleep: A Pioneer in Sleep Medicine Explains the Vital Connection Between Health, Happiness and a Good Night's Sleep, by William C. Dement. Dell, 2000. Expounds on what happens if we *don't* get enough sleep as well as the benefits when we do.

Sleep Thieves: An Eye-Opening Exploration into the Science and Mysteries of Sleep, by Stanley Coren. Free Press, 1997. In-depth, user-friendly scientific information about sleep, its necessity for peak performance, and how to overcome sleep difficulties.

www.sleepnet.com. Web site full of tips for improved sleep and overcoming sleep disorders.

STRESS MANAGEMENT AND DECOMPRESSION STRATEGIES

American Indian Healing Arts: Herbs, Rituals and Remedies for Every Season of Life, by E. Barrie Kavasch and Karen Baar. Bantam, 1999. Comprehensive volume depicting herbal medicines and rituals from several American Indian tribes.

Deep Healing: The Essence of Mind-Body Medicine, by Emmett Miller, M.D. Book version: Hay House, 1997; audio version: Hay House, 1999. Combines health education with guided visualizations to optimize self-care and heal stress.

Full Catastrophe Living, by Jon Kabat-Zinn. Delta, 1990. Introduction to meditation in a very easy-to-learn manner from the founder of the Stress Reduction Clinic at University of Massachusetts Medical Center.

Good Medicine: How to Turn Pain into Compassion with Tonglen Meditation, by Pema Chodrun. Sounds True Audio, 1999. Three-hour audio workshop teaches a simple, thousand-year-old breathing technique that instantly melts anger and aggressive feelings.

Medical Aromatherapy: Healing with Essential Oils, by Kurt Schnault. Frog Ltd, 1999. Filled with proactive self-help strategies that go back to ancient times. Author is an organic chemist.

The Native American Almanac, by Martha Kreipe DeMontano and Arlene B. Hirschfelder. IDG Books Worldwide, 1999. Offers healing remedies and rituals against a modern context.

The Pleasure Prescription, by Paul Pearsall. Hunter House, 1996. Uses Polynesian culture as a model for living more joyfully. "It's not too much stress, it's too little joy," says Dr. Pearsall.

375 Essential Oils and Hydrosols, by Jeanne Rose. Frog Ltd, 1999. Goes into great detail on the therapeutic uses of essential oils, their sources, and actions.

Timeshifting: Creating More Time to Enjoy Your Life, by Stephen Rechtschaffen. Bantam, 1996. Teaches breathing exercises for decompression that can be used throughout one's day.

When Things Fall Apart: Heart Advice for Difficult Times, by Pema Chodron. Shambhala, 1997. A powerful, compassionate psychospiritual text that will help you transform feelings of powerlessness brought on by loss and change.

Wherever You Go, There You Are: Mindfulness Meditation in Everyday Life, by Jon Kabat-Zinn. Hyperion, 1995. Offers a deeper experience of mindfulness meditation, bringing one's consciousness into the present moment so we can "be" rather than "do."

Who Dies? by Stephen and Ondrea Levine. Anchor Books, 1989. Teaches how to "die into life" using mindfulness, meditative breathing exercises, and spiritual approaches to our day-to-day reality.

www.HigherHealth.com. A virtual physical that provides health assessments and a customized action plan for your healing.

II. Nuts-and-Bolts Resources as You Leave the Job

LEGAL ADVICE

Firing Back: Power Strategies for Cutting the Best Deal When You're About to Lose Your Job, by Jodie-Beth Galos and Sandy McIntosh. John Wiley & Sons, 1997. Powerful legal advice to educate and support you through the legalese before your job ends.

Job Rights and Survival Strategies: A Handbook for Terminated Employees, by Paul H. Tobias and Susan Sauter. National Employee Rights Institute (NERI), 1997. Comprehensive guide from employment lawyers who are part of the nonprofit NERI. Can be purchased by calling (800) HOW NERI or through their Web site at www.ptobias@igc.apc.org.

Uncivil Rights: Protecting and Preserving Your Rights at Work, by Frederick T. Golder. Lyra Enterprises, 1999. From a labor and employment law professor, provides an extensive appendix of government agencies and support groups helpful to workers who want to file grievances. Loaded with fascinating case histories that detail what's involved (win or lose) in taking an employment case to court.

FINANCIAL ADVICE

Consumer Credit Counseling Service (CCCS). Provides free advice on eliminating credit card and installment debt. Call (800) 388-2227 to locate the office nearest you.

The Financial Peace Planner, by Dave Ramsey. Penguin, 1998. A straightforward guide to dumping debt and creating realistic budgets that keep you living within your means while showing you how to save.

Rollover Kit for Job-Changers. Free brochure from Fidelity Investments; order by calling (800) 544-8888.

www.fool.com. Popular Motley Fool Web site offers step-by-step advice on how to build a budget and develop investment strategies.

www.JobSmart.com. Provides salary surveys for a wide range of professions to suggest what your skills are worth.

www.money.mpr.org. Offers online tips and downloadable budgeting software originally presented by "Sound Money," a show on Minnesota Public Radio.

www.quicken.com. Offers budgeting software that's updated annually. *MS Money* and *Your Money* are other popular software packages for the same purpose.

BELT-TIGHTENING

The Complete Tightwad Gazette: Promoting Thrift as a Viable Alternative Lifestyle, by Amy Dacyczyn. Random House, 1999. The gold standard for money-saving tricks and tips.

Miserly Moms, by Jonni McCoy. Holly Hall Publishers, 1996. Suggests how to live on one income.

The Simple Living Guide: Sourcebook for Less Stressful, More Joyful Living, by Janet Luhrs. Broadway Books, 1997. Teaches wise and efficient use of our resources, including time and money management, to reduce stress and increase energy. From the publisher of *Simple Living Journal.*

Voluntary Simplicity, by Duane Elgin. Quill, 1993. Explores environmental consequences of excess. The sacred text for simple living.

Your Money or Your Life, by Joe Dominguez and Vicki Robin. Penguin, 1993. Presents a strategy for budgeting and simplifying your life.

www.frugalliving.com. Loaded with suggestions for belt-tightening and frugal living.

Find barter exchanges near you by contacting:

- •International Reciprocal Trade Association, 175 W. Jackson Blvd., #625, Chicago, IL 60604, (312) 461-0236, or online at www.irta.net.

- •National Association of Trade Exchanges, 27801 Euclid Ave., #610, Cleveland, OH 44132, (216) 732-7171, or online at www.nate.org.

III. Resources for Therapeutic Actions

CREATIVE PLAY

How to Trace Your Family Tree: A Complete and Easy-to-Understand Guide for the Beginner, by the American Genealogical Research Institute. Doubleday, 1975. Beginners' guide to launching genealogical research.

Places Left Unfinished at the Time of Creation, by John Phillip Santos. Viking, 1999. A beautiful memoir about a Mexican-American family; explores the drive to know about our families, our pasts, and our history.

Touching Tomorrow: How to Interview Your Loved Ones to Capture a Lifetime of Memories on Video or Audio, by Mary LoVerde. Fireside, 2000. A step-by-step guide to creating oral or written family histories.

Unpuzzling Your Past: A Basic Guide to Genealogy, by Emily Anne Croom. Betterway Publications, 1995. A basic guide; the author has also published a workbook and sourcebook for beginning genealogists.

www.i-craft.com. Web site of the Hobbies Industries Association. Helps you find hobby and craft ideas that are creative and relaxing.

www.learn2.com. Offers instructions ("2torials") on a range of hobbies, tasks, activities, and skills.

www.plantamerica.com. Inspires one to use horticulture as a means of reducing stress and harvesting new life.

VIDEO-THERAPY FOR OVERCOMING JOB LOSS

Office Space. 1999, VHS edition. A comic look at work in corporate America circa 1999; written and directed by Mike Judge.

Roger and Me. 1989, VHS edition. A documentary film of writer-director Michael Moore's efforts to track down General Motors chairman Roger Smith and show him what the General Motors factory closing did to Flint, Michigan.

ONLINE HUMOR FOR SUPPORT AND COMMISERATION

www.dilbert.com. Scott Adams's well-known Dilbert cartoons that boast, "I'm not antibusiness, I'm anti-idiot."

www.ditherati.com. Provides humor loaded with irony about work.

www.i-resign.com. A humorous site from Britain, offering funny resignation letters as well as other work-related laughs.

www.ishouldbeworking.com. Self-described "portal of slack," offering links to humor and gripe sites.

www.jobhater.com. Dubbed "the full-fledged site of hostility toward the workplace."

MENTORS AND MODELS

Awakening the Heroes Within: 12 Archetypes to Help Us Find Ourselves and Transform Our World, by Carol Pearson. HarperSan Francisco, 1991. Teaches a dozen classical patterns that can become paths to wholeness.

Creating Minds: An Anatomy of Creativity Seen Through the Lives of Freud, Einstein, Picasso, Eliot, Graham and Gandhi, by Howard Gardner. Basic Books, 1994. Analyzes each creator's breakthrough moments to synthesize and inspire creative thinking for all of us.

Creativity: Flow and the Psychology of Discovery and Invention, by Mihaly Csikszentmihalyi. HarperCollins, 1997. Study of ninety-one people to determine what makes them able to tap into their creative source. From the author of the original concept of "flow."

How to Succeed in Business Without Being White, by Earl Graves. HarperBusiness, 1997. Personal story of publisher and CEO of *Black Enterprise* magazine. Inspires anyone who wants to launch a business, but particularly targets people of color.

Leading People, by Robert Rosen. Penguin, 1997. Profiles of thirty-six inspiring corporate leaders whose creativity and ingenuity are great models for corporate and personal excellence.

The Virtues of Aging, by Jimmy Carter. Ballantine Books, 1998. The amazing journey of former president Carter from corporate refugee to international sage.

SUPPORT GROUPS

Forty Plus (40+). A nonprofit organization with chapters throughout the U.S. helping managers and other professionals over age forty. Find your local office of 40+ by going online to www.40plus.org.

www.mentalhelp.net/selfhelp/clrnghse.htm#states. Self-Help Clearing-house Web site; lists self-help support groups throughout the U.S., Canada, and overseas.

www.wsj.com. *Wall Street Journal* Web site, has a "Toolkits" section on its home page that lists self-help support groups all over the U.S.

REDESIGNING YOUR PHYSICAL ENVIRONMENT

Complete Illustrated Guide to Feng Shui, by Lillian Too. Element Books, 1996. Something for everyone, from beginners to feng shui experts. Too also has several texts on the art of feng shui as well as a kit that makes a game of redesigning your environment.

The Feng Shui Anthology, by Jami Lin. Earth Design, 1997. A beginner's sourcebook for understanding and experimenting with feng shui.

Lighten Up: Free Yourself from Clutter, by Michelle Passoff. HarperCollins, 1998. Suggests how piles of stuff can drain your energy. De-cluttering becomes its own art form as well as holistic release.

Use What You Have Interior Decorating, by Lauri Ward. Perigee, 1999. Inspires use of what you have but in creative new ways.

INSPIRING A NEW PERSPECTIVE

The Corrosion of Character, by Richard Sennett. Norton, 1999. Provides incisive commentary for corporate refugees on how "no long-term" workplaces damage the development of character. By reassuring displaced workers that they are not imagining the consequences of disloyalty and downsizing, this book inspires a philosophical shift.

Harold and the Purple Crayon, by Crockett Johnson. HarperCollins Juvenile Books, 1977. A children's book that's become a business fable.

Keep Your Brain Alive, by Lawrence C. Katz and Manning Rubin. Workman Publishing, 1999. Teaches "neurobics," brain exercises that increase mental fitness and use all of our senses, often simultaneously, to foster growth and creativity.

Learned Optimism: How to Change Your Mind and Your Life, by Martin Seligman. Pocket Books, 1998. Teaches the cognitive skills necessary to turn pessimism into optimistic, proactive thinking.

Soul Moments: Marvelous Stories of Synchronicity—Meaningful Coincidences from a Seemingly Random World, by Phil Cousineau. Conari Press,

1997. Shows how staying the course of your recovery journey will bring surprise benefits.

The Soul's Code, by James Hillman. Warner Books, 1996. Full of persuasive examples that inspire us to uncover and celebrate our own core gifts or talents.

Sukhavati: Place of Bliss: A Mythic Journey with Joseph Campbell (video). Mystic Fire Video, (800) 292-9001. Guides viewers through archetypal myths to help us identify our great possibilities.

Vision Quest: Men, Women and Sacred Sites of the Sioux Nation (CD-ROM), by photographer Don Doll, S.J. Crown, 1994. Takes the viewer on a Lakota vision quest that inspires creating one's own.

What Really Matters: Searching for Wisdom in America, by Tony Schwartz. Bantam Books, 1996. A personal search for meaning that vicariously guides us through the current "wisdom tradition of America" and helps us define our own deepest beliefs.

IV. Resources to Help Determine What's Next

IMPROVE YOUR PROFESSIONAL SKILLS

Toastmasters International. Organization that helps improve your public speaking skills. Call (800) 993-7732 to locate local chapters.

www.coachfederation.org. Listing of personal coaches by area from the International Coaching Federation, a trade group of 1500 private, executive coaches. They can also be reached by phone at (888) 423-3131.

www.edupoint.com. More than 500,000 real-world classes offered by brick-and-mortar institutions, saving you countless hours of thumbing through catalogs.

www.geteducated.com. Offers long-distance learning as well as consulting for product development.

www.hungryminds.com. In addition to online and offline course offerings on a huge number of topics, provides interesting study tools.

www.learnthenet.com. A primer for online networking and job searching; will teach you the ropes and save you lots of time using the Internet.

www.wcco.com/education. Lists online continuing education classes; sponsored by News Radio Channel 4000 in Minneapolis/St. Paul, MN.

www.youachieve.com. Nearly 200 "gurus" have created online courses offered in three formats: 60-minute workshops, 20-minute clinics, and 5-minute articles, for a fee of $399 for a one-year subscription.

EXPLORE OR TRAIN FOR A NEW VOCATION

American Management Association. Offers tuition-based business seminars on topics from information systems and sales management to finance and public speaking. Call (800) 262-9699 to learn more.

Callings, by Gregg Levoy. Three Rivers Press, 1998. Explores personal and philosophical grounds for honoring those intuitive messages that signify our vocational callings.

Creating a Life Worth Living, by Carol Lloyd. HarperCollins, 1997. Offers inspiring and practical career advice for artists, inventors, and innovators. Designed as a course, this book suggests "day jobs" for aspiring artists while they pursue their true passions.

Doing Work You Love: Discovering Your Purpose and Realizing Your Dreams, by Cheryl Gilman. NTC/Contemporary, 1997. Exercises to inspire ongoing creativity and motivation in your search for the right livelihood.

Do What You Are, by Paul Tieger and Barbara Barron-Tieger. Little, Brown, 1995. Introduces personality types based on the Myers-Briggs Type Indicator and suggests careers aligned with your personality type.

Is It Too Late to Run Away and Join the Circus? by Marti Diane Smye and Richard Chagnon. IDG Books Worldwide, 1998. Provides worksheets for obtaining a new career. Smye works for Right Associates as a change management specialist.

Making a Living While Making a Difference: A Guide to Creating Careers with a Conscience, by Melissa Everett. Bantam Books, 1999. Provides compelling stories and guidance for principled job seekers and those trying to change the circumstances of their current jobs.

Teamworks, by Barbara Sher and Annie Gottlieb. Warner Books, 1989. A follow-up to *Wishcraft;* offers creative networking processes to use individually or with family and friends.

What Color Is Your Parachute? by Richard Bolles. Ten Speed Press, 1999. Originally published thirty years ago, this venerable career-coaching manual is updated annually and offers traditional career decision tools.

Wishcraft: How to Get What You Really Want, by Barbara Sher and Annie Gottlieb. Ballantine, 1986. Offers great processes for identifying your passions and going for them!

Zen and the Art of Making a Living: A Practical Guide to Creative Career Design, by Laurence G. Boldt. Penguin, 1999. An inspirational, imaginative guide to determining your right livelihood.

www.careerlab.com. Offers fee-based vocational testing services.

ONLINE JOB SEARCH

Job Searching Online for Dummies, by Pam Dixon. IDG Books Worldwide, 2000. Lists meta-sites to help you save time.

www.careermosaic.com. Provides a "mosaic" of industry-specific job sites such as:

> www.accountingjobs.com
> www.EETimes.com (for engineering jobs)
> www.healthopps.com
> www.HRPlaza.com (for human resources jobs)

www.computerjobs.com. Provides "hourly updates" of jobs listed by region and skill set.

www.dbm.com/jobguide/local.html. A national jobs list categorized state-by-state from Riley Guide.

www.dice.com. A specialty site for tech jobs.

www.headhunter.com. Offers passive job-searching.

www.ipa.com. Called Recruiters Online Network; connects companies and job-seekers via international headhunters.

www.joboptions.com. A Web site on which you can search by job title.

www.monster.com. The granddaddy of career search Web sites; offers jobs, advice, networking opportunities, and more.

www.netshare.com. A recruitment site for senior executives.

www.100hot.com/jobs. Provides a hot-list that's updated every 72 hours, and includes state-by-state listings, jobs categorized by industry, and more.

www.resumezapper.com. "Zaps" your resume to hundreds of employers in your industry.

PRINT RESOURCES FOR SPECIFIC CAREERS

Civil Service Handbook: Everything You Need to Know to Get a Civil Service Job, 13th edition, by Hy Hammer. Arco Publications, 1998. Includes job descriptions and sample test questions with answers.

Green at Work: Finding a Business Career That Works for the Environment, by Susan Cohn. Island Press, 1995. A guide for "green" jobs, including contacts for green companies.

The Health Care Executive's Job Search, by J. Larry Tyler. Health Administration Press, 1998. A "how-to" book on conducting a job search in the health care industry, with a focus on senior-level positions.

Household Careers: Nannies, Butlers, Maids and More: The Complete Guide for Finding Household Employment, or *"If the Dog Likes You, You're Hired!"* by Linda F. Radke. Five Star Publications, 1993. Job searching advice for household employees.

Inside Secrets of Finding a Teaching Job, by Jack Warner, Clyde Bryan, and Diane Warner. Park Avenue Productions Publications, 1997. Advice for teachers from experienced educators.

Running from the Law, by Deborah L. Arron. Ten Speed Press, 1996. Supports disgruntled lawyers by providing fascinating case histories and many career change options.

Sunshine Jobs: Career Opportunities Working Outdoors, 2nd edition, by Tom Stienstra, Robyn Schlueter, and Janet Connaughton (editor). Live Oak Publications, 1997. Suggests many outdoor occupations.

Teaching English Abroad: Talk Your Way Around the World! 4th edition, by Susan Griffin. Vacation-Work, 1999. Lists short- and long-term opportunities, real-life experiences, salaries, red tape—and you don't have to be a trained teacher for this work.

STRATEGIC ADVICE FOR YOUR JOB SEARCH

Are You Paid What You're Worth? by Michael O'Malley. Broadway Books, 1998. Helps you compute the market value of any job and increase the compensation package accordingly.

Greener Pastures: How to Find a Job in Another Place, by Andrea Kay. Griffin Trade Paperback, 1999. Advises how to do a long-distance job search.

Guide to Executive Recruiters, by Michael Betrus. McGraw-Hill, 1996. A comprehensive directory of recruiting firms listed geographically and by occupational specialty.

High-Tech Careers for Low-Tech People, by William A. Schaffer. Ten Speed Press, 1999. A step-by-step guide for getting a job in the high-technology world with little or no background or training.

60 Seconds and You're Hired! by Robin Ryan. Penguin Books, 2000. A concise approach to packaging yourself and identifying your marketable strengths.

ADVICE AND RESOURCES FOR OLDER WORKERS

Age Discrimination on the Job, by the AARP. Publication #D12386, free. Offers advice about age discrimination. To obtain this booklet, write AARP Fulfillment, 601 E. Street NW, Washington, DC 20049.

National Employment Lawyers Association. Helps you locate a local employment lawyer in the event of age or benefits discrimination. Send a stamped, self-addressed envelope with your request to NELA, 600 Harrison Street, Suite 535, San Francisco, CA 94107.

www.monster.com. Offers several "toolkits" for older workers.

www.ncoa.org.maturityworks. Advice for older workers from the National Council on Aging.

www.shrm.org. Advice from the Society of Human Resource Management to HR professionals and job applicants regarding the hiring of older workers.

FINDING TEMP OR SHORT-TERM WORK

Executive Temping: A Guide for Professionals, by Saralee T. Woods. John Wiley & Sons, 1998. Guide to the preferred work style of millions of professional and technical workers. This proactive book makes temping very appealing.

www.aquentmagazine.com. Provides and advises on "temp-to-perm" placements.

www.hookupjobs.com. Web site of Hookup!, an agency that places mostly full-time workers in interactive media positions. This firm also places temps who are skilled at creating graphics content for print media and the Web.

www.kellyservices.com. Kelly Services' Web site; the second largest temp agency.

www.mactemps.com. Web site of Mac-Temps, which has offices in thirteen metropolitan areas nationwide and provides Windows and Unix temps as well as Macintosh specialists.

www.manpower.com. Web site of Manpower, which is by far the largest temp agency, with half a million temp workers worldwide.

www.mbafreeagents.com. Lists short-term project work for "virtual" companies.

www.natss.org. Web site of the National Association of Temporary and Staffing Services, with chapters in forty-five states; can refer you to member temp placement companies who agree to abide by the NATSS Code of Ethics and Good Practices.

BACKGROUND DATA AND COMPETITIVE INTELLIGENCE ABOUT POTENTIAL EMPLOYERS

www.companysleuth.com. Offers information about publicly traded, privately held, and international companies.

www.corporateinformation.com. Offers background information on thousands of international companies, indexed by industry, state, and country; also provides a huge collection of extensive links.

www.gartner.com. Provides background information and insights about information technology companies worldwide.

www.hoovers.com. Provides career advice, company information, and constant news about newly public companies.

www.industryinsite.com. Offers anonymous networking to learn what members have said about hundreds of companies, jobs, industries, and cities.

www.VaultReports.com. A "gripe site," where employees from various companies vent their day-to-day frustrations and thereby offer information on what it's like to work at those companies.

www.wetfeet.com. Offers informational interviewing online.

INSTANT BUSINESS AND ECONOMIC NEWS SOURCES ONLINE

The following Web sites offer a great amount of online business and economic information, both historic and up-to-the-minute:

www.businesswire.com

www.cnnfn.com

www.fastcompany.com

www.fortune.com

www.public.wsj.com/careers

www.techweb.com

www.washingtonpost.com

www.wired.com

V. Going It Alone

SMALL BUSINESS ADVICE

SCORE (Service Corps of Retired Executives) has offices throughout the U.S. and a Web site at www.score.com offering free advice on small business development and strategic planning.

www.garage.com. Offers boot camps for startups and a bank of resources for the high-tech entrepreneur.

www.inc.com. Web site from *Inc.* magazine offers books and free software (shareware) for writing a business plan. Also has a searchable database called "Virtual Consultant" for accessing forms, credit reports, businesses for sale, and ideas for doing business online.

www.msnbc.com/news/280213.asp. Aggregate page from MSNBC lists many great Web sites, some of which are industry-specific.

www.quicken.com/small business. Small business advice from the company that offers software to help small businesses manage all of their accounting functions.

www.sba.org. Offers advice and links from the Small Business Administration.

SOHO: SMALL OFFICE/HOME OFFICE RESOURCES

www.aquent.com. Provides resources, links, and articles for free agents and Independent Professionals (IPs).

www.hbwm.com. Site of Home-Based Working Moms, a trade association with yearly dues of $44; offers discussion lists, corporate discounts, freelance and work-at-home opportunities, print and e-newsletters, and great listserv links.

www.hoaa.com. Web site of the Home Office Association of America (HOAA), a trade association whose membership fee of $49/year includes group health insurance, legal advice, tips, and tools, both online and in print, for home-based workers.

www.liszt.com. Teaches the use of mailing lists and offers 91,000 mailing lists, as well as advice and discussion groups for direct mail strategies.

www.workingsolo.com. Offers consulting services to home-based entrepreneurs ("solopreneurs") as well as to large organizations hoping to reach solopreneurs. The organization presents an annual SOHO Summit, a conference providing the latest SOHO news and statistics.

www.workingtoday.org. Provides thirty minutes of free legal advice a year for $25 membership; also includes information on political advocacy, group health insurance, and pensions plus links to other associations for independent workers.

RESOURCES FOR CONSULTANTS, FREELANCERS, AND FREE AGENTS

www.forecastpro.com. Offers "MBA-ware," programs that help forecast the demand for your product and guide entrepreneurs in hiring, negotiating, and business planning.

www.freeagent.com. Allows freelancers and independent contractors to market themselves online via a specially designed "e-portfolio" and "gig-matching tools," and to receive money-saving deals on insurance, office supplies, billing services, and tax preparation.

www.guru.com. Offers project opportunities, career advice, and advocacy for freelancers and consultants.

www.netprocon.com. A free online exchange from Networking for Professional Consultants with 2100 members who want to network and exchange leads, forms, management strategies, and training.

www.scheduleearth.com. Lists conferences anywhere in the world at which you can present your wares.

The following Web sites offer contract work for e-lancers (electronically based freelancers):

www.advoco.com
www.elance.com
www.ework.com
www.iniku.com
www.ithority.com

VI. Resilience in the New Land and Beyond

SETTING (AND HOLDING!) YOUR BOUNDARIES

Difficult Conversations: How to Discuss What Matters Most, by Douglas Stone, Bruce Patton, and Sheila Heen. Penguin, 2000. Authors from the Harvard Negotiation Project use their mediation skills to provide an ingenious methodology for dealing with difficult people and situations. Also teaches how to communicate about issues before they become crises.

The Magic of Conflict, by Thomas F. Crum. Touchstone Press, 1987. Simple breathing techniques and movements to transform stress and conflict, from an aikido master.

The Tao of Negotiation, by Joel Edelman and Mary Beth Crain. Harper-Business, 1993. A primer for compassionate conflict resolution, whether at the breakfast table or in the bedroom.

When I Say No, I Feel Guilty, by Manuel Smith. Bantam, 1975. A landmark book on assertiveness and saying no that has stood the test of time. Setting boundaries is a key in managing stress.

Workaholics: The Respectable Addicts, by Barbara Killinger. Firefly Books, 1997. The definitive book on work addiction, the addiction to "doing," and what to do about it.

Your Perfect Right: A Guide to Assertive Living, by Robert Alberti and Michael L. Emmons. Impact Publishing, 1995. Gives the reader permission to set boundaries based on core human rights. These may seem self-evident at first glance, but stress, job loss, and the fear of having to go through it all again may make you less forceful in recognizing and enforcing these boundaries.

HEALTHY TIME MANAGEMENT

First Things First: To Live, to Love, to Learn, to Leave a Legacy, by Stephen Covey, A. Roger Merrill, and Rebecca R. Merrill. Fireside, 1996. Teaches you to apportion your limited time based on your highest values, rather than pushing you to do more faster.

www.coexpress.com. A well-organized site that provides every imaginable meta-link for news and resources—even humor, sports, and health. A great time-saver in your use of the Internet.

WORK-FAMILY BALANCE ISSUES AND RESOURCES

Good Enough Mothers, by Melinda M. Marshall. Peterson's, 1994. Gives working moms permission to be imperfect through exploration of necessary tradeoffs, creative compromises, and the testimony of powerful role models.

Living in Balance: A Dynamic Approach for Creating Harmony and Wholeness in a Chaotic World, by Joel and Michelle Levey. Conari Press, 1998. Includes good material on how the spillover of job stress affects the family and how to achieve work-family balance.

www.familiesandwork.org. Offers resources, articles, and support for working parents from the Families and Work Institute.

www.iVillage.com. Described as a "women's network"; offers ideas for work-family balance as well as general health for women.

www.nww.org. Provides ideas and resources from New Ways to Work for job-sharing, work-sharing, and flextime arrangements.

www.oxygen.com. Offers health and work resources via the Internet, cable television, and a new print publication called "O." Another women's online and cable network, this one has Oprah on its team.

www.womenconnect.com. Offers a cornucopia of business-related in-formation, from managing work-family balance to all kinds of how-to tools for launching a company, managing finances, interviewing effec-tively, and dealing with age or gender bias.

www.workfamily.com. A clearinghouse of resources and links for every-thing from childcare to eldercare, and work-family programs.

MAINTAINING RITUALS IN EVERYDAY LIFE

Everyday Magic: Spells and Rituals for Modern Living, by Dorothy Morri-son. Llewellyn Publishers, 1998. Describes creative rituals and remedies that combine ancient wisdom with modern technology.

The Power of Ritual, by Rachel Pollack. Dell, 2000. Suggests rituals for daily balance and inspiration.

The Sacred Pipe: Black Elk's Account of Seven Rites of the Oglala Sioux, edited by J. E. Brown. University of Oklahoma Press, 1989. Explores Native American rituals for change management.

Secret Native American Pathways: A Guide to Inner Peace, by Thomas E. Mails. Council Oak Distribution, 1988. A treasury of ceremonies by medicine men with instructions on applying them to modern life.

PRESERVING MEANING AND PURPOSE

The Heart Aroused: Poetry and the Preservation of Soul in Corporate Amer-ica, by David Whyte. Doubleday Currency, 1994. Inspires the use of poetry and creativity to connect work with soul.

The Last Word on Power, by Tracy Goss. Doubleday Currency, 1996. A powerful process for anyone seeking breakthrough visions of what they can create. Based on the author's Executive Re-Invention seminars for corporate leaders.

The Power of Flow: Practical Ways to Transform Your Life with Meaningful Coincidence, by Charlene Belitz and Meg Lundstrom. Three Rivers Press, 1998. Teaches sixteen techniques for fostering synchronicity in your life.

Raising Your Emotional Intelligence, by Jeanne Sega. Owl Books, 1997. Self-tests, case studies, and instruction from a veteran psychologist; helps readers experience and honor their feelings so they can live, work, and act from integrity.

A VIEW OF THE FUTURE

The Age of Spiritual Machines: When Computers Exceed Human Intelligence, by Raymond Kurzweil. Penguin, 2000. Predicts our future by looking at the impact of artificial intelligence and computers in every sphere of life.

New Rules for the New Economy: 10 Radical Strategies for a Connected World, by Kevin Kelly. Penguin, 1999. From one of the founders of *Wired* magazine, enthusiastically projects the economic and behavioral impacts of our increasingly networked society.

Who's Running Your Career? Creating Stable Work in Unstable Times, by Caela Farren. Bard Press, 1997. Using forty Leading Career Indicators, teaches you how to anticipate the impact of technological advances and maintain career resilience.